Teaching Naked

Teaching Naked

How Moving Technology Out of Your College Classroom Will Improve Student Learning

José Antonio Bowen

JOSSEY-BASS
A Wiley Imprint
www.josseybass.com

A Wiley Imprint
One Montgomery Street, Suite 1200, San Francisco, CA 94104-4594—
www.josseybass.com

Jossey-Bass books and products are available through most bookstores. To contact
Jossey-Bass directly call our Customer Care Department within the U.S. at 800-956-7739,
outside the U.S. at 317-572-3986, or fax 317-572-4002.

Wiley also publishes its books in a variety of electronic formats and by print-on-demand.
Some material included with standard print versions of this book may not be included in
e-books or in print-on-demand. If the version of this book that you purchased references
media such as CD or DVD that was not included in your purchase, you may download this
material at http://booksupport.wiley.com. For more information about Wiley products, visit
www.wiley.com.

Library of Congress Cataloging-in-Publication Data

Bowen, José Antonio.
  Teaching naked : how moving technology out of your college classroom will improve
student learning / José Bowen. — First edition.
     pages   cm. — (The Jossey-Bass higher and adult education series)
  Includes bibliographical references and index.
  ISBN 978-1-118-11035-5; ISBN 978-1-118-22428-1 (pdf);
  ISBN 978-1-118-23808-0 (epub); ISBN 978-1-118-26240-5 (mobipocket)
     1. Educational technology.   2. Education—Effect of technological innovations on.
3. School improvement programs.   4. Blended learning.   I. Title.
  LB1028.3+
  371.33—dc23

                                                                              2012016814

Printed in the United States of America
FIRST EDITION
PB Printing   10 9 8 7 6

Contents

Preface

The dogmas of the quiet past are inadequate to the stormy present. The occasion is piled high with difficulty, and we must rise with the occasion. As our case is new, so we must think anew and act anew. We must disenthrall ourselves, and then we shall save our country.

Abraham Lincoln

The future of higher education is deeply intertwined with new technologies. Technology has changed students and professors, how we access knowledge, the nature of community, the habits of learning, our understanding of patience, and virtually everything about education. It has also created an expanding global market for online learning that will continue to increase in quality, efficiency, and flexibility. Considering these changes, the value of a bricks-and-mortar university will remain in its face-to-face (i.e., naked) interaction between faculty and students. As the traditional model of college is challenged by changes in demographics and college preparation, for-profit institutions, hybrid class schedules with night and weekend meetings, free online learning, and even free certificates from the best traditional brands, it is widely predicted that there will be fewer students enrolled in expensive, inflexible, full-time, four-year degrees (Van Der Werf & Sabatier,

2009). If we want campus education to survive, then we need to focus on the experience of direct physical interaction in higher education and make it worth the extra money it will always cost to deliver.

We know from Alexander Astin's *What Matters in College: Four Critical Years Revisited* (1993) that student engagement and faculty–student interaction matter most in student learning. At the heart of *Teaching Naked* is the seeming paradox that technology can be harnessed to enhance the widely desired goals of increased student engagement and faculty–student interaction but that it is most powerfully used *outside* of class as a way to increase naked, nontechnological interaction with students *inside* the classroom. This book addresses the why and how of this paradox and provides specific guidance for faculty and administrators on how to leverage both technology and face-to-face classes to improve student learning and ensure the survival of the bricks-and-mortar university. Thus, the aim of this book is to connect the practical questions of immediate interest to professors with the larger managerial and policy challenges facing administrators.

The Tyranny of Common Sense

Abraham Lincoln argued against the tyranny of common sense, the invisible belief system that limits our imagination by mandating obvious and singular ways to do things. It is their "commonness" that makes these assumptions and attitudes transparent and therefore so dangerous.

Common sense tells academics that our students are learning *because* of what we do in the classroom. But it is a common misconception that *everything* that successful people do contributes to their success. A teacher might be successful because he is excellent at explaining complex problems in a simple manner, but after a few teaching awards it is easy to start believing that the soft voice and the no-late-work policy also contribute to his success, when in fact changing both of those tactics might make him even better. Since common sense tells him that he deserves his success, it is hard to convince him to change. Similarly, American education has been incredibly successful, but not everything we do has contributed to that success.

We were all taught with lectures, and we all give them despite a mountain of evidence showing that they are poor transmitters of content and even worse tools for learning. When our students learn, we attribute their learning to our current methods. We persist because common sense tells us that lecturing is working. But any analysis of how we might improve student learning has to start with the dissection of everything we currently do.

In America, for example, there is a deeply held assumption about modularity in the liberal arts. We believe that the order in which students take courses is only slightly important. We encourage students to take a majority of their general education courses in the first two years, but in reality we routinely mix seniors and freshmen in the same course and then do not expect more from the seniors in our grading. For the British, and most other academics around the world, this "common-sense" approach is nonsense that can only be justified by some economic necessity. A sequential curriculum is routine in most other countries: first-year students must master rudimentary skills before they move on to higher levels of thinking and analysis. Americans can see the logic of Bloom's taxonomy (Bloom, 1956, rev. Anderson & Krathwohl, 2001) that progresses from remembering and understanding to applying, analyzing, evaluating, and creating; even so, most American general education curricula are structured around content and continue to allow students to acquire that content in almost any order. Most college major curricula contain a modicum of progression, with "gateway" and "capstone" courses. However, few American institutions expect or assess integration of learning outcomes between general education and the major, so we have no idea if our modular curriculum structure is working or is just an old form of "common sense."

We believe that a liberal arts education works, but there is little evidence to support this contention and lots of evidence that we could be doing better. In *Academically Adrift*, Arum and Roksa (2011) conclude that the first three semesters of a college education have "a barely noticeable impact on students' skills in critical thinking, complex reasoning and writing" (p. 35). Of 2,300 students at 24 institutions, 45% showed no statistically significant improvement in these skills during the first year and a half of college. The Wabash National Study of Liberal Arts Education led by Charles Blaich confirms that while a majority of students show moderate improvement in some thinking skills, more than a third demonstrate a *decline* in these same areas. The majority of seniors actually graduate with *less* academic motivation and openness to diversity than when they started (Blaich & Wise, 2011).

We won't really know what works and how to do better until we embrace a culture of integrated assessment. Everyone in higher education is aware of the pressures for assessment. Like all human beings, faculty do not like being told what to do, especially by people from other professions who do not really understand the nuances of what faculty do. Nevertheless, until we embrace a culture of assessment, we will not know if anything we are doing is working.

Improving student learning requires articulating learning outcomes, collecting data, and embracing a feedback loop that uses results to inform change. Blaich and Wise (2011) also found that of the 19 institutions that participated in the initial 2006 Wabash study, nearly 40% had not communicated the findings to their campuses by 2011 and only 25% had tried to make any improvements as a result. Another characteristic of common sense (and a difficulty implicit in any significant learning) is that, when we are confronted with new data or ideas that might fundamentally challenge our core beliefs, if we can make no sense of them, we ignore them; if we have only round holes, we simply abandon the square pegs.

One challenge to common sense is to reconsider how and where to best use technology. I've chosen to focus on technology for four reasons. First, it is obvious and unstoppable. Our students arrive with laptops and iPads and want to know how they will be used in their education. No one would move to Spain and expect to teach only in English; we need to understand the language, habits, and assumptions of our students. Second, technology is driving the new global market; higher education's competition is now a flat screen. Third, technology has radically altered the availability of knowledge and thus changes the content delivery part of what universities were created to do. Our response should be to focus on core liberal arts skills—critical thinking, complex reasoning, and writing—but we need to understand how the importance and application of these skills are enhanced by changes in technology. Fourth, technology has shifted the nature of the classroom. Learning now happens in more mobile, customized, and varied ways. We need to consider how we can advance student learning by thinking equally about learning environments inside and outside the classroom.

Dual Audiences

This book is written for dual audiences—higher education faculty and administrators—with the dual purpose of illuminating both the why and the how of our technological and pedagogical future. It is crucial that both teachers and the administrators who support them understand the changes that technology is bringing and what practical steps are necessary to prepare.

Faculty need strategies for integrating technology. Therefore, this book contains practical resources and ideas for motivating students to engage with course content outside of class, thereby expanding the quantity and quality of interaction in class. Faculty will find many examples of "implementation," from expanding your repertoire of technological tools with Twitter and podcasts to using technology to facilitate more traditional pedagogies such as writing and active learning and even to make office hours easier.

Technology, however, is a means to an end. *Technology is a technique, not a strategy.* Strategies for learning have been the subject of exhaustive research, and new technology will not (at least not immediately) alter the way brains function and human beings learn. My goal, therefore, is to show how new technologies can support and enhance best practices in pedagogy. The principles of course design will not change, but technology creates many new ways to motivate student interaction with content and gives both students and faculty more control over the sequence of interactions.

Administrators who support faculty will find discussions of policy and administrative challenges resulting from the increasing quality and decreasing cost of online education. Increasing the value of bricks-and-mortar education will require more investment in student and faculty technology, different schedules and sizes of rooms, alternative pricing structures, new classroom furniture, and perhaps different definitions of faculty work and even different sorts of teachers.

Faculty are a heterogeneous group with a wide variety of talents; using this variety requires a flexible administration. Faculty who are comfortable with technology will find ideas for moving that technology out of the classroom or using it to increase interaction with students. Other faculty have been teaching naked all along but perhaps without knowing how to use technology to help students engage with content outside of the classroom. For both sets of faculty, this book will provide new ways to enhance current strategies. Not every faculty member will willingly embrace technology, but adopting such a position will make engaging 21st-century students increasing difficult. There are also many easy points of entry to this new world.

A wide array of new technology is available—some of it easy for faculty and cheap for administrators but others requiring more time, expertise, and money. I will emphasize the easiest and cheapest options for engaging students through technology first, but the point of this book is to make faculty and administrators aware of the range of available choices so they can select a practical mix that is appropriate for their situation, always keeping in mind that the goal is to enhance learning. Both faculty and administrators need to understand the arguments for and against using new technologies and the practical implications of going ahead or doing nothing.

Outline and Structure

Part One describes the new digital landscape in three chapters outlining the major changes—in technology and in students—with significant implications for education. Chapter One describes how the explosion of e-learning options is altering the marketplace for higher education. In Chapter Two, it becomes clear that today's college students consider physical proximity unnecessary for social networking, enjoyment (even sex), and, most importantly for our purposes, learning. Chapter Three describes how, with their ability to customize the challenge for the user, games have become the model learning environment and can teach us a great deal about the importance of customization in course design.

Part Two, the pedagogical heart of the book, contains five chapters that guide faculty through the design of courses that use technology outside of class to prepare students for face-to-face classroom interaction. Our most precious (and expensive) asset is student-faculty interaction, and "naked" pedagogy is an attempt to use technology in a new way to maximize deep learning. Chapter Four summarizes current research in the brain, learning, and course design and demonstrates that the courses with the most long-term effect create a sequence of learning experiences, involving both technology and classroom interaction, that changes the way students think. Chapter Five suggests practical ways to use the multiple formats and vast knowledge available on the Internet to replace the lecture as a point of first contact with course material. Chapter Six then discusses how to use e-communication and social networks to engage students with new assignments and constant learning. Chapter Seven makes the case that rethinking the processes and nature of assessment not only frees up class time but also motivates preparation for more transformative learning in class. With prepared students, Chapter Eight demonstrates how we can make our naked classrooms into interactive exploration spaces. The focus of Part Two is on practical advice for making both the online and live classroom experiences richer and better for all students.

Part Three turns to the institutional changes necessary to support these new course designs and to ensure that there is enough learning at our physical institutions to guarantee their survival against newer and more innovative competition. In Chapter Nine, the lessons of other intellectual property industries (music, books, and journalism) provide a framework for thinking about how technology may change not only the delivery of your product but also its very nature. The focus in Chapter Ten is on faculty, curriculum, and how we can motivate more innovation and more learning. Chapter Eleven considers the campus infrastructure: What is the difference between the product and the packaging for a university? How can face-to-face education be made worth its additional cost? What are the implications of naked teaching for the design and allocation of space and schedules?

Our product is learning, but its context has changed. Before the Internet, when knowledge was both rare and localized, universities could change lives simply by opening the doors of knowledge. Now that information is free and always available on students' phones, they need thinking and analytical skills more than ever. To survive in the digital world, universities will need to convince students and parents of three things: (1) learning takes place when students and faculty interact in classrooms; (2) this learning is different from the learning that happens when you learn on your phone; and (3) this learning is worth the massive expense of a face-to-face education. Technology makes it possible to improve learning in classrooms, but it is most effective when it is designed into out-of-class experiences and *removed* from classrooms. This book presents a new way to think about the relationships among higher education, learning, and technology.

Acknowledgments

Like most faculty, I have not been trained in pedagogy. I am, therefore, extremely grateful to all of my friends and colleagues who have supported my learning curve in a new field. Within my discipline, I've received tremendous support from the Musicology Pedagogy Study Group of the American Musicology Society (AMS), which has finally brought pedagogy to the table in our national society. Matt Baumer, Matthew Balensuela, Jocylen Neal, Jessie Fillerup, Mary Natvig, Mark Clague, and the rest of my AMS colleagues have taught me a great deal about teaching. Chapters Four and Six adapt some of the material from Bowen (2011), which Jessie especially encouraged me to write.

At Stanford University and the University of Southampton (England), I had chairs, friends, teachers, and colleagues who were ideal role models and also supported my teaching experimentation. At Georgetown University, I met Randy Bass, who introduced me to a real scholarship of pedagogy and who also supported the development of new technology in my teaching. I also had fantastic classroom role models and amazing teachers in Patrick Warfield, Anthony del Donna, and Robynn Stilwell. At Miami University I met Glenn Platt, who introduced me to the "inverted classroom," and Britt Carr, who, along with his wonderful team of visionary course designers and technology people, transformed my teaching. They helped me design and execute my first learning games in 2003.

At Southern Methodist University (SMU), I have been well supported by a dedicated team of technology folks including Jason Warner, David Sedman, Brad Boeke, Steve Snider, and Ian Aberle. I am grateful for comments on the early drafts or outlines from Tony Cortese, Laurie Campbell, Abby Bartoshesky, and David Chard. More SMU colleagues, Patty Alvey, Karen Drennan, Andrew Kaufmann, Marty Sweidel, Kris Vetter, and Deanna Johnson, either read sections, fed me ideas, considered tag lines, or provided support in the office. Thanks also to Afomia Hallemeskel, who alphabetized and checked the formatting of the bibliography (without the aid of advanced technology), and the other students who did support work.

David Brightman has been an amazingly supportive and thoughtful publisher who has shaped my thinking about this project. Judith Miller has been the ideal editor: responsive, thoughtful, knowledgeable, insightful, and patient. This book would be something very different without both of them.

Thank you to everyone who helped and encouraged me. I am deeply grateful to colleagues from all over the country who told me they were already teaching naked or helped me learn something new. Thank you to all of the course designers or directors of learning centers, like Lynn Jones Eaton, Rhonda Blackburn, Ben Wu, Suzanne Tapp, Jacki Thomas, Linda Roesch, and Harry Meeuwsen and many others, who were willing to teach me and allow me to learn with (i.e., experiment on) your faculty. My new pedagogy colleagues have also been very generous in putting up with my many questions: thanks to Ken Bain, Peggy Cohen, Catherine Wehlburg, Eric Booth, and especially James Rhem, who was willing to publish the initial "Teaching Naked" article (Bowen, 2006) when no one else would.

My college friend Kraig Robson has been generous beyond measure, keeping me going, reading chapters, and even building a website but mostly by being a challenging thinker and being willing to talk and think about hard problems. The suggestions and support from everyone were wonderful, but the errors and mistakes that remain are mine alone. I am also extremely grateful for all of the women in my life who put up with several long stretches of the same sweatshirt (you know the one), especially over the holidays. My very deep apologies and gratitude to Naomi, Kimberly, Molly, Daisy, Katie, Chloe, Tosca, and even Latte (our kitty-dog).

About the Author

José Antonio Bowen is Algur H. Meadows Chair and dean of the Meadows School of the Arts at Southern Methodist University. Bowen has taught at Stanford, Georgetown, Miami Universities, and the University of Southampton, England.

He has written over 100 scholarly articles, edited the *Cambridge Companion to Conducting* (2003), received a National Endowment for the Humanities (NEH) Fellowship, and contributed to *Discover Jazz* (Pearson, 2011). He is an editor of the 6-CD set, *Jazz: The Smithsonian Anthology* (2011).

He has appeared in Europe, Africa, the Middle East, and the United States with Stan Getz, Dizzy Gillespie, Bobby McFerrin, Dave Brubeck, Liberace, and many others. He has written a symphony (nominated for the Pulitzer Prize in Music in 1985), a film score, and music for Hubert Laws, Jerry Garcia, and many others.

He is currently on the editorial board for *Jazz Research Journal*, the *Journal of the Society for American Music*, the *Journal of Music History Pedagogy*, and *Per Musi: Revista Acadêmica de Música*. He is a founding board member of the National Recording Preservation Board for the Library of Congress and a Fellow of the Royal Society of Arts (FRSA) in England.

Bowen has been featured in the *Wall Street Journal*, *Newsweek*, *USA Today*, *US News & World Report*, and on NPR.

Bowen has also been a pioneer in active learning and the use of technology in higher education, including podcasts and online games <http://www.josebowen.com>, and has been honored by students and colleagues for his teaching at SMU, Miami, Georgetown and at Stanford, where he won a Centennial Award for Undergraduate Teaching in 1990.

Part I

The New Digital Landscape

1

The Flat Classroom and Global Competition

The new classroom is a flat screen. The leading edge of a transformation in learning through technology can be seen in corporate learning, military training, distance learning, K–12 education, and a plethora of medical, legal, governmental, and other certifications. In 2009, 29.3% of college students were taking at least one online course, up from 21.6% in fall 2007 (Allen & Seaman, 2010). New technology offers new learning environments, expanded potential for environmental and social good, and economies of scale. E-learning is the experience and expectation of our entering students, and it will continue to compete with traditional universities for eyeballs as well as dollars.

At the same time, higher education remains one of the few industries where the price, even though increasingly out of range for many consumers, fails to cover the true cost of delivering the product. A new for-profit sector has removed much of the "overhead" of traditional universities, and is delivering learning more cheaply. In higher education, the pricing gap between cheap and expensive products is colossal, yet there is little evidence that the price difference even remotely reflects the quality of learning. While a handful of elite universities will remain able to charge elite prices because of their brand equity, history, alumni networks, high demand, and limited supply, the vast majority of American universities are about to face a perfect storm of new global technological competition that will put even more pressure and scrutiny on tuition prices. In a reversal of recent trends, a likely outcome is a reduction in both what it costs to deliver a quality education and what people are willing to pay.

The Ubiquity of E-learning

Outside of the academy, online learning is well established. Corporations and professional organizations have been using video conferencing and e-learning for years in even the most sensitive areas. From Nestle to NASA, corporations and governments use online learning modules, live Web-based classes, and self-paced courses to train employees in equipment operation, sales techniques, emergency procedures, and performance reviews.

Complicated and important things are being taught online. The American Association for Thoracic Surgery has a large and up-to-date E-Learning Center (www.ctsnet.org) with articles and videos on a variety of procedures. Watching a video (available on mobile devices) seems a much better way to learn a new surgical skill than from drawings in a journal. The European Organization for the Safety of Air Navigation (www.eurocontrol.int) offers its Common Core Content for the Institute of Air Traffic Control as online modules. Over 2,000 online aviation schools will teach you to fly, maintain, or dispatch any size airplane or helicopter (www.aviationschoolsonline.com). Google assembled its tutorials, videos, and courses on Web programming into one place but then decided to make this "Google Code University" free, open-source, and available to the world (www.code.google.com/edu). There are courses on programming languages, Web security, and how to make phone apps. These courses are offered by universities, individuals, and companies around the world, but if you do not see what you need you can invent a new course and share it.

Even ethics is being taught online. Most research institutions have a commitment to the ethical treatment of human subjects and require ethics training for principal investigators even for unfunded projects. Government agencies mandate training in human subjects protection before funding can be awarded. Most institutions use the online course developed by the Collaborative Institutional Training Initiative (CITI), which began its Web-based training program in human subjects protection in 2000. By 2010, over 1.3 million researchers at 1,130 institutions and facilities had completed a CITI course. In 2004, Georgetown University created an online tutorial in scholarly research and academic integrity for all incoming freshmen to take *before* they started classes at Georgetown (https://library.georgetown.edu/tutorials/academic-integrity). It uses complex real scenarios to teach students the importance of academic honesty, the nature of scholarship, and how research fits into university life.

Developing online learning for corporations is big business. Many large companies have internal learning and development (L&D) departments. The global market for self-paced e-learning in 2009 was $27.1 billion and is predicted to grow by 12.8% a year (Ambient, 2009a). Not surprisingly, the technology industry has led the way; your computer support people take online courses before they install your new software, and Apple and Microsoft offer significant online resources and courses. Is your company ready for International Financial Reporting Standards (IFRS)? Deloitte has e-learning modules that feature "real life scenarios to demonstrate application of the standards, 'coach me' sections to explain the principles and theory, worked examples to show aspects of the standards in action, reference materials, and a printable certificate if you pass the assessment at the end of each module" (www.deloitteifrslearning.com). Deloitte's learning modules have been downloaded over one million times by major corporations and thousands of users in over in 130 countries.

As is the case with classroom instruction, the quality of online courses is uneven, but at its best interactive technology provides not only content, but also practice and individualized feedback that can be difficult to administer in a typical classroom environment. One small e-learning company (www.IsoDynamic.com)

specializes in online courses on complex subjects that require just this sort of navigated feedback. A six-hour course for the Maryland Library Partnership, for example, teaches customer service to librarians using role-playing scenarios that allow users to try new skills in a low-risk environment. Courses in the mental health area include tutorials on administering rating scales for autism and depression in which users practice their skills by observing subjects on video, responding to questions, making assessments, and receiving immediate feedback.

Foreign language learning is also well established on flat screens as a $1.3 billion industry in 2009 (IbisWorld, 2009). One of the largest areas in e-learning is English language learning, predicted to become a $1.69 billion industry by 2014 (Ambient, 2009b). Teaching Mandarin to Westerners using face-to-face instruction on Skype is such a major industry in China that the seventh (!) International Conference on Internet Chinese Education occurred in 2011. It will be no surprise to anyone who has called for technical help in the last few years that American accent training is another growing industry: voice recognition software has been used to teach correct pronunciation since 2005.

The U.S. government is also a heavy user of flat-screen classrooms. The National Institutes of Health (NIH) requires that all principal investigators pass an online clinical research training course (www.cc.nih.gov/training/training/crt.html). The U.S. Food and Drug Administration (FDA) offers online courses through its Center for Drug Evaluation and Research (CDER). CDERLearn (http://www.fda.gov/Training/ForHealthProfessionals/default.htm) offers online training as "one way to share FDA expertise with many more people than face-to-face classroom sessions would allow." Researchers can learn how to bring an unapproved drug into compliance, whereas physicians can learn how to communicate risk to their patients. Many state and federal agencies, like the federal General Services Administration, outsource their training, compliance, and professional development to Web-based e-learning companies.

The U.S. Army continues to use simulators with huge screens, realistic cockpits, and hydraulics, but it also now employs a wide variety of simulations that run on regular computers (including the free *America's Army*, www.americasarmy.com, which doubles as a recruitment vehicle) and mans its own gaming unit. The Department of Defense (DOD) has subsidized college tuition for active-duty service members since 1947; with over 400,000 men and women in the U.S. Army, Navy, Marines, Air Force, and Coast Guard the DOD spent $474 million on college tuition in 2008 (Golden, 2010). While traditional colleges still serve the majority of these students, many of these potential students are in remote areas, and online education and for-profit universities have been particularly aggressive in recruiting their business. Many service members already complete fully online degrees, but many others will be looking to transfer these credits toward degrees at four-year schools.

Learning management systems (LMS, formerly known as course management systems or CMS) software is now standard even in elementary schools. Parents expect daily updates on grades, but, more importantly, students expect to find assignments, tutorials, and help online. Today's students have been learning on-screen for years before they start school, and the homework tutor is more likely to be a flat screen than a parent. In addition to the millions of videos and podcasts from YouTube and iTunesU, there is also University of Illinois professor Bill Hammack, the engineering guy (www.engineerguy.com). From public broadcasting (www.PBS.org/teachers) to museums (www.moma/org/modernteachers), institutions of all sorts are creating, and often giving away, educational content and resources (see www.TeachingNaked.org for a growing list).

The most popular homework tutor, and in fact the most popular educator online (Young, 2010), is Salman Khan, a young

Harvard MBA with degrees in computer science from MIT whose online Khan Academy has 70,000 students a month from all over the globe watching 35,000 videos a day (www.KhanAcademy .org). Khan began with a complete math curriculum (organized into what he calls "playlists") from basic addition through calculus, linear algebra, and differential equations. With over 3,100 videos (now including his newer ventures into biology, chemistry, physics, finance, and even history), mostly in high-definition, Khan aspires to provide a free education to anyone in the world in 10-minute chunks.

With over two million lessons delivered per month and grants from the Google Foundation ($2M) and Bill Gates ($1.5M), the Khan Academy is a growing revolution. In addition to its huge body of content videos, Khan has introduced a (free) software package including a detailed knowledge map that can track progress and guide students to new problems tailored to their level. Students have to get 10 correct answers in a row to move on, and they collect badges for various levels of effort or accomplishment. For students, it is like a giant video game. Parents and teachers can get detailed and live information on students' performance, including every problem done, time on task, what videos they have watched, and where they might be stuck. Teachers can also see the progress and proficiency of an entire class on color-coded maps, with green for mastery, yellow for working on it, and red for students who might need teacher intervention. In trials, teachers have already begun to invert their teaching model. Rather than suggesting Khan lectures as a supplement, teachers are using Khan as the primary content, delivered online when students are at home so that they can do "homework" in the form of practice exercises during class time (Thompson, 2011).

For established schools, these resources are a wonderful new supplement, but for the estimated one to two million homeschoolers, online resources are a revolution. One million high school students were enrolled in online courses in 2007, and that number is growing even more rapidly than enrollment in college online courses (Van Der Werf & Sabatier, 2009). One study at Harvard predicts that half of all high school courses will be delivered online by 2019 (Christensen & Horn, 2008). That revolution will transform existing high schools and make the option of home schooling much easier and more attractive. Then those students will want to get college degrees.

The point here is not that online learning is better but just that it is here. Outside of traditional higher education, online resources have been transformative: you can already become a pilot, pharmacist, veterinarian, lawyer, or a rabbi online. With other industries believing that learning can take place on a flat screen, online learning challenges higher education's traditional course delivery model and its ability to increase tuition. The breadth of technologies, the capabilities of recent software, and the amount of free content will surprise most faculty. Most university professors and administrators are keen on additional resources for students, especially free ones. As long as these technologies expand what we already do (and since most do not threaten traditional colleges), we can probably be convinced to use online resources as a supplement. This tepid embrace, however, will change. With the high price of traditional models, new technology that puts interactive information, video, or gaming at the user's fingertips is already competing for some of higher education's traditional students. A large global market wants cheap, high-quality, online education, and American students increasingly want more flexibility and convenient schedules. Someone will meet that demand. American not-for-profit higher education needs to adjust to meet this new competition.

The Inevitability of Competition

The global market for online education is being most aggressively pursued by for-profit universities and e-learning companies. While

American higher education has recognized that online video content, LMS, e-mail, and educational gaming are transforming students and classrooms, we have been slow to recognize these same forces as a source of competition. American universities are eerily like General Motors in the 1970s. We are far enough ahead of the rest of the world, in both brand recognition and quality, that it will take time for the competition to make a serious impact. But like Detroit in the 1970s, our very success makes it harder for us to see how radical are the coming challenges, and few universities are yet taking seriously the threat of new products and changing consumers.

The advantages of a new technology are often hardest to see if you are surrounded by a previous technology that works. Americans, with our tremendously successful landline infrastructure, were slow to adopt cell phones, even though we had the money to invest in new technology. The benefits of cell phones were more quickly realized in poor regions of the world with no landline infrastructure. The importance of a cell phone (even a phone with poor reception and no Web or video) is most obvious to a person who has never had any phone. Likewise, the revolutionary importance of Wikipedia is much more apparent to the isolated individual in the third world than to university scholars surrounded by lecture halls and libraries. No one at Yale needs a virtual physics lecture, but for the majority of the world, Open Yale Courses (www.oyc.yale.edu) provides the first access to this experience. The Internet, like the book before it, is making a wealth of knowledge available to the people who could previously not afford the privilege of any higher education.

The Internet also enables increased competition between professional and amateur and between accredited, licensed, and unlicensed. There is still a wide quality gap between the best professional work and the worst amateur work, but before the Internet there was no way for even the best amateur, unaccredited, or unlicensed work to get into the public domain. In the past, only college professors could get teaching materials for college published: now anyone with an Internet connection can post review sheets or tutorials. As in all fields, some of the best amateur work is proving popular and highly successful. Most parents don't care whether the advice comes from a PhD; they care only if the kids can finish their math homework. Thus, the Khan Academy is popular because it works, not because Khan went to Harvard and MIT (although that probably helped with the early marketing). The Internet has challenged traditional universities with a completely new and global source of competition that cannot be regulated away.

Higher Education Online

Numerous new studies demonstrate that students want even more online learning and that even the most traditional colleges and universities will need to start providing it. The 2011 Sloan Survey of Online Learning received responses from 2,512 of the 4,523 degree-granting institutions in the United States. (Since smaller colleges are less likely to report, this response represents 80% of higher education enrollments; Allen & Seaman, 2011). Since 2003 (when the annual report began) the growth in online education (10.1% in 2010) has greatly surpassed the growth in overall higher education (0.6% in 2010). By fall 2010, 6.1 million students (31.3% of all college students in the United States) were taking at least one college course that was delivered at least 80% online, 560,000 more students than in 2009. Bad economic times generally drive more students to higher education, but online courses are attracting more than their share of students. While 48.8% of institutions saw increases in demand for face-to-face instruction, 74.5% saw increased demand for online instruction.

The Minnesota State College and Universities system plans to increase the percent of course credits delivered online from 9% in 2008 to 25% by 2015. The University of Minnesota has published two large studies, one about faculty and one about students. The student survey (Walker & Jorn, 2009b) discovered that students still wanted face-to-face instruction but were generally comfort-able with educational technology and were highly supportive of mobile technology. The percentage of students in Minnesota state institutions who had taken at least one online course soared from 11.3% in 2001 to 45.1% in 2009. In contrast, the parallel fac-ulty survey (Walker & Jorn, 2009a) found that the percentage of Minnesota faculty who are teaching online (about 9%) or even using online technology in their courses (about 70%) is virtually unchanged.

Large public institutions continue to offer the most online courses and enroll the most online students. The institutions with more than 15,000 students make up 14% of all institutions with online offerings, but they educate 64% of online students. Institutions with over 1,000 students make up less than half of the total insti-tutions with online offerings but educate 94% of online students. Smaller institutions may join the competition, but for the moment the online arena is for large players. While 65.5% of all report-ing institutions say that online learning is a critical part of their long-term strategy, a growing proportion are for-profit univer-sities, which now enroll 9% of all undergraduates in the United States ("Growth in for-profit," 2010). The for-profit sector has cre-ated new competition with an increasing number of fully online degrees, but a number of traditional nonprofit universities (includ-ing Boston University, Northeastern University, Penn State, and the City University New York [CUNY]) are now offering online bachelor's, master's, and even doctoral degrees. Online education is here and growing faster than traditional higher education.

The *Chronicle of Higher Education* report on the student of 2020 (Van Der Werf & Sabatier, 2009) predicts even more fundamen-tal changes. It concludes that there will be fewer traditional stu-dents to go around and that both three-year degrees and five-year programs (with a remedial first year) will proliferate. Students who choose a traditional four-year degree will be more likely to be part-time and will want the flexibility and convenience of hybrid class schedules with night and weekend meetings, online learning, and the ability to take courses at multiple universities at once—something that technology will facilitate. They predict that "**colleges that have resisted putting some of their courses online will almost certainly have to expand their online programs quickly**" (p. 4, bold in original). For universities that are largely residential, "hybrid" courses will dominate and become the norm: lectures, office hours, and assignments will be held online more and more.

Online products are only at their first stage: we've yet to see or even imagine what the luxury online education course will look like. Honda, Toyota, and Datsun hardly looked like a threat to the established Detroit brands in 1970. As gas prices stabilized, and with most Americans still wanting bigger cars and a brand they could trust, Detroit resisted change. No one in the American auto industry imagined the potential of improved quality and the introduction of luxury models on the part of the cheap competition. Honda introduced Acura in 1986, followed by Toyota's Lexus and Infiniti from Nissan (which replaced the Datsun brand) in 1989. The University of Phoenix is already the world's largest university and may be the Honda of our age. What will its Acura look like?

With less financial aid available at for-profit than at not-for-profit schools, student debt is much higher for grads of the former: in 2007 the average debt at graduation was $18,800 at a four-year public institution, $23,800 at a private nonprofit, and $38,300 at a for-profit. The for-profit world is results focused and growing exponentially (currently 4% of all BA degrees) and more focused on online education (Allen & Seaman, 2011). Students seem willing to go into debt for convenience, because for-profit education is attracting students despite higher cost. Whether because of results, convenience, or marketing, for-profit bachelor degrees are another new source of competition for traditional institutions.

With the economy and the public already putting pressure on traditional colleges, these huge technological shifts and the increased competition could hardly come at a worse time. But we can't turn back the clock. Now, before a market correction of falling demand and prices hits as well, would be the perfect time to examine our most fundamental assumptions (our common sense) about how higher education is organized, how learning is achieved, and how we pay for it.

Learning or Credentials?

While higher education is under pressure for change as a result of new technologies, equal pressure comes from increasing expectations from parents, students, and public officials, all of whom are interested in the value and quality of education: where do students learn the most? While teachers, parents, students, administrators, and policymakers have begun to understand that change is happening, the impact of technology has an unlikely accelerator in the completely nontechnological new interest in accountability.

U.S. News and World Report ranks American universities mostly on the basis of input factors (selectivity and SAT scores) with a nod to potential quality factors (class size, retention, and graduation rate). The current output factors are indirect at best, like the rate of alumni giving (which assumes that alumni give in relation to the quality of their experience). This is a bit like trying to buy a car by comparing which uses the most expensive materials; it is at best an indirect measure of reliability and does not tell you about workmanship or value. Parents, students, legislators, accrediting agencies, foundations, and even universities, however, are showing a growing interest in the quality and value of the education: at which institutions does the most learning take place, and how do we know?

As public trust has declined and parents worry about increasing tuition, accountability in higher education has become a part of the ongoing national political cynicism about schools in general. With Congress concerned about foreign competition, U.S. Secretary of Education Margaret Spellings formed a Commission on Higher Education in 2005. The report (Miller et al., 2006) focused on access, affordability, quality, and especially accountability. While they were controversial, the calls for accountability resonated, and universities, accreditors, and state legislators all began to look for ways to measure real outcomes. Several groups began collecting and publishing data, and the Collegiate Learning Assessment test of critical thinking and writing skills is now used by hundreds of schools. Studies on faculty productivity have taken this drive for accountability to new levels, especially in Texas, where published reports prompted the University of Texas System to make substantial changes. In August 2011, the system announced it would increase transparency, raise four-year graduation rates, expand the use of technology, and allocate $10 million for a Productivity and Excellence Framework that would give students, parents, and legislators access to an interactive, online database, with detailed measures of productivity and efficiency (Mangan, 2011). Further, as Congress moved in 2010 and 2011 to regulate the for-profit college industry, they extended many of the new regulations to all colleges. Accountability and regulation will continue to increase even for not-for-profit private colleges.

One result of the Spellings Commission report was the founding in 2007 of the Voluntary System of Accountability (VSA) by two large associations of public colleges and universities and with support from the Lumina Foundation. Members of the VSA commit to developing websites (www.collegeportraits.org) that deliver consistent information in a consistent format about student learning and experiences. Such transparency will help improve the comparison shopping experience, but will it become an accepted way to measure quality for either faculty or the public?

The increasing pressure for accountability cuts both ways. Current faculty common sense tells us that a four-year campus experience delivers more content knowledge with better writing, communication, and critical thinking skills than the online alternative, but we will eventually be forced to prove that our graduates have these skills. In an additional challenge to traditional higher education's monopoly on postsecondary learning, the idea of using online content or work experience as an equally valuable substitute for traditional college degrees has found advocates and developed an infrastructure. The paradox is that assessment, the very tool needed to assure wary parents that learning happens in expensive private colleges, will also allow the much cheaper competition to demonstrate the same benefit. A transparent and fair way to assess the relative skills of potential employees has long been sought by employers, and a grade point average and transcript are a poor substitute. E-portfolios and standardized assessment will level the playing field but also will suggest some radical unintended consequences.

In *DIY U: Edupunks, Edupreneurs and the Coming Transformation of Higher Education*, Anya Kamenetz (2010) demonstrates ways students can already assemble an education from the available free online courses. Those who work at (or paid for) high-tuition universities will continue to be skeptical; if a cheap for-profit degree can't be as good, how can a do-it-yourself degree provide real learning? For most people, however, self-teaching is a common path to success. Leonardo da Vinci, Benjamin Franklin, Abraham Lincoln, Thomas Edison, Herman Melville, Woody Allen, Frank Lloyd Wright, Bill Gates, Louis Armstrong, Steve Jobs, and J. K. Rowling all assembled skills and learned where they could. Now there are many more opportunities for self-learning, and we will soon have better ways to evaluate the quality of that learning.

E-portfolios have become a widely accepted way to chart and capture student learning on college campuses. Most common in schools of education, they are routinely used by school districts to screen potential teachers. Universities think of e-portfolios as administrative tools to track student or faculty performance, but they also provide a portable and potentially universal assessment tool that employers can use to hire graduates.

Learning Counts (a collaboration of the Council for Adult and Experiential Learning, the College Board, and the American Council on Education) and Knext (a Kaplan Higher Education project) are two new online portals for assessing workplace skills for college credit (Glenn, 2011). Credit for experience is not new, but these portals allow students to build a portfolio that is assessed by professors and then have (in theory) a portable and universal tool for demonstrating what they know. Why not, then, bypass the credit entirely and simply submit the portfolio to employers? (The Open Badges project from Mozilla, and funded by the MacArthur Foundation, aims to do just that; see Chapter Ten.)

Detroit in the 1970s did not predict that Japanese auto manufacturers could make better luxury cars or that consumers would want cheaper, smaller, and more gas efficient cars, and they certainly never imagined that consumers would pay more for hybrid or electric cars. Detroit resisted fuel efficiency standards that would have forced it to make better cars that could compete effectively. When the U.S. Department of Transportation and the Environmental Protection Agency began requiring window stickers with fuel efficiency for all cars in the late 1970s, consumers could decide for themselves. If an expensive university education is better than *DIY U*, we had better find ways to prove it.

A Pricing Structure That Will Not Survive

At the moment, the price of learning is radically differentiated. MIT Open University, the hundreds of schools on iTunesU, the Khan Academy, Google Code University, Udacity, Coursera, EdX, and many more are giving away content, while the brand-name products are increasingly unaffordable to most Americans. When free blogs and other sites began offering amateur content, the journalism industry thought that people would continue to pay more for their higher-quality product. Academia can hope that people value a traditional college experience more than they did newspapers, but in the meantime we need to examine our pricing structure very carefully. For the moment, higher education has a huge advantage in that we sell status and credentials and not just learning. But that advantage is temporary.

For the consumer, there is increasing choice in a new and largely unregulated free market. A high school student looking to take a three-credit introductory college course in economics, for example, has the choice of paying:

1. Nothing and taking the advanced placement high school course, which might or might not transfer as college credit
2. $120–300 ($40–100/credit) for an online course at a local community college, which combines the responsibility and flexibility of being more self-directed with the potential for transfer credit into a four-year college
3. $600–1,200 ($200–400/credit) for an online course at a for-profit college
4. $900–1,500 ($300–500/credit) at a four-year regional university
5. $3,000–6,000 ($1,000–2,000/credit) at a major private university

While it will certainly look better to see a transcript from Harvard University, most employers will focus on the institution that granted the ultimate degree, so there is limited value in paying full price for every course. Parents and students are increasingly looking for summer school courses at local community colleges with the idea of transferring the credit to their four-year home institution: it is simply a cheaper way of getting the same degree. One clever California father discovered that his sextuplets could each collect a year of college credits from the local community college while in high school and then a year of University of California credits while enrolled—and paying tuition—at the local community college. So each of his children received college degrees three years after high school and each received the coveted University of California degree, but he paid for only one year each of University of California tuition.

It is reasonable to ask where the most learning will occur. Is there really 10 times more learning at a four-year college, or is it just 10 times the price? Will a Nobel Laureate (or his teaching assistant) really be a good teacher for introductory economics? Will the course on a college campus have more interaction than an online course, or will the teacher just stand and deliver? Colleges need to be prepared to answer these questions.

University pricing resembles wine pricing: there is enormous price variation in the market, but it is difficult to tell how different the actual products are. Both wine and higher education are subject to complicated rating systems and a belief that the experts can truly tell the difference, but the abundance of exceptions seems to undermine the basic value proposition. With more than 6,000 blind tastings as evidence, the relationship between wine ratings and price is small and actually *negative*: on average even wine experts enjoy more expensive wines *less* when they do not know the price (Goldstein et al., 2008)! It does not matter if expensive wine is not actually better, but it tastes better if we think it costs more. Similarly, it ultimately does not matter if a student learns more with an Ivy League education. As long as everyone else believes that a given education is better, it will be in high demand and continue to bestow genuine benefits. In the same way that a bottle of wine is about the quality of the experience, a college degree, in the current market, is really more about buying a credential or a degree than it is about buying learning. Both consumers and providers have been willing to continue their shared misconception, since little else could justify the massive price variation in both wines and education.

Value, however, is an increasingly important proposition in the college marketplace. Parents and students already make decisions based upon cost. As competition increases and accountability provides easier ways of comparing outcomes, traditional education will need to provide justification for its added expense. Knowledge is now freely available on the Internet, and physical campuses cannot beat the online competition for cheap delivery of content by providing live versions of online lectures. Fortunately for colleges, employers clamor loudly for graduates with better communication and thinking skills, exactly the stated focus of many college curricula. Competition in a free market is a good thing, and in many ways physical colleges are ideally placed to provide a better learning experience.

Creating Value

American universities, however, need to reexamine core beliefs. A liberal arts education was genuinely transformative for faculty—that is why we became faculty—but this is not generally true for undergraduates, most of whom find that a liberal arts education only confirms the beliefs and assumptions they had when they entered college (Blaich & Wise, 2011). A liberal arts degree (the BA received by most American undergraduates) can indeed prepare students for a life of in-depth analysis and critical examination, but we cannot take it for granted that our curriculum or teaching methods are producing these skills (Arum & Roksa, 2011; Palmer, Zajonic, & Scribner, 2010).

If critical thinking matters, then developing it needs to be one of our central learning goals. It is at best a paradox, at worst appalling, that although we say we want to develop critical thinking skills, we structure most of higher education around delivery of content. The reason for this mismatch is that college teachers in general have no formal preparation for teaching, so they teach as they were taught, going back in an unbroken chain to the founding of Bologna, Paris, and Oxford universities in the 11th and 12th centuries (predating the invention of the printing press). We need to adjust our classrooms to focus less on content and more on application of material to new contexts, development of intellectual curiosity, investment in the material, evaluation, synthesis, challenging personal beliefs, development of higher-level cognitive processing, oral and written communication skills, construction and negotiation of meaning, information literacy, connection of information across disciplines, teamwork, and reflection on the significance of content. The Association of American Colleges and Universities has, in fact, already developed a set of essential learning outcomes as part of its Liberal Education and American's Promise campaign (AACU, 2007). All of these skills are best developed through interaction with faculty in small group situations (Astin, 1993; Kuh, Kinzie, Schuh, & Whitt, 2005). Technology, largely used outside the classroom to deliver content, can be an important tool to prepare students for classroom discussions and to increase the class time available for those discussions and other active learning. A college education can (and should) change minds and lives, but it will require some curricular and structural changes to make this happen.

The central argument here is that to add value and compete in the next centuries, universities will need to do much more than just deliver content: that will be done more efficiently and cheaply online. To provide the sorts of critical thinkers that employers, governments, and the public now insist on, universities need to rethink both the use of technology and the design of the liberal arts education. The accountability movement will only increase the importance of achieving and demonstrating student learning. But even without external pressures, as faculty, we should care if our methods are working. Knowledge can open minds, but research demonstrates that application, integration, and personalization of content opens more minds more effectively (Fink, 2003; Zull, 2004). We need better pedagogy; only more learning will provide the extra value to justify the high cost of a bricks-and-mortar education. While the top 20 brands may be able coast along without much immediate change, most universities need to both provide and demonstrate that they deliver better learning to survive in the new competitive environment.

Education in the New Global Marketplace

There is still a difference between listening to an MIT professor on your iPod or completing an MIT Open CourseWare course and attending MIT. Open CourseWare, however, has dramatically reduced the value of a bad lecture. In 2007, if a student were sitting in a bad or boring lecture in freshman European history or physics—the kind given in large lecture halls on almost every campus in America—the student had few options. There was always the textbook, and there might be a learning module online somewhere that explained the material or a set of notes posted by another student or perhaps even an eager teaching assistant, but there were few alternatives to sitting through the actual lecture. Now there are dozens of competing lectures from the most prized teachers at our most elite universities.

Technology has changed the marketplace, and traditional universities face competition from both directions. On one hand, large public and for-profit universities bring an economy of scale to a huge new online learning market. On the other hand, universities can and should play an important role in free projects designed to do social good (like the Khan Academy or Udacity) or simply to harness the potential of social networking (like YouTube and Wikipedia). An online MIT course might not be the same as attending MIT, but it still provides a resource that can improve lives and help the global economy.

There are, then, four current business models for higher education, not all of which will survive. The first is the free model, which major universities, governments, and philanthropists seem willing to support: the University of the People founded by Israeli entrepreneur Shai Reshef with $1 million of his own money has hundred of professors volunteering to teaching students from all over the world (www.uopeople.org). After 23,000 students (of the initial 160,000) completed Sebastian Thrun's free online artificial intelligence course (which he offered simultaneously to 200 paying students at Stanford), Thrun gave up tenure at Stanford to start the free Udacity.com. In February 2012 he launched the first two free classes, both in computer programming, with the goals of attracting 500,000 students. These projects will continue.

The second is the elite university model in which the product is really a brand and a credential. A large or powerful alumni network does indeed have career value, so the investment may pay for itself in networking. This model will survive as parental and employer demand continues to be higher than supply, and there may be no need to demonstrate learning as a return on investment. The third is the model that for-profit and community colleges have adopted: results-oriented, flexible, convenient, jobs-focused training. Students are clearly willing to pay for it, and demand will continue to rise.

The vast majority of U.S. colleges and universities, however, are none of these and continue to pursue a fourth model that is about to change. Traditional institutions without an elite national brand are increasingly expensive. They are often residential, and their business model has relied upon the number of 18- to 24-year-olds increasing every year. In every region except the South (due to a growing Hispanic population) this demographic trend is over, and the number of high school graduates will continue to fall (Van Der Werf & Sabatier, 2009). The only enrollment growth will come from older learners, part-time students, and students who want online courses. Such a shift will pit traditional universities that have historically been slow to adapt against new free resources or largely for-profit institutions that have made flexibility and adaptability a trademark.

The future will surely bring more convenience and more options for students. The marketplace will contain more for-profit and global and even free universities. State system tuition will continue to increase faster than private university tuition in the short term, but some state systems are aligning with their community colleges to offer more ways to get cheaper four-year degrees. Faculty may object to universal articulation and transfer agreements, but legislators and parents love their efficiency and low cost. While elite institutions may be able to increase tuition, most traditional universities will face the choice of either freezing or even reducing tuition to compete with cheaper options or demonstrating that there is additional learning and value that comes with the additional cost.

One way or another, new technology is drastically changing market conditions and the nature of our product. The good news is that the worldwide market for education is enormous. The bad news is that a large swath of American higher education (whatever its additional value) simply costs more than most of the market can pay, and our current financial model requires constant tuition increases that exceed inflation. In the short term, American higher education (especially the strong regional universities) can carry on selling a high-priced product to the elite few who can pay or using dwindling state subsidies while they last. Ultimately, however, the unique set of circumstances that has allowed both a lack of accountability and constant tuition increases is disappearing quickly. Technology has created new competitors, new expectations, and a global market for higher education. We have a window of opportunity to reinvent ourselves, but with a culture that values process and self-governance, universities are not good at rapid response to market conditions.

Technology offers an abundance of content. Technology also offers myriad new learning environments, multiple points of entry to every concept, an easy and cheap way to increase instantly the diversity of our student populations and our course offerings, instant connection and constant interaction with students, massive quantities of data about what students are doing and how they are learning, and more resources for improved teaching than ever before. The challenge for universities is to take advantage of the new possibilities that e-learning provides to improve and prove learning across the curriculum.

2

Social Proximity and the
Virtual Classroom

As described in Chapter One, technology has changed the availability and value of knowledge. We have moved from a world in which we walked around with the knowledge we could carry in our heads or in books to one in which we can access much of human knowledge from our pockets. Similarly, our interaction with our friends and colleagues used to be limited by proximity. Now, our constant connectivity with other people regardless of physical distance has become an indispensable part of our lives, but it has also redefined community.

On the prairie, your closest friends were apt to be those physically closest to you. When families moved from Europe to America, they often brought Grandma too. Although the letter and the telephone offered some important exceptions, being connected socially used to require some physical connection. Today, human beings are experimenting with new definitions of social proximity. Online social networking means that relationships and communication no longer depend on physical contact. Those who know the most intimate details of your life are not necessarily those you see daily, or even at all.

Instant access to knowledge and to each other has changed the nature of community and the speed of work, life, and, most importantly, thought. Time for reflection and interaction is a casualty of the digital age, and one of the primary goals of higher education should be to reclaim this time. The paradox is that the same technology that glues us to flat screens can also be the primary tool for reclaiming this lost time for human interaction and thought. The ability to reach our students wherever they are means that we can extend the classroom and hence the conversation; we can recreate the ideal of students discussing Plato in the dining hall, but virtually.

Virtual Communities

The very definition of what it means to be alone has changed. To be physically alone is still relatively easy, but many of us struggle daily to turn off e-mail, computers, or cell phones. For many of us, going to concerts, lectures, the movies, or social activities provided time to be disconnected from other demands. Our students, however, find requests not to text during these activities strange, annoying, and downright silly.

While most public schools still ban the use of cell phones, they allow phones to be carried. Most students can text without looking (with their hands on their phones inside a purse or their jeans) and have a hard time resisting a glance at an incoming text. (Faculty tip: Few people just look down at their crotch and smile—unless there is an incoming text message there.) More comprehensive bans have sparked opposition from parents. Campuses used to have a monopoly on wireless technology—we could isolate students by turning off the wireless connections in classrooms—but the technology and expectations have overrun us. It is possible to confiscate cell phones physically during class, but most of us do not want to work as security guards. (As a dean, I also get complaints from students about faculty who answer their cell phone during class.)

All of this connectivity has changed our students. It is now possible to go away to college and text, chat, share pictures and video, be on Facebook, and even talk as much to your high school friends or parents as you did when you were living close together.

This does not mean college students do not make new friends, but they communicate constantly with friends both near and far and no longer see proximity as essential. Even online dating has morphed into virtual dating; that person at the next table looking longingly into the computer may be on a date. The term *social proximity*, defined as the "cumulative trust between members" and measured by the number and length of friends, is the concept behind the popular dating site www.meezoog.com. Virtual sex is clearly beyond the scope of this book, but Travelodge plans to have it by 2030 (Pearson, 2011) and it made an appearance in Season 5 of the hit television show *Big Bang Theory* (2011).

Although it is easy to see potential harm here, most of us would hardly trade virtual communication for the alternative. Would you really rather be limited to living within driving distance of your parents? Would you really give up talking to your children by cell phone or Skype? Would you really prefer discussing your research only with the colleagues who live in your city? As scholars, most of us use e-mail and the phone for exactly the same reasons as our students do—we want to be connected to a community of others with similar interests, regardless of where they live. Social networking has allowed the most dispersed global communities to connect online. Such groups can be trivial, but they can also be academic and scholarly. We have always lived in a world of overlapping communities, but now we also live in a world of overlapping virtual communities.

Most faculty belong to at least one professional society. Conferences remain important and useful, but we all benefit from online communities. Professional discussion boards and listservs include job postings, ideas for new courses, teaching tips, scholarly discussions, requests for information, gossip, and everything else we would do at a live conference. It has never been easier to find out who in the world is doing research on what or who might be interested in collaborating. Hopefully these technologies influence scholarly communities to become more collaborative. But even if they have not, social networks improve research and learning.

As faculty, we want every class to be a community of learners, and now we have the opportunity to make that dream a reality. With 79% of American students commuting, creating a community on campus has become harder. However, even if your students are living on campus, there is no guarantee they are discussing class in their dorm room. Social networking offers faculty the chance to change how much and how often students think about course content outside of class. Social networks are a chance to create communities, connect with students, integrate ideas, apply knowledge, influence student culture, and improve student learning.

Embracing E-Communications

Teaching is about making connections, and the first thing we need to do is connect with our students. Relevance and credible analogies are critical for good teaching; being unable to understand a fundamental premise of your students' lives will make it harder for you to teach and relate to them. Worse, it makes you uncool, so when you do try to demonstrate that your discipline is relevant, your inability to answer your cell phone has already convinced them that you cannot possibly have anything important to teach them. If you do not have both LinkedIn and Facebook profiles, if you do not tweet or blog (or know that a tweet is like a Facebook status update), if you do not routinely use iTunes or YouTube, if you do not know how to use GPS, or if you do not share photos on Flickr, Snapfish, or Picasa, then you have an immediate credibility problem with your students.

Second, the ability to use technology to find information and people is an essential skill of the 21st century. If you have not searched for a job since the Internet, you may not realize that the amount and sources of information about everything, including jobs, has changed. Virtually all jobs are now posted online, and knowing there is an unofficial blog about your new faculty search process is a critical piece of information. This does not mean that that all previous ways of finding information are irrelevant, only that they have been augmented. There are certainly times when the old way is better, but in the same way that you probably want your doctor to have the latest and least painful new technology (would you like the new outpatient microsurgery or the old hospital stay?), your students will need serious convincing if you want them to embark on the more painful pretechnology path for doing something. Are you fully convinced that what is familiar to you is really the better way?

Third, it is impossible to critique something well that you do not fully understand. If you want to convince your students that texting or playing *Angry Birds* is a waste of time, you had better first understand the allure.

Finally, e-communication can help to bridge the power differential inherent in education. Students, especially those from less privileged backgrounds, are afraid of teachers. Even the youngest, hippest film teacher is a little intimidating for a student fresh out of high school. Both because stress inhibits learning and because fear will keep students from seeking you out for help, finding ways to appear ordinary and human can enhance student learning. There are clearly nontechnological ways to connect with students. In a small town you may see students at the grocery store, or you might attend athletic or arts events of students in your class. But social media is normal for today's students. By 2010 many of their parents had joined Facebook. They talk online to clergy and follow tweets from the president of the United States, and 80% of them sent a friend request to a school admissions officer (Ruiz, 2011). They will be concerned that you may be from another planet if you are unfamiliar with modern life.

Implementation: Your E-Communication Strategy

Students no longer want to come to office hours, and for commuter students the requirement to do so can be a serious barrier to getting help. Relying on e-mail alone is not a viable strategy. A clear e-communication plan for the semester can stimulate your community of learners and make you more available to help your students.

- Establish in the syllabus how you will communicate. This should include your maximum e-mail response time and if you accept chat, Skype, Facebook friend, or other network requests. How to contact you is vastly more important to most students than your office hours.

- Limit the forms of communication. You probably do not need to do both Facebook chat and Skype. Don't try to do everything at once. Ask students for casual feedback after class, but stick to your plan for a while before you try different or multiple channels at once. Do not randomly change your mode of communication.

- Create a schedule for yourself, follow through for an entire semester, and then reevaluate. When is the best time or the best day of the week to announce new assignments or provide your feedback on the last test?

- Do not mix the personal and the professional. (This is also an excellent principle to model for your students.) If you are going to post summaries on Twitter, do not add a post on your new puppy. Keep your personal information on a personal channel, which can be another Twitter feed or Facebook or some other network.

- It is fine, and even useful, to employ multiple methods of communication as long as you are clear and consistent. You might, for example, let students know that e-mail is used for announcements and information about the readings but

that you will tweet study questions. You could just as easily
reverse this, but be clear and consistent. Students are used
to filtering (i.e., blocking) certain stimuli, so it is essential to
let students know that information coming on their phone can
affect their grade.

It is equally important to consider how students will communicate with each other outside of class. Long before Facebook,
teachers recognized the importance of social networks for discussion and study, and we now understand that it is one of the
(perhaps the most) important ways to level the playing field for
minority students (Treisman, 1992). We have also increasingly
recognized the importance of peer-to-peer learning. Discussion
sessions and study groups are all radically easier to do in cyberspace, but the technology creates a new set of challenges.

Do you (or your teaching assistant) want to monitor these
conversations? In a physical discussion you are either in the room
or not, but in a chat room or a discussion board there are more
shades of gray and more options: you can approve posts before
they go public, participate in the conversation, observe but not
participate, scan simultaneous discussions, or just allow students
to argue on their own.

Before e-mail, we had two modes: in the classroom or one-
on-one. If we wanted to move a discussion from our office to the
classroom, we had to wait. E-mail offered a third mode, but it is
not a good group discussion tool. It is now much easier to move a
conversation into this middle space. If a student sends you a question via chat on Facebook, you might decide that this is a more
general question that will benefit more students. Instead of asking the student to repeat the question in class, you might allow
other online students to join the conversation. This strategy is
immediate but limits the conversation to those who are currently
online. Another option would be to move the question to an

asynchronous discussion board, which would keep a record of the discussion and allow other students to read or join in later.

E-communication technologies lower the barriers to communication but also make it easier to play favorites. Most of us are very careful about physical student social invitations and would not meet students for drinks, for example. A late-night online chat, however, seems both less and more dangerous. Twenty-first century students have radically different ideas about "friends" and online relationships. Like keeping your office door open when meeting with a student, an open discussion board is often safer. Many of the conversations you have most wanted to have with students can now be done, perhaps even more comfortably, without proximity.

Facebook

Facebook is ubiquitous; virtually all your students have profiles and spend daily time on this site. Its ubiquity makes it potentially useful for you and your classes, but it also creates many challenges. Creating a class group can be an effective supplement for your LMS. However, it needs to be handled carefully, and there are probably better options.

Students see Facebook as both public and private, and faculty should too. Facebook has convoluted privacy settings that allow you to control what each individual or group sees. You can allow your high school friends to see your pictures but not your relationship status, and you can prevent your students from seeing if you have children. Students are masters at manipulating privacy settings, and most will simply block you from seeing all of their party pictures.

The advantage of using Facebook to extend the classroom is that it is where students live. In this way, it is very much like the living and learning communities at many colleges, where faculty live in residence halls with students. In a great deal of ways,

Facebook duplicates and even extends both the advantages and disadvantages of this system. Encountering students in the hallway can make faculty more accessible and can lead to academic discussions, but faculty who live in dorms have their own apartments: neither we nor our students want to share showers. Be clear about the potential disadvantages: Facebook will take you into students' bedrooms and beyond, and your presence may be a little creepy.

Implementation: What to Do with Facebook

Most of what can be accomplished on Facebook can also be done on any number of other sites. However, assuming you have now created a professional Facebook profile (see www.TeachingNaked .com for more on Facebook and privacy) and you are interested in more than just being social with your students, here are some things you can do:

Create a Facebook group for your class or a special project

Students can join without becoming your friend. If you send an e-mail to all students announcing this class Facebook group, even before the first class, you may find that nearly all of your students join within hours. If you want the group to be an integral part of your class, you need to post there on a regular basis and encourage students to do the same.

Extend the Classroom

Since most students will follow Facebook on their phones, this is a good way to get to your students where they are—quickly. Connect what is happening in class to what is happening in the world to create relevance and motivation. If you teach a course on earthquakes and there is an earthquake, make the connection with a quick post and a link.

Online Discussion

You can use your class group to post announcements, links, photos, video, or study questions, but it is most useful as an interactive tool that allows students to respond in a place (the group "wall") where everyone can see both their question and answers from you or other students. It is basically another discussion board, and if you set it up with you as the administrator, you can remove any post you want. Unlike the discussion boards in most LMS, Facebook does not have tools for sorting threads, but it is immediate and everyone knows how to use it. It also allows students an easy way to post video, photos, or links.

Chat Office Hours

You can have an exclusive chat within a group on Facebook. Instead of having physical office hours, try virtual hours on Facebook.

Take a Poll

While you can post a question as a status update, you can also post something on your group or personal wall as a question and add answer options. You can even set it up so anyone can add an answer option. You can allow any student to poll the class as well.

Questions

Having a group is a great opening for student questions. Any member of the group can post to the group wall, and everyone (or just you) can see it. You can also see which of your friends is online at any moment and ask to chat with other group members who are online too. This is a great way for students to connect to others in the class and form their own study groups.

Your Wall

Be aware that students who are your Facebook friends will post questions to your personal wall if you give them access. This is a great public forum since everyone can see your response, but

I think this is best done on the class page and not on your personal wall. If a student asks you when the midterm is on your personal Facebook wall, I suggest deleting the posting, sending the student a private Facebook message, and asking the student to ask questions on the group wall.

Facebook Events

You can create events that are open, by invitation, or for a group on Facebook, and this is the perfect way to organize a field trip.

Most of these features are duplicated on LinkedIn, and, since LinkedIn is designed to be a professional networking site, students are much happier to connect with you there. For a class, however, LinkedIn offers no advantage over the LMS: it is another site to check.

On Facebook, your virtual community was initially set for you: you joined based upon your school. It has gradually become easier to join multiple networks and sort friends by education, location, and workplace, but in 2010 and 2011 Facebook repeatedly had to update its privacy tools to allow users to control who could see what. The redesign of the groups feature helped, but social needs continued to move faster than Facebook could keep up. The recognition that people live in layered communities (physical as well as virtual) has led to the introduction of Google+, which aims to capitalize both on the distrust of Facebook (with its spooky targeted ads) and its clunky privacy settings. In Google+, you begin by adding friends to "circles." I can add you as a friend to more than one circle; they can overlap, but my friends, colleagues, students, and family now live in different virtual places with different virtual access to my life. As with many new technologies, we now have a new way to manage a very old problem. Google+ is a better academic tool, and its "circles" design could easily solve the Facebook faculty "creepiness" problem. (Facebook groups also provide a way to do this, but it seems less organic.) However, as long as everyone is checking Facebook daily or hourly, it will remain the central virtual place in the life of our planet.

Twitter

Most of us did not "get" Twitter at first; it seems like an end-less stream of what people had for breakfast and when they took a shower. It can be something mundane about your day, or it might be the latest news about a topic of importance to you. With 50 million tweets a day, there is plenty of nonsense being posted, but it can still be a useful tool, and you need to know how it works.

Twitter is a messaging system for short 140-character bulle-tins. You can create an account (www.twitter.com) and ask your students to follow you. (Facebook has friends, and Twitter has fol-lowers.) You can also include a link in your tweet. All of your fol-lowers will get your short message immediately—on a phone if you set it up that way. You can also retweet (RT; i.e., forward) a mes-sage. By including a unique hash tag for your course (the symbol # followed by a unique identifier) or anything else, you can create a exclusive learning community centered on any topic or course.

Classroom Application: What to Do with Twitter

Microblogging

The original and still most popular use of Twitter is as a personal microblog. In this case, personal does not mean any personal infor-mation. If you teach a course in psychology, you might do daily or weekly tweets about how psychology helps to understand a celeb-rity or news story. Or you might ask your students to do so.

Twitter Conversation

Twitter is another way to converse. It happens in real time, so it can be used in as well as out of class. In a large class, you might ask a few students to summarize an article or identify key talking points and tweet to the class to stimulate discussion.

Current Events

Since Twitter is instant, it is all about timing. Use Twitter to connect and apply what is happening in class to breaking news.

Twitter Questions

Send students a study question once a week, timed to coincide with a weekly event like after a favorite TV show.

Twitter Lists

This is a feature in Twitter that allows you to create groups that you want to follow (or your students to follow). If you are teaching finance, you could create a list of the best finance Twitter users. An art history professor might want to create a list of art experts or museums that tweet. This is a good way to model how experts matter (see Chapter Seven).

Backchanneling

If you are brave, you can allow students to tweet questions to you (or better, your teaching assistant!) during class. You can maintain your flow but know there is a question. Students can also share links or other information in real time.

Twitter Search

You can search for a keyword and see what your students are saying about you or your class.

A new study demonstrates that using Twitter to augment a class can improve student engagement and grade-point average (GPA). An experimental group of prehealth majors used Twitter as a microblog for discussions, sending questions to professors in and out of class, receiving feedback and reminders, and review-ing course concepts. This group more frequently participated in class, sought out professors, discussed course material outside of class, and had an average GPA half a point higher than their counterparts in a non-tweeting control group (Junco, Heiberger, & Loken, 2011). Content analyses of sample Twitter exchanges showed that students and faculty were both highly engaged in the learning process in ways that transcended traditional classroom activities.

Skype

Laptop computers and phones now come with cameras, as do most tablets. Programs like Skype, iChat, or MSN Messenger are free and need only a stable internet connection to work. Facebook and the iPhone also have video chat features. All of these allow for free face-to-face conversations anywhere in the world using the Internet.

Skype (www.skype.com) is the most common of these and is basically a free video phone on your computer or mobile device. For two people, Skype is easy. You can talk to multiple people at once, but in the free Skype version you lose the video when you do this. The video, however, is very useful. You can draw a picture and show it to a student just like you would in person. If you are having a bad hair day, you can turn the camera off, but seeing each other allows for more of the normal social cues and makes Skype much more like a conversation in your office than a phone call.

Skype also allows two users to look at the same screen (i.e., screen sharing). If you are used to looking over a student's shoul-der to edit a paper or problem set, you can now both look at the same image, paper, or problem on both of your computer screens. Most students already use this feature, and it can dramatically change the way faculty interact with students.

Implementation: Using Skype for Virtual Office Hours

Most student rating forms ask students about faculty accessibility outside of class, and most of us dutifully sit in our offices waiting for students to visit. We have all read, "Professor X is never in his office, and I stopped by multiple times during the semester," and laughed or cried. Perhaps there is a better way.

Millennial students are much more interested in the speed of your response than in your physical presence. The term *office hour* conveys two antiquated propositions: (1) a student would need to visit a physical office; and (2) time is measured in hours. For most 21st-century organizations, customer service has become proactive and immediate. If I am 20 years old and want to buy new mobile phone service, I might make a phone call, but I'd rather just get online and wait for the chat window of a salesperson to pop up. Here are some different ways to do office hours:

- Pick a time frame when you will be on Skype and available for calls from students. This will limit you to one student at a time (unless you want to create a conference call). Much like a regular office visit, you and the student can see each other.

- Pick a time frame for a Skype session, but combine it with a chat technology (Facebook has a separate chat feature that works very well for this). You can use the chat to keep a queue for your Skype calls. When there is no Skype call, you can talk to as many students on chat as you can handle. With a bit of practice you may be able to Skype and chat at the same time.

- Pick a time, and give students a few choices. Tell them they can contact you on Skype or by text, or post questions to the class Facebook group and you will respond. Such multitasking may be tricky, but it allows you to give a group response to the entire class and also to send an individual response to a student.

- Finally, don't overlook the value of (nontechnologically) getting out of the office. Your physical presence and a little casual small talk with students are good for both of you, but it is much less likely to happen in your office. Instead of staying in your office, set up your hour somewhere else: try a local coffee house and offer to buy students coffee, find a student lounge and park yourself for an hour, find a spot next to your class and get there an hour early, tell your students where you sit for a football game (or better yet, find out where they sit and go say hi), eat lunch in the cafeteria once a week. You can even require that students have lunch with you, perhaps in groups, once a semester; you don't have to buy them lunch. All of this will make you more approachable and will increase your understanding of student issues and improve their learning.

The Virtual Classroom

The video conference call is also a form of virtual classroom. Skype allows multiple video conversations at once if you upgrade to Skype Premium and pay a monthly fee. Adobe ConnectNow is free and allows for three participants. A host of third-party products (like VuRoom) allow for true multiperson video conferencing, and they work like a video conference call. Despite being designed largely for business uses, commercial video conferencing products offer many more features that can truly create a virtual seminar. Vidyo, WebEx, Nefsis, and many others designed for live interactive training all allow multiple-user video conferencing (often in HD) along with simultaneous sharing of documents. Adobe Acrobat Connect Pro (formerly Breeze) allows for video conferencing with up to 80,000 people (giving new meaning to the term *large class*) in a variety of virtual meeting rooms (think classrooms), with breakout sessions (you can pass notes or talk independently to anyone or any small group in the meeting), shared screens and content, shared whiteboards and tools, recording, notes and polling. It also comes with a suite of e-learning tools for tracking, quizzes, content libraries, and course management.

LMS like Blackboard, Scholar 360, and OLAT initially focused on reporting and content and offered only asynchronous communication. New systems (e.g., Elluminate, now BB Collaborate 11, Fronter Platform, eCollege, or desire2learn) offer all of the old tools plus synchronous communication like chat and video, and features like shared content. Some of these tools are merely convenient, for example, "Click here to arrange all of your students into new discussion groups." Other tools like document sharing, whiteboards, simultaneous discussions, and the ability to mix live content, faculty, and students from all over the globe have barely been touched.

Implementation: The Virtual Seminar

With current software, the virtual seminar (sometimes called a *webinar*) is a reality: you can share conversations, documents, images, music, videos, whiteboards, and ideas in real time across continents. You can sit at your computer and do everything you can in a real classroom in real time, and more:

- You can look at a single student, a few students at once, or the entire classroom to see who is still awake by changing the format from lecture hall to seminar table with a click.

- You or any student can present content or documents, images, music, film, or PowerPoint.

- You or any student can write on the whiteboard. You or your students can also write on any image or document and file it on your computer or share it live with any group.

- You can ask and receive questions in any form (audio, video, or text) and have live, simultaneous, or threaded discussions with the whole or any subgroup.

- You can have students work or talk simultaneously in small groups of any size and then share their work with the entire class. You can also eavesdrop on any student group.

- You can poll your students and share or hide the results of any questions.

- Virtual seminars also create multiple new learning opportunities.

Guest Speakers

The costs of a guest speaker have just been drastically reduced. If you want your students to get another perspective from someone who lives in another city or country, you don't need your guest to travel. You can talk to an eyewitness of a recent world event or opposing sides of a conflict. Your class on the Holocaust can now talk firsthand to a survivor, regardless of where your campus is. You can also ask Professor Smith, who teaches on the coast, if she will substitute for you when you are in the hospital or on a topic she knows better than you.

Classes During Faculty Travel

Most universities are working on a contingency plan for H1N1 that involves faculty working from home, but the virtual seminar is also an option if you need to present a paper at a distant conference. You can bring your laptop and meet with your students during the regular class period or can leave a podcast for the week you are traveling.

Visiting Faculty

The pool of adjunct or visiting faculty just became worldwide and cheap. If you need that one advanced course and Professor Jones is on sabbatical, you can still hire an expert from another university or city. The same applies for teaching assistants. Some universities have already outsourced grading to India, but now live tutorials and office hours can also be hired globally.

Team Teaching

If you teach in a small school or the colleague you have always wanted to collaborate with lives across the globe, you can now offer that seminar to your students with one or more virtual professors.

Students Abroad or Summer School

One of the biggest issues in studying abroad is the availability of classes in the major. Now your students can travel and still take that advanced engineering seminar on your campus that they need to graduate.

Cross-University Seminar

Suppose you want to teach a small graduate seminar, but you have only a few students at your home institution who are interested in the subject. Opening up your class to students in Finland and Japan both provides a critical mass to offer the course and adds a global perspective for discussion.

Real-Time Simultaneous Chat

In a physical classroom you can have only a single conversation at once, or if you do buzz groups you are limited to one group at a time. But in a virtual classroom, you can have dozens of conversations, even on different topics, going on at once and can quickly scan the texts and jump among them.

Global Discussion

Imagine teaching introduction to ethics in collaboration with professors in Denmark and Australia. Suppose the three professors taught each others' classes once a month. Think about how it would change the discussion to have your students talking to the foreign students instead of their usual classmates. You could use live video conferences, but even just sharing some asynchronous chat or a discussion board, it is much easier than ever before to get a diverse mix of student-to-student discussion.

Interactive Real-Time Virtual Tour

You have a former student who now works at the Large Hadron Collider or the Louvre. Perhaps they can give you a tour and take questions live from students.

While teachers may not yet be comfortable meeting online, students already feel right at home there. Students' new understanding of social proximity therefore creates opportunities and problems in tandem. Our students now live online in many ways, and while we can now use our LMS to prevent cheating or check if students actually accessed a reading, do we really want to use our network control to determine where they are or what photos they have posted on Facebook? Students are already e-mailing anyone, especially professors or deans, from their desks, and soon they will be just as comfortable requesting a video conference from their phones. The new access is good for interaction and learning but is also more work for faculty. Social networks and e-communication will extend learning, but we will need to consider carefully how to create and perhaps teach new social boundaries.

It will be fun to teach in your socks the first day, but the real reason to offer virtual seminars is that you can offer classes, material, faculty, experiences, and a mixture of students that you otherwise could not. The real revolution will come from redesigning courses to take advantage of technology that offers exponentially more resources. Your students can now literally travel to the most remote jungles and deserts. They can talk to Palestinians one day and Israelis the next. They can have daily practice in a language that no one in your state speaks. They can work collaboratively with students in New Zealand and Nigeria. They can help design a new anything anywhere and talk every day to the people building it. All of this has the potential to improve learning but also to change the structure of higher education.

Economic and Curricular Implications

If schools are going to invest in new technology, we must do more than just increase convenience. Most colleges (and I suspect many corporations) use e-communication tools only for talking and meetings. While most universities are thinking about how technology might bridge the gap during a pandemic, few are taking advantage of the real educational possibilities and considering their economic and curricular implications.

Faculty will need to adjust both the content and social mechanisms of courses. E-communication (whether it is Twitter, Facebook, or Skype) can increase the frequency of faculty–student interaction; more contact is not automatically better contact, but the potential for increased reinforcement and application is there. More contact is more work, however. At the same time, the need for faculty to be a content provider is diminishing. As faculty become less oracle and more curator (see Chapter Ten), the workload will shift. Design of courses and the mechanisms of communication will be more important. Further, the availability of content discussed in Chapter One means not just that there will be a global marketplace for lectures but also that as knowledge proliferates, the need for analysis and critical thinking will only increase. The talking head is dead, but the need for thought and reflection will only increase.

As technologies create new types of virtual classrooms and new ways for students to work and play together, new definitions of social proximity will change the norms of human interaction. Even something as individual and interactive as a music lesson can now be given and taken anywhere on Earth. Hundreds of music lesson websites give you a wide choice of options from a live teacher (via Skype), interactive software, free video, or a combination. The new employment world accepts these new forms of communication, and millions of employees already telecommute, but what will be the new normal in the classroom?

The virtual classroom completely changes the market for adjuncts. In the same way that call centers can now be located anywhere, professors and students can now connect from anywhere. I recently interviewed a candidate for a job whose resume said she had taught at a university in Chicago for three years, so I asked how she liked Chicago. She had never set foot in Chicago: "I live in Moscow, Russia, and do everything online," she told me.

As for everyone else with a microspecialty, the Internet allows access to a much wider market (Anderson, 2006). If a small department or school wants to offer a course or even a major in an obscure area, it can pool resources with institutions anywhere. Individual students no longer have to be limited by the course offerings at their physical location. If your school does not offer a course in contemporary Mexican painting, either you can hire an adjunct to teach a course for you remotely or your student can enroll in a course in Mexico. It will be easier for schools to collaborate and also for schools to compete.

The rising price of gas in summer 2007 helped increase online enrollment, but substituting online classes for physical ones is a lost opportunity. Campuses were designed for a social education as well as an academic one, and most students and researchers agree that students learn more outside of classrooms than in them. So we will need to think holistically about virtual campuses and begin to design a learning environment that deals with the changes in society that new communication technology has wrought.

The power of proximity remains. Given the extra expense, however, we will need to think carefully about how to use and articulate the advantages of physical classrooms and especially how to design courses that use those advantages. The physical classroom can become a crucible of contemplation and critical thinking, but only if we do not clutter it up with too much delivery of content, too many announcements, and poor uses of technology. We engage and provoke students best face-to-face if we focus on human interaction. The best courses will make the best use of both social and physical proximity

If teaching is largely about faculty–student interaction, then we have to recognize that human interaction is changing. Our interactions with students (and with each other) are now all hybrid. (Should I send a text to my roommate who left the door open or wait until I see her?) We will need an equally hybrid strategy for creating courses that leverage the best of each world. Higher education is hardly alone in this; we have all bad experiences with automated (so-called) customer service on the phone but probably also with people who would not, or could not, help us. There are times when we want a better website and times when we want to talk to a real person. Getting the balance of humanity and technology right is everyone's new mission, but we often want both and we want it now. This drive for both simultaneous and customized information may be a defining characteristic of human expectation in the next century; its implications for higher education are the subject of the next chapter.

3

Games, Customization, and Learning

Technology has changed education by increasing the availability of knowledge and opportunities for communication and interaction. Another new technology has changed the way students learn: computer and video games are now our most common teacher. The average American 21-year-old has played 10,000 hours of games, about as many hours as they would have spent in perfect attendance from fifth grade through high school (McGonigal, 2010; Prensky, 2010)—more than enough hours to become a concert musician (Ericsson, Krampe, & Tesch-Römer, 1993) and Malcolm Gladwell's (2008) magic number of practice hours for success. Five million Americans spend more than 40 hours a week playing games (McGonigal, 2010, 2011). At the same time as authored encyclopedias were becoming crowd-sourced Wikipedia, games were changing focus from acquiring rote skills to forming relationships, and Google was customizing knowledge, a parallel paradigm shift from teaching to learning was happening in education (Barr & Tagg, 1995). Higher education has shifted its focus from the professor to the student and from knowledge given to knowledge created. As learning has become more interactive, gaming has become the ubiquitous model for understanding and delivering interactive learning.

Games were always a part of childhood and have always been used to teach, but two changes in games are profound. Computer and video games have displaced other forms of imagination, including pretend play with nonresponsive objects, books, and even films, video, and television. Portable electronic devices (including cell phones, iPods, laptops, DVD players, and portable game platforms) allow users control over their personal space and reduce the time available for imagination, distraction, or inter-action. We can bemoan these changes, but they have happened. Just as most faculty would not want to give up our cell phones or laptops, students will find learning without control or connection to electronic stimulation to be a new and frustrating experience.

Although we may not think of video games as a learning activity, they are designed to be learned, and without recourse to any manual or textbook. If a game can't be learned, it fails in the marketplace. So while the purpose of the video game business might be profit rather than learning, the ability to be learned at different speeds by a vast population of users with a wide array of learning preferences and abilities is critical to a game's success. Unintentionally, the video game industry was forced into creat-ing the best electronic teaching tools available. Games are ideal teachers, in part because they address different learning styles in sophisticated ways. Video games adapt instantly to the player; they learn about how we learn as we learn. We may not like the content of some popular video games, but they have taught an entire generation. Few teachers can respond instantly to the plethora of backgrounds, learning habits, and styles in a typical classroom, but digital tools can. Students now arrive in college accustomed to this level and speed of adaptation. Increasingly, we expect customization in the rest of our lives as well: we want intuitive controls on our microwave and a car that learns how we drive. Customization and gaming are changing the human condi-tion and will change education too.

Customization

Customization begins with choice, and recent generations of American consumers have seen an incredible growth in choice. From books to bread to cars to clothes, the choices of formats, grains, styles, sizes, and a multitude of options have exploded.

If a store is out of a color, we rarely settle anymore: we simply check online and get exactly what we want. Despite the tens of millions of iPods and iPhones sold, it seems as if each has a unique cover.

The Web offers another exponential increase in customization. It is not enough that we can select a background photo or a home page; we can customize exactly how our environment works. Think of the difference between having the local newspaper delivered—with whatever content in whatever font the editor decided upon—and customizing your iPad to combine the finance section of one paper with the sports from another plus analysis from your favorite blogger, all in whatever format you want. My phone knows which movie theaters I like and how I like my coffee. While the loss of privacy seems threatening and often creepy, most of us enjoy recommendations of books from Amazon, movies from Netflix, and even the way Facebook prioritizes the newsfeeds from the friends we most actively follow.

Pandora (an internet radio site that boasts of over 50 million users) will teach you things about yourself you may not want to know. Pandora plays songs it thinks you will like based upon any information you provide—as little as one artist or one song—and then learns what you like as it feeds you a series of new material. You can train Pandora to deliver as little or as much variety as you like. If you want to listen only to the Eagles all day long, it will let you, but the magic happens when you allow Pandora to play something other than the Eagles that an Eagles fan might enjoy: perhaps a long forgotten song by an artist you once knew or a brand-new recording in the style of the Eagles. It is truly like having a personal DJ who cares only about learning your personal tastes and desires and will never, even decades from now, forget a preference as it simultaneously watches your tastes change.

Along with new opportunities, customization creates paradoxes. If Amazon.com knows who you are the instant you enter their site, why would they force you to follow a generic path past the best sellers, when they can pave your way with books on topics they know you like? Loading up your iPod with the podcasts of your favorite radio shows is convenient, but you may miss stimulating accidental discoveries. The same argument surfaces when libraries talk about moving books to storage, eliminating opportunities for casual browsing. Future research will need to ask if structured databases, keyword searches, library geography, or dumb luck are more useful to human intellectual exploration.

Customization and Education

While most of us enjoy creating a unique drink at Starbuck's, we chafe at students who want faculty to be as customizable as ringtones on a phone: the demand for customer service can be tremendously annoying in the classroom. Think, though, about the possible benefits for learning. While it used to be the case that people were flexible and technologies were rigid ("select one for billing and two for technical support"), new technologies are becoming far more flexible than most people ("select one for English and two for Spanish"). Teachers have been asked for years to connect with the different auditory, visual, and kinesthetic learners in our classroom, but they are rarely able to do it well (Kolb & Kolb, 2005; Lachenmayer, 1997). Only through technology can such customization be done simultaneously for more than one student. Instead of a bilingual teacher who speaks two languages (neither of which the child may speak), a computer program can read in multiple languages to thousands of children at once. For example, Academic OneFile, one of the large online journal services, now provides instant translations of journal articles into a dozen languages. While the translations may not be perfect, surely the academic community will benefit from the ability to share more research more easily.

Technology presents teachers not only with more content than ever before but also more routes into that content. Although most efforts at customization have focused on assessment at the end of the learning process (largely accommodation for learning disabilities with extra exam time), the most important moment for customization actually occurs before class. At present in higher education, most first exposure to content happens during class, and the material is therefore presented in only one way at a time. Assigning a reading before class (if students do the reading) increases time spent on learning, but it substitutes one modality for another. Reading followed by lecture is a useful way to teach reading and note taking, but it may not be the best way to introduce content. Even if reading followed by lecture were the best way to reach the most students, it would still be teaching only the students whose learning preferences favor reading and listening. With technology, we can do more to ensure that all students can find a way into the material. The number of billionaire dyslexics tells us there may be multiple paths to financial success; however, it will probably remain the case that the ability to read well and quickly will remain the most important asset in college. If improving students' ability to read is a declared learning objective, then other strategies truly aimed at improving reading can be employed.

We can almost certainly improve learning by offering more choices for preclass first exposure. If the point is to introduce material or learn content, then offering students a choice of preclass reading, an audio podcast, a video podcast, or an activity will improve their preparation for class. In a recent Educause poll, "Listening to audio or watching video content" topped the list of how students like to use technology to learn ("Information technology on campuses," 2011). Giving students choices for first exposure seems an easy way to use customization technology that can improve learning. Chapter Five offers a range of preclass preparation techniques.

In a fascinating test of the possibilities for customization in education, the New York City Department of Education began an experiment in 2009 at I.S. 339, a middle school in the South Bronx. In the School of One, each unit of content is presented in a variety of learning modalities: large group live instruction, small group live instruction, self-paced podcasts, individual prac- tice, collaborative activity, virtual activities, individual virtual tutor, or group virtual instruction. Instead of a single teacher using one modality at once for 25–30 students, School of One uses technology to offer multiple modalities at once, custom- ized for each student. If it takes a student five or six exposures in a collaborative setting to grasp a concept but the same stu- dent exhibits mastery after one podcast, then the school switches the first exposure modality for this student. In higher educa- tion, individual teachers also customize learning opportunities, albeit on a small scale. I routinely offer my students a choice of textbooks and let them know that one is more analytical or another has more charts and pictures and that they should read the one that holds the most interest for them. In the School of One, however, the rapid (technological) return of data allows for detailed monitoring: each student receives a new schedule (a playlist) each day. Teachers pay as much attention to how students are learning (what School of One calls the *learning algorithm*) as to what they are learning, so they can adapt their lessons almost instantly.

Such customization is long overdue in the classroom. School of One is an early experiment, and the only results (while promis- ing) are those in news reports and media stories (Dubner, 2010). We know that boys and girls often learn differently and that boys tend to be more competitive and girls more collaborative (Belenky, Clinchy, Goldberger, & Tarule, 1986; Kulturel-Konak, D'Allegro, & Dickinson, 2011). Experience matters: girls (unless they play baseball) have a hard time understanding physics when male teachers talk about torque using baseball bats as an example. We assign boys and girls different summer readings. What is stop- ping us from going further?

The one-room schoolhouse with one teacher and 25 students was based on practical need, not pedagogical theory. But teachers today still tend to teach to the middle. We love our best students, but we know that we have an obligation to help all of our students learn. We can offer individualized instruction some of the time, but even in a small class we are really using a mass production model: what teaching modality will reach the most students?

New technologies of customization, therefore, will give students more choices. If one explanation does not work, there are many others to try. Students who prefer a chart can use that while others can memorize songs or listen to a lecture. Students are likely to know, or learn, their own preferences, but experiments like School of One will tell us if indeed learning can be improved by monitoring and catering to learning styles. On the flip side, we are creatures of habit, and it might be better to change the modality from time to time. Few people change news sources once they find one with which they agree, but exposure to different perspectives might be a good thing. In any case, the technology will not force us to choose.

Implementation: Foreign Languages

Language teaching is highly specialized and requires knowledge of the specific language; few German language teachers can also teach Welsh. Students at all schools, therefore, are limited by the languages that school offers. The Internet can teach you any language you want to learn. Rosetta Stone offers 28 languages in its home school program, and surely no high school can compete with that number of choices.

Language learning also requires a wide variety of skills and, as such, highlights individual differences in learning. Some learners grasp grammar easily but struggle with accents, whereas others can read but cannot remember vocabulary while speaking. This has led to an abundance of pedagogical approaches, but none can meet the needs of all learners simultaneously. Language teachers often pick whatever textbook they think works for most students and then individually tailor the experience as much as possible, with flash cards for one students and more time in the language lab for another.

Virtually all foreign language textbooks now come with some digital or online component. Students can now use digital workbooks or flash cards, listen to native speakers, drill endlessly, or record dialogues online. Digital tools learn students' strengths and weaknesses, remember progress, and have limitless time and patience.

The potential for virtual language instruction is equally obvious: why be pen pals when you can have a daily conversation? The website www.mylanguageexchange.com has over one million members in 133 countries practicing 115 languages and will pair you with a native speaker who is learning your language. American universities can't seem to find enough Arabic or Mandarin teachers to meet the demand, and many small or remote colleges have neither the faculty nor the student numbers to offer more than a handful of traditional languages. Think virtual teachers, and the problem is solved—and cheaply. The site www.fluentfuture.com offers the choice of free exchanges, paid individual lessons with rated teachers, or online courses. If you have two students who want to learn Vietnamese or one student who needs Finnish to read articles for a thesis, there is a teacher somewhere available for the job, now in cyberspace.

Beyond daily conversational practice and teaching obscure languages, the Internet gives students a chance to speak with people with different regional accents or from different social classes. Why stop at conversing on a flat screen? New mobile video conferencing tools open up new possibilities: take your Spanish class to a party in Chile, a bullfight in Spain, or a soccer match in Mexico.

Customizing Learning with Games

Video game designers want to create products that people will buy and enjoy, and players want games that are easy to learn but not easy to play. Good video games are challenging, long, hard, and complicated, and they engage the player in active learning. In fact, good video games do everything that we want from a good learning environment: they may even inspire optimism about how human action can change the world (McGonigal, 2011). Games are really just an endless series of tests, a constant stream of problem solving and assessment. Future educators will need to understand how games take the part of school that most students dislike the most and make it fun. Gee (2003, 2004, 2005a, 2005b) describes the qualities of good games and the learning principles that make them such good teachers, and they are outlined in the following subsections.

- *Customization.* Good games allow lots of different types of learners to play. Good games not only have different levels of difficulty but also allow different ways to solve problems. In role-playing games, players can even experiment with different talents and characteristics.

- *Risk-Taking.* Good games lower the consequences of failure and encourage risk-taking. Failures can immediately be used against a new challenge.

- *Performance Before Competence.* As in language acquisition, a good game allows players to create, control, and perform before they have complete competence. A good game needs no instruction manual (think textbook).

- *Pleasant Frustration.* The sweet spot for engaged learning is providing students with a surmountable challenge. In school, students are often forced to endure lessons that are either too hard or too easy. In contrast, a game that fails in either aspect will fail in the marketplace.

- *Interaction.* Even Plato (in *Phaedrus*) complained that books are passive and cannot talk back. Games provide a constant stream of feedback and reaction.

- *Agency and Identity.* Learners want to see value in what they are doing and feel a sense of control. A good game gives players an identity and a stake in the outcome.

- *Challenge and Consolidation.* Games offer the player a limited set of pleasantly frustrating challenges and offer infinite time for consolidation before changing the problem just enough to force players to reexamine their recent mastery. Learners are forced in games to explore thoroughly before moving on, thus encouraging mastery and expertise.

- *Situated Meanings.* School is often full of definitions, words defined by other words. But students learn better in context, and games are all about the relationships between words, images, and actions.

- *Just in Time or On Demand.* Textbooks are inefficient largely because the student gets too many words at once. Games aim to deliver words, new concepts, and information exactly when the player needs them and can immediately apply them.

Gee (2003, 2005a) also points out how games often focus on many of the skills that global employers most want in the 21st century:

- *Systems Thinking.* Games require learners to think about relationships and how each action or acquired skill affects future events and the other players in the game. Games require the application of what you have learned. Unlike in school, isolated facts are rarely useful.

- *Sequential Problem Solving.* Games are a series of problems to solve. Like a good curriculum, the sequence of problems (levels) is critical. Games that encourage creative and multiple solutions tend to be more fun but are also better training for future employees.

- *Lateral Thinking*. Creativity and mastery require rethinking goals periodically, and games encourage this constant reassessment of aims. Game outsiders may see only the external goals (points or levels), but if games were only linear they would not be fun. Exploration is an integral part of the enjoyment.

- *Distributed Knowledge*. In many games, the characters have skills and abilities that the player does not, but the player also knows and can do things the character cannot. Thus, knowledge is distributed. In multiplayer games, knowledge is distributed even more widely. The ability to create teams that are smarter than any individual is a key skill not generally taught in school.

- *Cross-Functional Teams*. In multiplayer games, the abilities, cultural backgrounds, ethnicities, class, gender, and specializations of the players and characters are often highly diverse. Teams are affiliated only by their desire for a common goal. Using these shared resources for a common goal is another highly valued global skill.

- *Production*. Learners do not want to be just consumers. They want to write and create their own worlds. Many games allow players to modify and create new environments for the game itself.

It is a common mistake to disparage video games simply because of *what* they teach. Even the worst general wants to learn from his enemies. If you believe that games are responsible for increased violence in teenagers (a finding not supported by the most recent academic studies; see, e.g., Kierkegaard, 2008), that would be more evidence that games do, in fact, teach.

Gee (2004) is emphatic that games teach more than how to play the game in the same way that learning biology is more than just learning its facts. As Mazur (1996) discovered in his physics courses at Harvard, students can learn a lot of facts and still be completely unable to apply them to solve new problems. When you learn physics, you learn to play physics. You learn rules, relationships, variables, disciplinary assumptions, and thought patterns. Distribution requirements for liberal arts degrees are designed not so much to give students a sampler of content but rather to introduce students to different disciplinary thought patterns. Like games, our disciplines come with rules, often unstated. Learning to become a physicist involves more than just the acquisition of lots of facts about small particles.

It is vital that educators understand video games more fully. Even if we disagree with the content and the method, we have an obligation to meet our students and parents where they are: 68% of parents believe game play provides mental stimulation or education, and 45% of parents play with their children weekly (ESA, 2011). Like it or not, the gaming industry is growing and the number of high school graduates is declining. The video game industry continues to expand into all ages and is no longer an activity just for boys or teenagers (Fahey, 2008). The Entertainment Software Industry estimates that women over the age of 18 represent a much larger share of the playing population (33%) than boys 17 or younger (20%; ESA, 2010); 99% of teenage boys and 94% of teenage girls play regularly (McGonigal, 2011). While students at our most elite universities have discovered the rules of success in school, even they often think games are fun and school is boring. They have been learning from games their entire lives, and increasingly they want school to be just as engaging.

Customizing Information with Apps

The Internet is huge and offers us everything, but everything is more than we need most days. Phone applications are little slices of the Internet. Higher education can learn something from the fact that people will pay for little slices even though the entire pie—the whole of human knowledge on the Internet— is available for free. An app is a refined and limited amount of information; it offers *less* than the Internet does but in a *customized* form. This should have been predictable: in an age where information is abundant, quality and specificity of information have become increasingly important.

American Airlines, for example, offers an app that does only some of what I can do on its website, but in a format that gives me only the information I need and quickly. I do not want to know how many flights will be late today; I want to know only if my flight is delayed. My phone app knows who I am because it is on my phone, so when I touch the app icon it instantly and automatically shows me information only about my next flight.

If you have a Web-enabled phone, the app duplicates the functions you already have through your Web browser, but it is optimized for your phone and easier to use. The same is true for the many apps that deliver movie information, previews, and screening times and now also allow you to buy a scannable e-ticket on your phone. News, weather, traffic, sports, realty, stock, and radio apps are also just Internet content delivered in a simplified form to your phone or iPad.

Some apps make use of phone technology, so Barnes & Noble allows you to use your phone camera to take a picture of a book cover, and the app automatically finds the nearest place to purchase it. The Chase Bank phone app is a streamlined version of its online banking website, except that it also allows deposits to be made using photos of a check you make on your phone—you never have to send the physical check to the bank. A traffic app is slightly faster on your iPhone than on a computer, since the phone can use your GPS to find your location yet on a computer you have to tell the map where you are.

Museum and library apps for the Louvre, the New York Museum of Modern Art, and the Library of Congress all duplicate content that is on their websites, but they limit what you can see to what might be useful while you are physically in the museum or on your way. Some apps are beginning to make better use of

GPS, and soon *place* will become a part of social media functions. Louvre patrons, for example, will be able to leave observations about the Mona Lisa that are accessible only from a particular angle near the Mona Lisa.

Technology is taking us in two directions at once. The explosion of information has created a wealth of primary data that is a wonderful resource for learning activities. But the trend toward less quantity and more customized information increases the importance of authority (who is doing the customization), and it also provides an opportunity to rethink the relationship between content and thinking in our educational models. Students who can categorize and analyze will be in ever more demand in a world where knowledge is instantly available. We have always wanted students to learn to apply knowledge; however, the balance between content and application has shifted, and we need to adjust both how and what we teach.

Apps are by nature a compromise between unlimited and targeted information, and they may also be a fundamental metaphor for how education needs to change. The Internet can do more, but apps have proven popular and useful precisely because they limit what you can do at one time. This is an important lesson for faculty: when do students need less? Giving students content in smaller chunks and getting them to apply it before more content is provided is how both good education and good apps work. We judge apps not by how much content they deliver but by how useful they are at solving our immediate problems: we should judge teaching not on how much content it delivers but on how useful it is in advancing the capabilities of our students.

Customizing Education with Games and Apps

Many faculty have a favorite memory from elementary school. Perhaps you made the model volcano, won a spelling bee, or watched a chick hatch from an egg. College students today, however, are more likely to remember playing *Oregon Trail*, the immensely popular education game in which a player guided a party of Conestoga wagons in 1848 from Independence, Missouri, to the Willamette Valley in Oregon. Originally developed in 1971 and widely released in 1978, it sold 65 million copies, one for every four to five Americans, and most people played it in school and never even bought a copy.

Although educational gaming has become big business, many games are now online and even free and increasingly designed for college content. Games teach everything from the geologic processes that formed the moon (*Selene*, free from Wheeling Jesuit University's Center for Educational Technologies, http://selene. cet.edu/) to empathy in the banking bailout of 2009 (*Layoff*, free from Tiltfactor Lab and the Rochester Institute of Technology Game Design and Development program (www.tiltfactor.org/play-layoff). There are games for social change (www.gamesforchange .com) and games to teach people about the discoveries of Nobel Prize winners (www.nobelprize.org). The game *Nephrotex* is part design course, part apprenticeship: undergraduates role-play engineers in a fictitious company to design a next-generation dialyzer that incorporates carbon nanotubes and chemical surfactants into the hollow fibers of the dialyzer unit (www.Epistemicgames.org).

Games offer limitless possibilities for customization. The Tiltfactor Center at Dartmouth (www.tiltfactor.org), supported in part by the National Endowment for the Humanities, Microsoft Research, and the National Science Foundation, develops games for health, social issues, and educational initiatives and has created one to help middle school girls learn math. The market has been branching out from K–12 learning, and the Serious Play Conference in 2011 included tracks for games in health and medicine, business and corporate training, consumer games, social good, government and military, and learning.

Games teach professional skills that cannot be taught in other ways (like flight simulations of crash situations). *Air Medic*

Sky 1 (www.airmedicsky1.org), designed by University Medical Center Utrecht in The Netherlands, is a patient safety game in which doctors learn how to control their own physiological stress responses to avoid patient harm. Players (doctors) wear sensors on their fingers that monitor their heart rate and skin conductance. Players use biofeedback from the sensors to manage their stress levels while navigating complex patient situations. This game provides a safe way for doctors to learn how to apply their knowledge and practice decision making under extreme pressure.

A number of academic centers produce free games. *Virulent*, the first game from the Morgridge Institutes for Research at the University of Wisconsin–Madison allows players to experience how a cell is infected and how the infection is replicated and escapes to other cells (www.discovery.wisc.edu). The Education Arcade (www.educationarcade.org/) is home to the popular multiplayer game *Revolution*, which puts players into historical events in Williamsburg on the eve of the American Revolution. Designed to be played in a 45-minute classroom session in a networked environment, students role-play from one of seven social perspectives, from an upper-class lawyer to an African American house slave. The game responds to player choices, so actions have consequences. You can find more free games at Education Games Research (www.edugamesresearch.com), Emerging Ed Tech (www.emergingedtech.com/), and Teaching Naked (www.TeachingNaked.com).

The intrinsic motivation in games is already being used to alter our behavior in many other areas. Games are full of small reward systems, and the collection of these points or bonuses is now a common business practice. We collect rewards or points for using credit cards, buying groceries, or staying at hotels. The dashboard of the new Ford Fusion and Lincoln MKX hybrids includes a leaf-and-vine EcoGuide, but it is really a game: gently accelerate, and the leaf grows and blooms. In the hugely popular Facebook game *FarmVille*, the points matter only in the game, but tens of millions of people still spend real money to buy virtual money. (The U.S. market for virtual goods in games reached $1.2 billion in 2011, with half of that coming from Facebook games; Hudson & Smith, 2011.) Points and games change behavior. Jessie Schell (2010) imagines a future where we will get points for almost everything: our toothbrush will know if we brush our teeth for three minutes and award us points, with bonus points if we brush five days in a row.

Many faculty award points in class, but Lee Sheldon (2010; 2011) designed his entire course on multiplayer game design in the nomenclature of a game:

> This class is designed as a multiplayer game. Class time will be divided between fighting monsters (Quizzes, Exams etc.), completing quests (Presentations of Games, Research etc.) and crafting (Personal Game Premises, Game Analysis Papers, Video Game Concept Document etc.). . . .Your level will be determined by experience points (XP) on a 2000 XP scale. You gain XP by defeating mobs, completing quests and crafting.
>
> Solo: Craft your own game proposal. (Written, 50 pts.)
>
> Solo: Present your game proposal to the class. (25 pts.)
>
> Solo: Sell your game proposal to the class. (Extra credit. 25 pts.)
>
> Raid: Guild reading presentation (75 pts. each person, 1 of these per guild)
>
> Pick-Up Group: 2-Player reading presentation (150 pts. each person, cannot team with fellow guild member) OR
>
> Solo: 1-Player reading presentation (150 pts. but easier than above)

> Solo: Craft 3 page report on MMO article (Written, 75 pts.)
>
> Solo: Craft 3 page analysis of MMO-based research topic (Written, 100 pts.)
>
> Solo: Craft 5 page analysis on MMO of your choice (Written, 125 pts.)
>
> Solo: Defeat Five Random Mobs (5 written reading quizzes, 250 pts. total, 1 extra credit question per quiz)
>
> Solo: Defeat Level Boss (Midterm Exam, 400 pts.)
>
> Guild: Paper Prototype Presentation (50 pts. each) . . .

Terminology is important, although awarding points, using levels instead of grades, and even forming groups of complementary talents are techniques that many faculty already use. Sheldon (the game master) has gone further by giving students more choices about when and which quests (i.e., assignments) to face and making the playspace (i.e., classroom) more collaborative, with students creating presentations and activities for each other (Sheldon, 2011).

A further experiment at Louisiana State University used gaming nomenclature in two (mostly female) introduction to education classes in a hybrid format that met face-to-face once a week and then in an asynchronous Moodle discussion site instead of the second class session. While not all of the nomenclature was familiar to students or successful in this subject, students did report that they put more work into assignments and that they seemed less like work when they were called *quests*. The use of avatars (a character or representation of the user, or simply a screen name) also produced more productive and honest discussion (Broussard, 2011). Avatars might be more generally applicable: we all adopt a teaching personality or a persona, and sometimes in class we play devil's advocate. We know that we can't reach all students from the same perspective: Black students might not trust a White professor, or a woman might think a man can't know certain content. An avatar could extend possibilities.

Game design is also being used to solve complicated problems in a fraction of the time anticipated. On December 5, 2009, the U.S. Department of Defense Advanced Research Projects Agency (DARPA) offered $40,000 to the first team that could identify, using social networking, the locations of 10 red weather balloons spread around the United States. A total of 4,000 teams signed up, and the Pentagon allowed nine days for the treasure hunt. A team from MIT used small financial incentives to complete the task in nine hours (www.networkchallenge.darpa.mil). University of Washington AIDS researchers announced a breakthrough in the journal *Nature: Structural & Molecular Biology* with the help of an online game: after a decade of trying to solve the crystal structure of M-PMV retroviral protease by molecular replacement, biochemists challenged players of the protein folding game *Foldit* (www.fold.it), who solved the problem in days (Khatib et al., 2011) even though few of the players had any kind of background in biochemistry.

Games and gaming concepts are entering higher education. The Web is full of higher education learning modules, many of which would be even more valuable as games or apps. Some, like *Virulent*, are already available for iPads and Android tablets. (Developing new games and finding specific new games is covered in Chapter Seven.) But faculty should start by asking, first, "What pedagogy do I want students to have on the go?" And second, "Does my phone offer some technology that I might use? Could I use my camera to take photos of rock formations, maintenance problems, or other material I might gather in the field? Could I record accents or airplane noise? With GPS, could students test the accuracy of maps? What about sending students to a museum with an iPad so they could compare the experience with those at other museums using the Google Art Project virtual museum tours?"

In a classroom situation, apps can be very useful in limiting the range of content. Students with a Web browser open can do almost anything (including stay connected to Facebook), which can be distracting. However, a class set of iPads can keep students engaged but also focused on the specific app that is available. Instead of asking students to search for ancient maps, cell structures, or Beethoven sketchbooks, you can create an app that has only the information you want students to access. Since learning, like gaming, usually works best when beginners start with simpler scenarios and move to more complex ones, games or apps are an excellent way to introduce a student to an area of internet content in a structured way and then gradually increase that information or change the situation. For example, Level 1 might limit searches to academic journals, .edu sites, or professional journalism before Level 2 allows students to see bloggers.

Another advantage of an app is that it is with you when you are waiting in line at the grocery store or sitting in the stands at a football game. We might want our students to come to the language lab and practice their French with no distractions, but if the app is with them they will do it more often. If the app is interactive and uses sound and video, they might do it more often still. Apps can also exchange data with a learning management system, so music students could practice identifying composers or genres all night long and in the morning see extra points show up in the online course grade book.

We often complain that our students are distracted by all of the electronic communication that bombards them, but they are rarely distracted from a good game. Games hold our attention because they offer a chance to gain competence, autonomy, and connectedness to others (Rigby & Ryan, 2011), plus they are fun. If we can design games and apps that create the same possibility of expression, excitement, challenge, discovery, fun, success, and progress, then students will want to use them (Schell, 2010). It is a habit: students reach for the phone when they get bored, but often what they start to do is not very interesting. If your app is even slightly more interesting than feeding their *FarmVille* pigs, and perhaps also a little more useful for them, then students will use it instead.

We are only beginning to see the ways virtual environments, games, phone apps, and customized technology can improve higher education. The for-profit education sector is outspending nonprofit higher education by three to one in technology (Waters, 2011) and will soon have a serious technological advantage. Although for-profit higher education has made mistakes, it has outpaced traditional higher education in responsiveness to student demands for flexibility and technology. For-profit rapid growth will continue if the rest of higher education does not realize the importance of customization for its future.

Video games offer one final lesson for higher education. We know that video games are pleasantly frustrating in part because they offer a graduated series of challenges customized for each user. Similarly, college should provide a customized but structured path through progressively more challenging learning. In theory, traditional four-year colleges should do this well but often do not. If American education remains completely modular and students simply collect the right types of content and credit to graduate, then predictions about the increased number of part-time students taking courses at a number of different universities will surely come true (Van Der Werf & Sabatier, 2009). In this scenario, taking a series of high-quality online courses from important professors at major universities might be an improvement over choosing random courses out of the university catalog with the help of an overworked adviser. If the levels of college courses do not really relate to increasing challenges, as they do in a video game, then all the fraternity parties and recreation centers in the world will not be enough to justify the $200,000 cost of a campus education. So the next chapter focuses on the macro issues at the heart of higher education: creating progressively challenging low-stakes learning opportunities. In other words, we need to make college more like a video game.

Part II

Designing 21st-Century Courses

4

Designing College More Like a Video Game

Learning requires change. Complex learning requires a series of changes that build upon previous changes. Video game designers understand that challenge alone is not enough and that it must be combined with practice and the motivation that results from steady progress. Start almost any activity (yoga, cooking, reading, or even a game) at too high a level, and you will soon become frustrated and lose interest. If we want our units of content and our courses to add up to significant change in our students, then we need to think not only about the progression of individual courses through a semester, or even the progression of a major course of study, but also about a four-year curricular progression as a long, engaging, and increasingly challenging game.

If college were designed like a video game, everything in the environment would be designed to promote change (i.e., learning). The student–player would be pleasantly frustrated by constant attempts to integrate increasingly foreign and complex ideas into their mental map. Mastery of each level, topic, or course would be required before moving on, but failure would be utterly inconsequential, with infinite opportunities to start over. An intermediate player–student would have learned how to reflect on two opposing ideas at once, and the highest levels could be reached only when a player–student was able to abandon a previously held belief in the face of new evidence. The progression through levels would reflect the consensus of research about the developmental capabilities of adolescents to maximize learning and engagement.

Part Two of this book is about how to integrate technology into course design, but in this chapter I put technology aside. Like designing games, designing better courses starts with designing a structure that motivates and enables learning. Technology can increase the possibilities for these experiences, but only if it is thoughtfully placed into a larger context. This context needs to be courses designed with outcomes, activities, and feedback that take account of the large body of research about why and how college students learn. This chapter examines key research findings about brain development and learning and asks how we might apply them to designing courses. Chapters Five, Six, and Seven demonstrate how technology can amplify each area by delivering content, enhancing engagement, and providing feedback. Chapter Eight then considers how we might rethink class time if our students arrived prepared and motivated.

Brain Development

Few of us would assume that simply watching other people cut hair, do surgery, write a book, or play football would qualify us to do the same, but we assume that you can become a good college teacher just by watching other people do it. Rather than seeking out the existing research, most of us base our teaching methods on the discipline-specific models we observed as students. We make assumptions about what techniques are appropriate or effective based only upon our own experience with science courses, which had labs, and political science courses, which did not. However, there is extensive research into how young adults learn and how they develop as well as how we as professors can have the long-term impact we desire.

Recent studies of the brain have come to important conclusions that inform design of learning experiences. Zull (2004) summarizes how the basic conceptual model of the brain as fixed has been completely replaced over several decades by new evidence that the architecture of the brain is flexible and is constantly shaped by experience, even before birth. The mechanism is simple; use causes neurons to fire:

> If a neuron fires frequently, it grows and extends itself out toward other neurons, much like the branches of bushes in your backyard reach out and touch one another as they grow. Particularly in the cortex, neurons that fire more frequently will also reach out more frequently.
>
> Neurons do more than reach out, though: They actually connect. The branches of our backyard bushes don't do this. Each bush remains independent, even when many branches touch one another. But neurons can actually begin to send signals to one another if the places where they touch can transport those signals.
>
> These signaling connections are the famous synapses. Synapses convert the isolated neurons into a buzzing network of neurons. The bushes begin to talk to one another. In place of individual bushes, we have an entire hedge of neurons sending signals back and forth through millions of synapses. These networks are the physical equivalent of knowledge, and the change in the connections that make up the networks is learning. (p. 69)

Two things cause these networks to form: practice and emotion. When learners practice, the brain grows. This may seem obvious, but only recently did Draganski et al. (2004) demonstrate through magnetic resonance imaging that the part of the brain that controls vision and responses to movement became denser in subjects who learned to juggle. Tellingly, when the subjects stopped juggling, the brain reverted to its prior state, a finding that foreign language teachers could have predicted.

Emotion is equally important, because adrenaline, dopamine, and serotonin modify our neuronal networks (Brembs, Lorenzetti, Reys, Baxter, & Byrne, 2002). Zull (2004) argues that "the thinking part of our brain evolved through entanglement with older parts that we now know are involved in emotion and feelings. . . . We feel our emotions in our body, and the way we feel always influences our brain" (p. 69). Zull cites the work of Damasio (1994), who labels the feelings we have about our pleasure at solving a problem or our frustration at failure as *somatic markers* and concludes that the implications for student motivation are clear: the best and most lasting learning is motivated by emotion and solidified by practice. A lecture can indeed motivate students and stimulate emotion, but it does not give them much practice at forming their own explanations and networks or much control over their progress.

Neurologists have helped us further understand that the brains of college students are not fully grown. The memorization required in high school uses the striatum, but the frontal cortex necessary for higher-order thinking is still increasing in size during college. Specifically, the dorsolateral and ventromedial parts of the frontal lobe that quickly comprehend situations and make judgments do not reach full maturity until we are in our 20s (Reyna & Farley, 2006). Adolescents require about a sixth of a second longer than normal adults to answer no to questions like, "Is it a good idea to set your hair on fire?" (Baird & Fugelsang, 2004). When designing courses (or planning a field trip), it is useful to remember that most of the neurons of judgment that adults take for granted are still growing in college students.

Models of Intellectual Development

Perry's (1999) classic model (originally published in 1970) of how college students develop intellectually predates the confirming brain scans, but he observed many of the same behaviors that

Zull (2004) and others have confirmed with recent brain research. Perry discovered that male Harvard freshmen exhibited dualistic thinking, characterized by the beliefs that ideas are either right or wrong, that the professor's job is to provide facts, and that learning is about taking notes and memorizing for exams. These students resisted drawing their own conclusions and were uncomfortable with disagreement between authorities. Perry showed that students grow into a second stage, multiplicity and subjective knowledge, in which they believe that knowledge is just opinion and that all opinions are equally valid. Students in multiplicity may chafe at the audacity of faculty who do not recognize their right to an alternative perspective. Perry wanted faculty to coax students into *relativism* (a word most academics dropped after the culture wars of the 1980s), in which the evidence upon which conclusions are based makes some conclusions better than others. These students understand that faculty have informed opinions and can teach them how to make their own judgments about different arguments.

Researchers in a wide variety of fields with different approaches have come to similar conclusions about how adolescents develop a more sophisticated relationship with knowledge. Kuhn (1999) labels the three stages as absolutist (completely objective, assertions are facts), multiplist (completely subjective, assertions are opinions), and evaluativist (an integration of the two where assertions are judgments and the better supported position is "more right"). Kuhn applied her analysis to the teaching of critical thinking and noted that development of more sophisticated positions lasts well into adulthood. Belenky, Clinchy, Goldberger, and Tarule (1986), Baxter Magolda (1992), and others investigated gender-related patterns and modified the stages but supported Perry's (1999) basic trajectory. They also emphasized that progress is at best slow and requires more than just a single course (see Erickson, Peters, & Strommer, 2006, for a summary).

Society and states have conflicting views about the exact age of adulthood. However, most of the rights and responsibilities of adulthood (voting, military service, trial as an adult, and even the administration of death penalty) are bestowed immediately at 18 years of age, yet alcohol is reserved for 21-year-olds and three states try 16-year-olds as adults. Developmentally, though, adolescents enter adulthood much more gradually than the law assumes. Arnett (2004) terms the early to late 20s *emerging adulthood*, characterized by identity exploration, instability, focus on self, feeling in transition, and openness to possibilities. College, therefore, is largely about trying to change a growing brain while it still has a lot of growing to do.

Understanding and motivating change are at the core of all learning theories. While there are legions of different models and theories, from cognitive dissonance (Festinger, 1957) and double loop learning (Argyris & Schön, 1974) to social learning (Bandura, 1977), Gestalt theory (Wertheimer, 1923), radical behaviorism (Skinner 1953, 1954), and Piaget's (1970) theory of cognitive development, the differences are largely in the *strategy* they suggest for how to get individuals to change. Festinger argues that when we perceive a discrepancy between our attitudes and behaviors, we attempt to create consistency, usually by changing our beliefs to match our behavior. Argyris and Schön instead propose that learning involves the testing of values in action. The correction of errors requires a double loop where the initial assumptions or *governing variables* are reexamined and changed. Bandura thinks that learning is more social and that change is stimulated by modeling the behavior of others. The consistent theme is that learning requires more than just new facts; it is motivated by forcing students to confront, analyze, and articulate compelling discrepancies that require change in what they believe.

Models for Designing Educational Experiences

Bloom's (1956) taxonomy of educational objectives was designed for higher education, but it is now pervasive in curriculum design—even dog trainers use a version of this structure. Anderson and

Krathwohl (2001, pp. 67–68) revised the taxonomy into the form most widely used today. It classifies cognitive skills into six levels of increasing complexity, and, like a video game, each higher level assumes mastery of all of the previous levels:

- **Remembering**: Retrieving, recognizing, and recalling relevant knowledge from long-term memory
- **Understanding**: Constructing meaning from oral, written, and graphic messages through interpreting, exemplifying, classifying, summarizing, inferring, comparing, and explaining
- **Applying**: Carrying out or using a procedure through executing or implementing
- **Analyzing**: Breaking material into constituent parts and determining how the parts relate to one another and to an overall structure or purpose through differentiating, organizing, and attributing
- **Evaluating**: Making judgments based on criteria and standards through checking and critiquing
- **Creating**: Putting elements together to form a coherent or functional whole; reorganizing elements into a new pattern or structure through generating, planning, or producing

---

Implementation: Developing Learning Outcomes

Bloom's (1956) levels are a common vocabulary in learning outcomes. This taxonomy helps articulate how defining, classifying, critiquing, and composing represent a progression. Most campuses want to develop higher levels of thinking, and Bloom's taxonomy breaks down the process into stages. Students need to learn to identify the parts of a poem before they learn to evaluate how they fit together.

If faculty do nothing else, they should take the time to consider seriously what students will be able to do by the end of every course because this will improve learning. Clear learning outcomes contain verbs that correspond to each level:

Remembering (define, know, repeat, describe, identify, recall, list, tell, locate, match)

Understanding (compare, comprehend, convert, explain, summarize, predict, discuss,)

Applying (classify, demonstrate, modify, arrange, solve, relate, apply, examine, illustrate)

Analyzing (infer, estimate, order, separate, subdivide, distinguish, contrast, categorize)

Evaluating (judge, argue, critique, justify, discriminate, support, conclude, verify, assess)

Creating (construct, synthesize, design, formulate, revise, compose, invent, imagine, propose)

For example, each of the following learning outcomes has been further specified as stages of learning using Bloom's (1956) taxonomy. The smaller, more specific stages can guide the formation of individual units and assignments in courses.

Example A

Students will learn about the importance of scientific, social, artistic, or political innovations or discoveries. In this course or major, students will learn to:

- List important discoveries from the past
- Explain the basic disciplinary concepts underlying each discovery
- Apply the concepts of the discipline to classify discoveries

- Analyze novel aspects of each discovery

- Evaluate which current discoveries will have the greatest impact

- Design a strategy to address an important unanswered question in the field

Example B

Students will learn about musical styles and historical periods.

In this course or major, students will learn to:

- Define the different conventions operating in each style or period

- Compare examples of each style or period

- Classify key practitioners using examples

- Infer the style of unknown practitioners using typical characteristics

- Judge if the most typical exemplar is the most interesting

- Construct an argument as to how and why certain thinkers/ artists/authors/leaders cross boundaries

In individual courses, the increased specificity and the progression of cognitive skills can help students understand what they are supposed to be learning. For faculty, the process of connecting content to levels of thinking can help clarify the order and purpose of specific activities. At the program level, articulating learning outcomes with detailed levels and specificity allows departments to have the necessary and serious discussions about what students need to learn, when, and how. Designing course sequences, for example, becomes much easier when objectives are articulated. If, for example, creation of a business plan is the desired senior project, then identification of the parts of a plan and analysis of risks will need to be addressed in earlier courses.

Fink's (2003) taxonomy of significant learning (see Figure 4.1) extends beyond content to context. Unlike Bloom's (1956) linear hierarchy of increasingly more complex sorts of thinking, Fink's taxonomy is circular to show how each type of learning enhances all the others. The more a course or program can integrate all six conditions, the greater the potential for a significant learning experience for the student.

Foundational knowledge remains important here, but Fink (2003) helps us understand that we need to pay more attention to the frame in which that learning occurs. Fink's work is also enormously practical, and more detailed discussions of how he uses this theory to design courses and feedback occur in the following section.

Figure 4.1 Fink's Taxonomy of Significant Learning
Source: Fink, 2003, p. 30

Contexts for Learning

Research from neurology and developmental psychology reinforce the observations of educational researchers: content has to be integrated; practice and growth take time; and motivation, control, and emotion all need to be part of our teaching strategies. Research that looks further at the relationship between student engagement and student success also points to a broader web of supporting practices.

Chickering and Gamson (1987) summarize a generation of quantitative research in "Seven Principles for Good Practice in Undergraduate Education" that are still a cornerstone of pedagogy. According to them, good practice:

1. Encourages contact between students and faculty
2. Develops reciprocity and cooperation among students
3. Encourages active learning
4. Gives prompt feedback
5. Emphasizes time on task
6. Communicates high expectations
7. Respects diverse talents and ways of learning

While many of these principles apply directly to the classroom, the title underscores that learning requires a broader context that supports the student in multiple ways. Laird, Chen, and Kuh (2008) identify institutions with higher than expected persistence rates based upon the demographics of incoming students. Using the National Survey of Student Engagement, they discovered that high-persistence institutions were characterized by higher levels of academic challenge, active and collaborative learning, and supportive campus environments. The findings suggest that campuses with better than expected persistence emphasize the social and collaborative aspects of learning.

Bain (2004) used a different research method: he sought out teachers who had a lasting effect on students and interviewed the students decades after they had left the classroom. He then observed classes and talked to the teachers. He, too, discovered that although there is no one magic technique or style, the best college teachers teach facts "in a rich context of problems, issues and questions" (p. 29). They understand that learning is emotional and that mental models (often called deep learning) change slowly.

This emphasis on context is also confirmed by a large study by the National Research Council's Commission on Behavioral and Social Sciences and Education 2000 (Bransford & Brown, 2000). This report confirms that student motivation and preconceptions are important, and that if they learn new information for the purpose of a test, they quickly revert to their old ways of thinking. The authors recommend a metacognitive approach, which combines factual knowledge with an emphasis on conceptual frameworks, applications, and dispersal to students of control over their learning. Zull (2004) argues that brain-based research gives us an additional physiological understanding of these phenomena; teacher explanations often fail because not only the context does not align but also explanation or lecture does not create enough opportunities for practice or emotion. "Neuroscience tells us that the positive emotions in learning are generated in the parts of the brain that are used most heavily when students develop their own ideas. These areas include the frontal cortex and the pleasure centers deep in the brain that are control centers for voluntary movements... The biochemical rewards of learning are not provided by explanations but by student ownership" (Zull, p. 70).

Implementation: Facts and Context 1: Analogies

A wonderful way to generate ownership is to get students to make their own analogies: to teach and explain something they know to someone who has a different context. This helps students not only conceptualize the information but also see how malleable facts are to context.

I ask students to articulate what they hear in the voices of Sarah Vaughan, Ella Fitzgerald, and Billie Holiday by describing the sonic differences of these three singers to someone who works in a different context. Some notable student creations are that Sarah, Ella, and Billie relate to each other like:

- Velvet, silk, and burlap (at the fabric store)

- Cabernet, champagne, and whiskey (at the liquor store)

- Shag carpet, hard wood, and stained concrete (for the builder)

- Chocolate mousse, angel food cake, and key lime pie (for the cook)

- The first drink, beer pong, and the morning-after (for the fraternity brother)

Students cheer and laugh but also start to see that this works only if you know the metaphor. Most of them understand there are no right or wrong answers here (multiplicity) and may start to see that better and more insightful metaphors add meaning and understanding (relativism).

This technique works well in lots of subjects: ask students to compare different experiments, chemical bonds, management systems, or ways of solving logarithmic equations to rock bands, football teams, or lunch offerings in the cafeteria. If nothing else, you will gain some insight into students' world and how they think about yours.

The problem of teaching, therefore, is getting not the facts but the *context* from my brain to yours. Doing so requires an understanding of the complexity of what we know and how we know it and of what and how students know. Students and teachers alike have a hard time learning things that contradict their current understanding of the world; most of us believe that the new information we receive confirms our earlier beliefs, theories, interpretations, and arguments. When confronted with information that seems contradictory to what we believe, we try to force it into the mental model we already have and perform "all kinds of mental gymnastics to avoid confronting and revising fundamental underlying principles" (Bain, 2004, p. 23). New facts change very few minds.

Implementation: Facts and Contexts 2: Hermeneutics

We don't simply absorb facts. We place them into our own contexts, and our ability to assimilate new information is constrained by our context, goals, beliefs, and our individual cognition about the nature of knowledge—what Hofer and Pintrich (2002) call a *personal epistemology*. The reverse is also true: when we learn something new, it changes everything else we know. This constant reinterpretation of our knowledge and its relationship to the world is known as the *hermeneutic circle*. Hermeneutics has its origins in biblical exegesis and later textual interpretation. In the 20th century (when everything became a text), Heidegger (1927) and Gadamer (1975) demonstrated how our understanding of the whole is dependent upon our interpretation of the particular in an iterative cycle: the more we learn, the more we reformulate our view of the world.

I introduce my students to hermeneutics and ask them to ponder how we learn new things. They understand the idea that we learn new things by comparing them to things we already know (see "Facts and Context 1: Analogies") but quickly discover the paradox. A truly foreign or different concept means nothing. With no context for understanding, we can't make distinctions. All the music you don't like sounds the same. We compare new tastes to things we already know and often find that they "taste like chicken." Everything new, at first, seems simply a variant of what we already know.

Since college is full of new experiences and encounters with people from different backgrounds, I often extend the analogies assignment by letting students regale each other with first-week anecdotes of roommates who had never encountered something they consider ordinary. "You've never used conditioner on your hair?" "What do you mean you don't know who Keith Urban is?" Once students notice that understanding requires that the sender and the receiver share some experience, they can see the ramifications for learning. Explaining that Ramadan is a little bit like a month-long Yom Kippur works only if your roommate is Jewish. If your roommate is Catholic, a comparison to Good Friday might be more useful. Students soon learn that good teachers need to know something about their audience. Teaching your roommate about fry pie requires an extra step of considering what other references she might already have: do you describe it as a sweet peach calzone, chimichanga, beerock, kreplack, or char siu bun?

Discussing hermeneutics is challenging, but it also helps students understand that change is not subversive—although if Perry (1999) is right, not all students are developmentally ready to accept this. Learning to think in new ways is hard, but students perform better when they understand both what and how they are supposed to be learning.

Contexts for learning include student apathy, contradictions to belief systems (personal epistemology), religious or political beliefs, educational background, and psychological development. In other words, the context for learning is the context our students bring with them. The brain is not an empty bowl waiting to be filled. Zull (2004) suggests that educators "engage the whole brain: Instructors should provide experiences and assignments that engage all aspects of the cerebral cortex: sensory cortex (getting information), integrative cortex (making meaning of information), integrative cortex near the front (creating new ideas from these meanings), and motor cortex (acting on those ideas)" (p. 71). Fink (2003) calls this significant learning, but Zull's metaphor that neurons are like bushes is apt: we want the bushes (neurons) not only to grow larger but also to talk to one other and form new connections (synapses).

According to Bain (2004), the best professors model change because change is part of the context. They teach the history of their subject and demonstrate daily how knowledge changes. They present problems instead of solutions and model how to suspend judgment until they have a better understanding of the context. They focus on big questions, show how scholars disagree, and provide many opportunities to practice revising judgments and taking risks. The best professors, in other words, use change in the discipline as a model for individual change: our disciplines change because great thinkers took on the biggest challenges and sometimes failed. Faculty need to demonstrate that engagement with big issues matters and that students can do it too.

Bain (2004) provides the example of Ken Seeskin, who wants to convince students that the issues in his philosophy class are still worth fighting for. He pits ancient authors against each other (Plato vs. Aristotle) and forces students not only to learn but also to choose. This strategy to motivate learning would please any video game designer: the player–student has a stake in the process and an incentive for change.

Implementation: WGAD

Another of Bain's (2004) star professors writes *WGAD* (who gives a damn) on the chalkboard each day. Students are allowed to interrupt at any moment with "WGAD!" I have coupled this highly motivating offer to debate anything with the requirement that students keep an open mind and honestly debate both sides of every WGAD objection. The result is a more intense and intellectually open atmosphere.

Another way to stimulate motivation is to question constantly the relevance of your own subject. Students do this anyway, and doing it yourself invites them into the academic clan. After all, we dismiss (or simply ignore) many of the papers at our annual conferences simply because they are irrelevant to our own interests. Why not make the judgment of relevance an explicit part of the course? For example, music history teachers struggle with relevance when they teach required courses for music majors. Music majors are mostly performers who see every hour away from the practice room as a loss and history as tangential at best.

I respond by matching a particularly controversial theory to an important piece and asking if the work of theorists and historians makes any difference to the way they would or could perform the piece. We read contradictory interpretations of the same works and ask if the alternative meanings of the beginning of Beethoven's Ninth Symphony affect how it might sound in performance. I ask students to read Tchaikovsky's letters to Nadezhda von Meck, knowing that a student will always ask, "WGAD, how can it possibly matter if Tchaikovsky was gay?" This usually leads to an engaged discussion about how we might imagine a gay performance of the Symphony No. 4. I keep my word and often interrupt with my own WGAD. Does theory ever improve our performance? Does cultural context or biography ever affect a performance? Should we abolish program notes? Can your personal story with a piece of music influence an audience? These are the questions that students debate after WGAD interruptions. As Bain (2004) predicts, by giving the students the authority to have opinions about fundamental issues and by valuing their interests, all of a sudden my obscure discipline of musicology matters to them.

Motivating Change with High Standards and Low Stakes

We can open doors, but students have to walk through them. How then do we motivate students who have been highly successful in high school (using one part of their brain and one way of thinking) to abandon that mode of thinking and learn to think in new ways using new parts of their brain that are not yet fully developed? We are asking students to discard the very patterns of thought that have led them to success. We are asking for substantial change under conditions (awarding grades) that punish failure and at a time (the beginning of college) when anxiety about change and failure is at its fullest.

Pintrich, Marx, and Boyle (1993) demonstrate that motivation is an important factor in leading students to conceptual change. After failure it is natural to ask what went wrong, but few of us do so after success. Thus, it is easier to teach change after failure than after success, so we need more planned failure in the college experience.

Thus, the traditional passive method of college teaching (i.e., lecturing) is less effective than active learning in developing higher-order cognitive skills. Delivering content alone has virtually no effect on students' beliefs about the world. Students can memorize data that conflict with their beliefs, but without active engagement with the new material, in the form of discussions, writing, debates, projects, and hands-on application, they do not really confront the implications of the new content.

For example, Mazur (1996) discovered that his Harvard physics students were very good at memorizing but not at learning to understand. Students liked him, did well on his tests, and were able to recite formulas but left his courses with little ability to solve problems, virtually no conceptual knowledge, and certainly no love of physics. Improving the quality of his lectures did not improve student learning, so he created a new method of peer instruction that begins with giving students a reading before class. In class he asks students to think about a question, then to answer, and then to convince a neighbor of the right answer. He then asks students to answer the question again and provides an explanation before starting the process over with a new question.

He found that even when he never worked a problem in class, he could improve students' ability to solve problems by allowing them to practice on each other. Embedded in Mazur's methods are high standards—conceptual understanding instead of mere memorization—but low stakes, in the form of no penalty for wrong answers in class.

Empirical evidence confirms that the combination of high expectations and low stakes (exactly the conditions of a good video game) matter for learning. Arum and Roksa (2011) even quantify how high the standards need to be: demanding faculty require over 40 pages a week of reading and more than 20 pages of writing per semester (p. 93). Even at highly selective American colleges, they found that only 68% of students experienced both standards in any one semester (p. 73). They also discovered, however, that the best faculty not only expected and demanded more but also were approachable (p. 93). There are structural ways to reduce the stakes (e.g., have more exams worth fewer points or allow students to retake exams), but being approachable and supportive also improve learning.

Bain (2004) came to the same conclusion: The best teachers focus on challenging students in a supportive environment where failure is tolerated. The combination is essential; just having high standards is not enough to help students learn. Bain discovers repeatedly that the best teachers expect more of their students yet treat them with genuine caring and give them a sense of control. Students learn best when they believe that the professor wants them to succeed.

We know that the brain is most easily changed when different parts are engaged and students feel they are making progress. Students have to be motivated and feel safe. Understanding and reconciling these two seemingly disparate concepts of high standards and low stakes is critical for successful course design: Bain (2004) concludes that we need to combine "faith in abilities, concentration on outcomes, rejection of power in favor of creating opportunities, and the perception that external factors do make a difference" (p. 83). The personal and the intellectual are intertwined.

Practically, our ability to lower the risk of failure while maintaining high standards means we have to rethink what and how we assess. Walvoord and Anderson (1998) point out that grading and assessment not only are about evaluation but also are an important part of the environment and motivation for learning. We can reduce anxiety and increase the opportunities for change by combining clear learning outcomes with lots of low-stakes assessment. Lowering stakes can consist of more exams worth fewer points each, more chances to practice skills and experiment with concepts, more drafts, second and third chances for resubmission and regrading of assignments, feedback on drafts, practice tests, less time pressure, discussion that rewards risk, reduced competition for grades (e.g., pass–fail grading or grading against a fixed criterion instead of using a curve, which increases competition), and an environment of shared interest and exploration. It is precisely the combination of challenging engagement and low consequences for failure that has proved so potent in the video game industry: if games do not provide both enough pleasant frustration and positive feedback, they do not succeed in the marketplace.

Good assessments also need to motivate students, but motivation is complex, variable, situational, and personal. Motivation varies with our interest but also with our expectations of success, effort, and intrinsic value of the task (Pintrich, 1988, 1989; Wolf, Smith, & Birnbaum, 1995). As a group, faculty are highly motivated by intrinsic value of a task (Froh, Menges, & Walker, 1993) and feelings of competency (Blackburn, Lawrence, Bieber, & Trautvetter, 1991), but it may also be useful to remind ourselves of the importance to our students of other types of motivation. High expectations can be motivating; if someone else believes we can do this, then perhaps we can. The relationship between motivation and lower-stakes assessment, however, is more complex.

Wise and DeMars (2005) determined that, on average, motivated students outperformed unmotivated students by one-half a standard deviation. Raising stakes can actually be a motivational strategy; increasing the consequences—the strategy of the U.S. Internal Revenue Service—raises test motivation and test performance. Grades, therefore, motivate some students. However, raising stakes also increases anxiety, which can offset any motivational gains (Smith & Smith, 2002). Importantly, students in these studies felt that they could exercise some control over motivation but not anxiety: I can decide to do better, but I can't decide not to be anxious. Low-stakes assessment can reduce anxiety, and that will clearly help some students: about a third of students in Wolf and Smith's (1995) experiment did better on the test that did not count toward the grade. But lower consequences also lower motivation for some students. Others in education (Bain, 2004), psychology (Weiner, 1990), and neuroscience (Goswami, 2008) all find that stress inhibits learning. If we can lower anxiety and increase motivation at the same time, we will create optimal conditions for learning.

There are ways to increase motivation with encouragement, rewards, or recognition that do not also raise anxiety. Financial rewards, although impractical for schools, work for most parents. Having an honor roll or dean's list is another way to increase recognition and importance.

Assessments that promote learning combine low-stakes and high-quality feedback. Both foster change and are highly motivating; it is easier to try something new if the stakes are low and easier to change when you are being encouraged and when you know exactly what change is needed. Fink (2003) defines high-quality feedback as being frequent, immediate, discriminating, and loving (FIDeLity).

Creating time for quality feedback takes time and needs to be part of course design. Walvoord and Anderson (1998) suggest separating commenting from grading: offer comments but no grade for an assignment, and then grade the final product without commenting, since at that point most students will ignore the comments (p. 120).

Since effort is inversely related to motivation, making tests and assignments easier and less work improves motivation. Essay questions are perceived as more mentally taxing, so they produce lower motivation compared with multiple-choice questions. Wolf et al. (1995) found that less-motivated students worked harder on questions that seemed less mentally taxing, but this strategy, of course, also lowers standards. Spreading out the same material over multiple tests, however, maintains high standards while lowering the consequences of any individual failure, thus increasing motivation for each assessment. If we want to stimulate and evaluate the critical thinking skills of students, we need ways for students to try this dangerous and life-changing practice in a safe space.

Implementation: Fifty Great Classroom Assessment Techniques

Angelo and Cross (1993) provide 50 excellent classroom assessment techniques (CATs) that will broaden your view of assessment. Try the minute paper (p. 148), done at the end of class on an index card. (You can also give students five minutes and a larger piece of paper.) Many faculty use this as a diagnostic tool by asking, "What is still unclear after today's class?" or "What is the most important thing you learned today?" But it can also be used as a tool for low-stakes practice in critical thinking. Instead of asking students just to summarize, ask them to go beyond the class content and evaluate the arguments used today or describe how the last two topics are connected. I often tell students that at the end of class they will be required to posit a new question on their index card, for example, to define a new research project or a new question that scholars have neglected to investigate. Such low-stakes assessment motivates students to think and interact with the material in a particular way.

Video games are really just a series of tests, but unlike most college tests they are designed to be intrinsically motivating. Players and students alike are more motivated by tests that are pleasantly frustrating (Gee, 2004) or moderately challenging (Pintrich & Schunk, 2002). Like game designers, we can also create tests that follow a narrative or tackle a problem: in other words, make tests more fun by giving them a story line or having them relate to a problem that will motivate your students. While we tend to focus on creating tests that are fair and reliable, we need also to construct assessments that are focused, moderately challenging, and intrinsically interesting. By giving consideration to the format of exams and the examples we use, faculty can increase motivation and lower stress.

As described in the following chapters, technology creates more opportunities for low-stakes tasks that double as motivators and assessment; we can literally turn courses into video games. The fundamental conclusion from this research, however, is that high standards, low-stakes assessment, and motivation all need to be integrated into course design. Constant low-stakes assessment provides opportunities for practice, risk, and even failure but needs to be paired with ambitious and clear learning outcomes in the context of a broader course strategy and tasks that motivate students to persist.

Implementation: Motivation and Course Design

I teach a history of opera, one of those surveys that aims to fill students' heads with repertoire and maybe some knowledge of different styles. When I realized that learning repertoire was mostly a matter of motivation (and fairly easy to do), I began to focus my course first on Wagner and then on Wagner's monumental *Der Ring des Nibelungen*. The goal was to give students a passion for opera and a desire to learn more about its complexities. To change their view of opera, I needed to stimulate all four areas of motivation and all six areas of Fink's taxonomy. Choosing only one opera allows for development of more thorough foundational knowledge but also more consideration of the relationship between the cultural context and how it was performed. We look at set and costume designs for different performances and listen to dozens of different sopranos sing Brünnhilde. Rather than give a final exam, I put students into production teams and ask them to come up with a new interpretation of the *Ring* and pitch it to the artistic team from the local opera company. I tell them they need to take a position and argue for their new production concept. This makes it personal—they care about their own design concept—but it also allows them how to learn about becoming better students. Next time they can learn about any opera on their own. Having them grilled by a panel of passionate experts raises the importance and increases motivation but hopefully without raising the stakes too much. The aim is to create an assessment that will also contribute to learning and motivation.

I give each group 45 minutes to explain how they will produce the *Ring*, but they could go on for hours. I still have some of the models of sets they have made. These students, many of whom had never been to an opera, now have a passion for and an investment in this art form. It does not matter if their designs are never used; this piece of art is now a part of their own lives. They have integrated its network of connections with their own and created personalized interpretations and meanings.

We understand why it is better to teach a starving man to fish, but a repertoire course is worse than handing a fish to a starving man. Our students are not starving; if anything, they are drowning in an ocean of information. So a survey course is more like handing a giant box of chocolates to a fat, rich man. However tasty, it is unlikely to be memorable. Change requires not just exposure but also motivation and integration. My students could certainly learn more about Mozart and Verdi. However, if instead they develop a passion for opera and the self-confidence to learn more themselves, then in the end they will change more.

Integrated Course Design

Fink (2003) points out that there are two related but distinct activities of teaching: (1) the choices we make in designing our courses; and (2) the student–teacher interactions we have. Since we have little or no training in course design, the first factor tends to limit our effectiveness (p. 23). Most of us can easily conceive of how to arrange content, but the research is emphatic that student success depends on a broad combination of factors. Fink created a 12-step process for integrated course design (p. 61) that accounts for the six factors in his taxonomy of significant learning. (Fink, 2004, is an essential and free online workbook.)

Fink (2003) suggests limiting yourself to what you want students to remember in a few years: integration is more important than volume of content. Do not shy away from grand goals just because an easy assessment method does not spring immediately to mind. Despite all of the emphasis on assessment, teaching only what you can assess directly or easily will not lead to significant learning. Fink also suggests that you focus on your own dreams. If you want students to "'find a lifetime of joy in continued learning' about your subject, you need to translate those dreams into explicit goals for the course you teach" (p. 81).

Figure 4.2 shows how learning outcomes, class experience and activities, and assessment should be aligned. Long before we start on a syllabus, we need to think about how these three activities will interact with whatever situational factors we encounter;

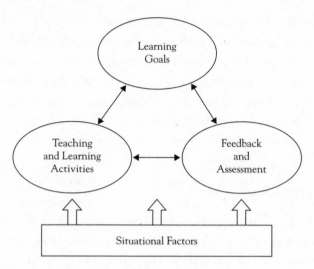

Figure 4.2   Fink's Key Components of Integrated Course Design
Source: Fink, 2003, p. 62

only then can they be assembled into an integrated instructional strategy, course structure, and finally a sequence of what happens inside and outside of class (see Figure 4.3).

It is at this point that technology changes everything because of the flexibility it adds. Walvoord and Poole (1998) note that in traditional lecture-based pedagogy class time is primarily used for first exposure. Students are then sent home to process, analyze, and synthesize the material by writing, studying, and solving problems, that is, to do most of the actual learning at home. Then they return to class for a response to this integration (i.e., exams).

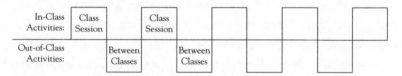

Figure 4.3   Fink's "Castle Top" Template for Creating a Teaching Strategy
Source: Fink, 2003, p. 132

Walvoord and Poole argue that first exposure could be moved to the students' own time, "perhaps assisted by technology such as books, computer-software packages, and CD-ROMs or by graduate or undergraduate assistants" (p. 39). Books? Then the Internet exploded; Walvoord was writing in the same year Google was founded. Lage and Platt (2000) proposed that technology would soon allow us fully to invert the traditional classroom paradigm of classroom first exposure, out-of-class learning, and finally in-class testing by pushing first exposure and examination onto the Internet and reserving class time for rich learning experiences. Indeed, technology now allows faculty to put first exposure anywhere we want it and to create better learning opportunities both in and out of the classroom.

We know that Millennials are relentless time shifters. They hate to wait and experience e-mail lag anxiety if you fail to respond with a few minutes or even seconds (McHaney, 2011): "Just checking, but did you get my email from 10 minutes ago?" While we may not want to foster this sense of urgency in all communication, faculty should use student enthusiasm for video, instant communication, and feedback and even reading on small screens to educational advantage. If students can watch lectures at home, we can have more discussion in class. Or we can lecture and have chat discussions and provide peer feedback, all online. If students can run virtual labs from their phone, then we can analyze more data in class. First exposure, learning activities, and feedback are no longer limited to the classroom or class time.

Fink's (2003) actual Step 1 (even before Step 2, *identify important learning outcomes*) is to identify important situational factors; in the 21st century, such factors will always include technology and student assumptions about instant access to content, learning, and feedback. Our content and learning outcomes may stay the same, but teaching strategies will have to change. With so much content available online for free, course design, and not just course content, will matter more for future faculty.

Some faculty think of course design as a syllabus with a sequence of topics and readings. This subject-centered approach, however, is not designed to maximize learning or change in our students. The best course designs motivate change (like a video game) with a combination of high standards and an environment that supports risk and failure. Traditional courses support only the accumulation of knowledge, but 21st-century courses need to provide a scaffold for the experiences (including both technology and in-class interaction) that enable change. A learning strategy is "a particular combination of learning activities in a particular sequence" (Fink, 2003, p. 130). Ultimately, delivery of content (by lecture, book, video, or podcast) is only a technique, not a learning strategy. Like the printing press or the copy machine, technology gives us many more possibilities for learning activities and many more ways and times for stimulating and connecting with our students; we now need to determine which technologies can most enhance learning and when and how we can use them to motivate change.

5

Technology for Information Delivery

We have established that knowledge is abundant on the Web (Chapter One), that students are comfortable and even crave constant e-communication (Chapter Two), and that customization and control can improve learning (Chapter Three). We also know that research on significant learning demonstrates that good course design needs to integrate content with student contexts, motivation for change, and the confrontation of discrepancies (Chapter Four). So how can we get students to learn content as a basis for discovery rather than being satisfied with receipt of knowledge? In other words, how can we use precious classroom time for more than first exposure to content? These middle chapters (Five, Six, and Seven) demonstrate how a few outside-of-class technologies (often the simplest ones) can improve student learning. In Chapters Six and Seven I advocate for more complex uses of technology to motivate change, demonstrate relevance, foster practice, guide application, stimulate critical thinking, engage students, and improve assessment. Here, however, I begin with the most basic uses of technology to deliver content and improve student preparation for class.

Both Walvoord and Anderson (1998) and Fink (2003) postulate that most faculty want to teach students (1) to "master the content of the course" and (2) to "learn how to use that content in some way" (Fink, p. 130). Most of us wish we had more time to spend on the latter; however, class time gets taken up with the former, and higher-order processing of the content gets sacrificed. The simplest way to use technology is as an out-of-class content delivery system that frees up class time for higher-order processing of foundational knowledge—applying, analyzing, evaluating, and creating.

One of the most common faculty complaints is that students are unprepared for class. We lecture in large part because we have suffered through discussions or activities that failed because students had not read the material before class. Too often, rather than looking for creative ways to improve the situation (Chapter Seven offers an easy way to test before every class), we simply do what we think we must: deliver content directly.

Technology can deliver content in better and more varied ways than we can do live. Most students are already much more comfortable watching online video or extracting information from online sources than from reading books. Some faculty might find the live delivery of information more compelling, but the Millennial generation, for the most part, does not share that view. They are used to finding content online. Students might not enjoy long, written texts in any format, but they are not bothered by reading on a screen. They will search for information online before they even consider heading to a library.

Ultimately, any course strategy needs to consider the connections among learning goals, activities, and assessment, and later chapters (Six and Seven) will demonstrate how technology can be an integral part of a broader learning strategy. In this chapter, technology is considered merely as a content delivery technique, like lecturing, only better. We may think of content delivery outside of class as being limited to Web-based information, but e-mail and podcasts have a role to play. By providing resources to students in advance of class sessions and requiring that students engage with those resources, faculty will have more time in class to spend on other things.

Creating Class Time with E-Communication

The simplest and most basic use of new communication technologies is to create more class time for engaged learning: every announcement, clarification, footnote, or reference that can be done electronically frees up class time for interaction and discussion. You can communicate with students using e-mail or the Web. I recommend getting into the habit of doing both: send e-mail and simultaneously create an accessible record of all your e-mails in a blog or on an announcements page on a website or learning management system (LMS).

Like a Web posting, e-mail is not the most immediate form of communication. Twitter, text messages, and Facebook postings arrive immediately on students' cell phones but have different purposes. Most students can get e-mail on their phones as well, but they are unlikely to check it as obsessively as they do Facebook, Twitter, and text messages.

Implementation: E-Communication

- Start with a policy: Decide how you will communicate and how often. Put this policy in the syllabus.

- Be consistent: Post on a regular basis. If there is a Twitter or Facebook group, decide if participation is mandatory and keep up with your own participation.

- Be dependable: Deliver on time. If you say the paper topics will be posted at 10 a.m., students will start checking at 9:45 and will refresh the page every 6 seconds. Post any delay by 10 a.m.

- Don't bombard: Limit communications to one a day.

- Be brief: You can include a link with more details. Twitter has a limit of 140 characters, so it enforces brevity. (Both text and Twitter make it easy to embed a Web link.)

- Be transparent: Tell everyone before you tell individual students. If you tell a student in the hall that you have decided to make the test a take-home, they will tweet this to everyone; it is better coming directly from you.

- Use the right channel: Some forms of e-communication are more passive and less urgent. You can post a news story as your Facebook status, but if you want to remind students where the exam is, use a more active communication (like tweets, or text).

- Archive: You should keep a record of every message (and the initial channel used) and keep this log posted either in a blog or in an LMS.

E-communication can be the vehicle for many kinds of routine communication that would otherwise take up class time.

Announcements

Students don't really have questions about where the final is, and announcing an extra class session verbally is not terribly reliable. Most of us want written confirmation of meetings or movie times, so put everything in writing. Even if you get only five minutes more per class, you've gained a couple of hours every semester for learning. Students will soon learn to check e-mail or the website instead of asking you.

Summaries

Students don't sleep with your syllabus. It is reasonable and useful to send a summary after each class or a reminder of the upcoming topic and what preparation is needed. Short, interesting summaries can be learning tools in their own right (see next section), but also save time in class for other things.

Readings, Files, Notes, and Handouts

Many students still like writing on hard copies, but as students move to laptops and iPads that they bring to class there is less of a need to print hard copies. Try the Notability app for the iPad: it allows users to integrate audio, image, and text in real time. I can annotate a pdf or take a picture of the board and then draw, type, or erase and share this with my neighbor. Students want easy access to pdfs and files. Putting something in an e-mail will make it available for class, but it also wastes storage space and makes it harder to keep track of things. It is much easier to create a website or use an LMS to keep in one place all of your handouts, files, links, and anything else students might need for either study or class. If you must have hard copies, then establish a system where students pick up things as they enter your classroom. Remember, though, that distributing hard copies in class wastes precious class time and the departmental copying budget.

Dropbox is an easy-to-use free cloud service. It works well as a repository for class pdfs and documents, but be aware that if you also use Dropbox for student papers they are visible to everyone. Notability syncs with Dropbox, so every student in class can type a response or make a drawing and share instantly with the entire class.

Additional Content

Students and faculty rarely remember the lectures that went perfectly and got through all the material. Knowing that you can use e-mail, a blog, or Dropbox for additional examples that you forgot (or ran out of time for) in class can help you stop obsessing over covering the material and focus on what is happening in the moment of each class.

E-mail as a Teaching Technique

Most faculty still think of e-mail as informal (and it is), but it is also more formal than texting or tweeting. More importantly, students perceive it as a little old-fashioned. It is precisely because e-mail is less immediate and allows for slightly longer and more detailed conversations (and attachments) that it is useful as a teaching technique. If you use e-mail for longer learning conversations and reserve announcements about class being canceled for tweets or text messages, you can create the expectation that e-mail is a content delivery system.

Show Your Passion

Communication is highly motivating and has a direct impact on students' learning. Students want to know that you love your subject and that you care about their learning. Use your e-mail style to demonstrate that this subject matters to you.

Digress and Make Connections

We all do it: We suddenly think of another interesting tangent or example, and soon students are wondering how far off topic our lecture will go. If you can catch yourself, you can make connections via e-mail between today's topic and current events and have more time in class to stay focused on the topic at hand.

Introduce Readings

E-mail is a great way to prepare students for a reading, acquaint them with a video, or introduce their first exposure to a new subject. Some of the most common complaints from students are that there is too much reading for the course, the reading is boring, or there are too many readings that say the same things. While all of these things might be true, and students often do not like to read, the problem may be that students have not been properly introduced to the reading.

In the traditional model, students are assigned readings before a class. We assume, incorrectly, that students will figure out why the readings are important and how they contribute to class lectures or discussion. Readings are an important way for students to get detailed information and to hear extended arguments, but they are often the worst starting place. Faculty know why they have assigned the reading and what they hope it will say to students, but most students lack the interest and the ability to read the disciplinary and professional clues needed to guide them through the reading. (Students who are really good at interpreting reading tend to become faculty later in life.) It is much better first to get students interested in a question that matters to them and then to introduce them to a reading that might provide the answer.

Implementation: Sample Reading Introduction

This is an example of an e-mail that I send to students a week before this reading is due. Motivation to read a difficult text is one of my goals, so I tell them some of what Rousseau is trying to say in advance and then ask questions that can open our discussion. I also try to supply some of the author's agenda and demonstrate relevance to contemporary issues as well as those we've been discussing in class. Clarity is another goal: what are we reading and why?

Hi all,

Here is an introduction to our reading for Wednesday. We will be reading Jean-Jacques Rousseau's "Letter to M.D. Alembert on the Theatre" from 1758. You do not need to read the intro or appendix, but I'd like you to read the entire letter (pp. 3–137) before you come to class on Wednesday.

I should note that, because I am sending you this e-mail, I will NOT provide an introduction to the text in class. These are the issues I hope we can discuss together, so come to class with some answers to the questions I've raised below and some views about the big questions Rousseau asks. Deal?

Rousseau's letter is a response to the article D'Alembert wrote about the city of Geneva for the seventh volume of the *Encyclopedie*. For D'Alembert, all Geneva needed to become a great city (like Paris) was a Théâtre Comique. For Rousseau, Geneva is the modern ideal of the great polis, Sparta. Why? What does this tell you about Rousseau?

Rousseau's letter is a public attack on the fundamental assumption of the Enlightenment: that reason was, or should be, the core essence of humanity and human dialogue. For Rousseau, the *Encyclopedie*, his response, and indeed any discourse is also governed by rhetoric, passion, and persuasion. Rousseau is particularly disdainful of philosophers or scientists trying to pretend they are above politics or emotions. The implications are that society can never be fully rational: trying to make society entirely rational only perverts and corrupts. So this is a text about the importance of persuasion. Do you agree with Rousseau? How important is emotion in any discourse? Note the similarity to today's prevailing notion that logic is all it takes. (With a presidential campaign in full swing, think about the importance of symbols and passion in politics. Does the music or drama of a convention matter? How would Rousseau advise the candidates?) Note, too, that Rousseau takes his own advice, and his letter is deliberately rhetorical and public and not just logical.

Some other key issues:

VIRTUE. This is a key concept for Rousseau. Do you care about virtue? In the end virtue versus art is an impossible choice; is it better to be miserable and art-loving or happy and ignorant? That virtue is boring in the essay adds to the difficulty.

WOMEN. It is hard to argue that Rousseau isn't a misogynist or at least a chauvinist, but the feminists are having another look. Sadly, his position on women is an important part of his critique of the theater that we can't avoid. The basic argument is that when female modesty declines (according to Rousseau) men stop loving women as women and distrust builds (why is she dressing up so much?). Odd, yes, but his fundamental question is interesting. Is there something about modern society that makes women want to be less modest and what are the consequences? Will the men in class be wearing "guyliner" and "manscara" next week?

EDUCATION: This is also an attack on the value of education! Rousseau argues that science, as well as art, show people how stupid and unsophisticated they are. He asks if education will make you happier. Is that a reasonable question? What is his answer?

HABITS: Rousseau believes that habits are really what govern human society and that we won't change habits with reason. Habits come from (and can be changed) only through law, pleasure, and public opinion. Which do you think will work best? Do your own habits help or hinder you?

In the end, this is a difficult and thorny text, but that is the point. In many aspects of life (including the arts, business, higher education, politics) we often recognize the most important thinkers as those who ask the really big questions, even if they get it totally wrong in the end. (This is how I will grade your papers: I would rather you wrestle with a big issue and fail than be unambitious!)

Rousseau did not resolve all of the problems he saw, but he was a critical thinker and saw new problems and issues. Many of the issues he identified are even bigger issues now. Many critics have noted that there is even more access to art and entertainment today and that this might be bad. (Someone needs to defend *Real Housewives* please.)

In short, Rousseau should make you question a wide range of art, media, politics, and even religious experiences. But you don't have to agree with Rousseau. I should note that he calls into question all of the basic assumptions I routinely like to make about school and the importance of art in society! This is a humbling work, and I hope you enjoy it.

See you in class.

Technology for First Exposure

Great lectures can be an important motivational tool, but they are poor at delivering content, creating high-level questions, encouraging deep learning, and getting students to reexamine their assumptions. Using lectures for first exposure forfeits class time that could be used for more advanced activities and may not be the best way to get students started in any case. Technology offers a better way to get students started on the path to learning.

First exposure to material before class is not a new idea; many of us routinely assign readings, papers, or problem sets as preparation for class. For some students and for some topics, such pre-class assignments work. Videos and podcasts, however, have become ubiquitous and offer some new learning paradigms. A 21st-century college student who wants to learn how to do laundry or solve quadratic equations is hardly going to assume he needs a book and really wants to avoid having to *read* the answer. Do a quick search for how to do almost anything, and you will surprised: you can still find printed recipes and the owner's manual for your car, but you will also find videos on how to deep-fry a turkey or change your oil. As the phone replaces the laptop as the device of choice, it becomes even more likely that students will start a search for knowledge with a mobile video explanation.

Huge numbers of online resources such as video lectures and short videos are available on most subjects; some are more academic, like those of the Khan Academy, but a host of sites (e.g., ehow, howcast, wikihow) also will show you how to thread a needle, buy a car, find venture capital, do a lesson plan, design an app, become a Buddhist, or even remove a bullet from yourself. You can find hundreds of thousands of lectures and podcasts from iTunesU (many from the most respected universities and most honored scholars) or Utubersity.com (Utubersidad in Spanish: do you have students who could benefit from first exposure to a new concept in Spanish?), which is a growing site of educational videos, mostly college lectures. Other sources, like YouTube or Merlot, include archives of lectures but also plenty of songs, photos, primary sources, documents, diagrams, interactive websites, games, and a huge body of other material. And of course, there are books, articles, flash cards, DVDs, CDs, workbooks, and everything the copy machine and the previous generation of technology gave us. The key is to think about your particular situation and students before selecting materials that will provide both a personalized and diverse introduction to the material.

Podcasts Are Better Than Lectures

A podcast can be an audio or video creation of any length. The original idea was that audio (and later video) files would be pushed directly to your iPod (and later your phone), where you would have them whenever you wanted them. As devices became more connectors than storage, *podcast* became a misnomer. You do not need to copy any of your favorite YouTube content to your phone; all you need is a Wi-Fi or cellular connection, and you can connect to the videos as you need them. We will all soon store everything in a cloud (a shared common server for storage) like Dropbox and simply access what we need as we go.

Students like the flexibility of anything mobile, and they use podcasts and video to study for exams (Fernandez, Simo, & Sallan, 2009; Winterbottom, 2007). Even in 2007, students believed that podcasts were more effective tools than their textbooks and more efficient than their own notes in helping them to learn (Evans, 2007). Students tend to access recorded lectures just after live lectures and before an exam (Copley, 2007). All of the hype about students not coming to class seems exaggerated at best, and the current research indicates that even regular lecture capture does not negatively affect student attendance (Bongey, Cizadlo, & Kalnbach, 2006; Brotherton & Abowd, 2004; Dale, 2007; Harrity & Ricci, n.d.). Attendance will be even less of a problem when your lectures become podcasts and class time becomes more interactive.

Podcasts are better than lectures, or even lecture capture. A lecture capture video is just a recorded video of a live lecturer, with all of its flaws, interruptions, and technical failures. Edited lectures (like the TED lectures) are better, but a podcast is more like a film created specifically for a flat screen or a mobile device than a video of live theater. You can make these yourself or use someone else's. In either case, a podcast is better because it can do more things at once and offers many more possibilities for customization.

First, you never run out of time: a podcast allows you to use many more examples than you would in class. Most of us teach to the mean, so if most students can understand a problem after two examples, we do two examples. We would hesitate to help just a few struggling students with more examples in class when the majority of students seem ready to move on. The best podcasts, when played in iTunes, have chapters that allow students to move about easily and allow you to include parallel or redundant material. For example, I have one podcast on the Blues but include dozens of different (i.e., extra) chapters, each with an additional example. (Instead of chapters, the Khan Academy sorts its short videos into playlists, which has the additional positive association with the ordered groups of songs in iTunes.) The ability to create redundancy and alternative explanations that can be easily sorted is an important feature of the best podcasts and makes them more than just an audio or video file. Research demonstrates that students do indeed use the ability to skip or repeat sections, and they use the podcasts mostly for the topics that give them trouble (Dey, Burn, & Gerdes, 2009; Lane, 2006; Soong, Chan, Cheers, & Hu, 2006). A podcast allows for more examples but also different types of pedagogies. You can put in every possible different perspective or analogy and still have plenty of time left.

Second, the reverse is also true: the advanced student can fast-forward and skip the easy examples. Instead of being bored while you work through the same example again with different numbers or answer questions she already understands, the advanced student can stay engaged by moving forward to the part she does not yet understand. Podcasts, when built with chapter titles and multiple examples or pedagogies, are powerful tools for student engagement and control.

Third, podcasts can provide a host of further resources for students. You can archive lectures from visitors or reference videos of the topic by other professors. You can add a more complex or unusual case. You can add detailed tutorials for procedures or techniques: how to diagram a sentence, find the meniscus, or conduct an interview. Different students need different approaches, and podcasts allow for customization. Instead of one lecture or podcast on how to create a business plan, you can have one for art majors and another for engineering students. Your physics or psychology lectures might include different examples for men and women.

Fourth, podcasts give students flexibility in how they absorb material and take notes, which leads to deeper engagement. Some students take notes by stopping and writing things down, while others simply review the podcasts multiple times (Coghlan et al., 2007). Having all of the material on podcasts encourages students to stop taking so many notes during class, in the same way that providing a handout with dates and names or formulas allows students to stop copying and concentrate on concepts and ideas. Undergraduate students report that podcasts keep them focused and make learning more informal and independent (Duke University Center for Instructional Technology, 2005; Edirisingha & Salmon, 2007).

Fifth, podcasts have the potential to allow you to raise standards. Since podcasts move content delivery to out-of-class time, they should give you more time in class for interaction, integration, and deep processing. Study time has fallen drastically for all groups of students since the 1960s (Arum & Roksa, 2011, p. 4). If podcasts did nothing but increase student study time outside of class, they would allow you to raise standards. Students at the University of Michigan who viewed recorded lectures believed that they helped clarify misunderstandings, review for exams, and improve their grades (Brittain, Glowacki, Van Ittersum, & Johnson, 2006; Pinder-Grover, Millunchick, & Bierwert, 2008). One study suggests that students tend to look at the professor in a live lecture so that in equation-heavy courses audio podcasts with slides result in more student learning (Dey et al., 2009, p. 391). If students learn more simply by watching recorded lectures (Brotherton & Abowd, 2004), then the gains should be magnified when we stop also making them sit through the same live lectures. We should be able to raise expectations for higher-order thinking by replacing in-class lectures with interaction, discussion, and writing.

Sixth, podcasts allow a low stress way for students to help each other and learn by teaching. Encouraging students to share their own insights or find relevance is motivating and gives students an important sense of control, but it can take valuable class time. You might have students comment on your podcasts or make their own videos of how they studied for your exams or found a research topic. Combining those into an indexed podcast of student tips will help your next set of students and also provide valuable feedback for you.

Note that having a video available and showing one in class are very different things. Students rate professor preparation as one of the most important variables in good teaching. Intensive use of homework raises student ratings, and the use of video in class lowers them (Cochran, Hodgin, & Zietz, 2003). Even before the widespread use of computers and phones to watch videos, students disapproved of spending class time just watching. Showing a video in class today is like paying for your groceries with loose change; the experience may be valid and even important, but you will need to make the argument explicit and beware of the wrath of those behind you in line.

Existing Podcasts and Video

Using existing content videos will save you tremendous amounts of time, effort, money, and technology involved in making your own. Like textbooks, the most material is available for the most popular undergraduate survey courses (see the following Implementation box). Finding material is easy: start with iTunesU, YouTube, Utubersity, Merlot, Khan, and a general Google search (using a generic course tag like "University Political Science 101" or a specific topic like "how to pass a bill"). Then check the sites of the major university providers: Yale, MIT, and the Open University. Every course is different but if you teach a basic course that is in any way similar to courses offered at other institutions, then the resources available to you and your students have exploded in recent years. (See www.TeachingNaked.com for links to both general sites and subject specific resources.)

Implementation: Lectures and Web Content for General Chemistry

Here is an example of online content delivery resources for a popular course that is taught almost everywhere with a professor in a large lecture hall, teaching assistants (TAs), and (if times are good) a bevy of live demonstrations between the chalk and talk. Your discipline may be vastly different, but I include one long example here to demonstrate (1) the astonishing quantity of material already available and (2) the vast array of formats and different kinds of sources, from university websites to iPad applications, that might provide first exposure to content.

For Introduction to Chemistry, the list of topics is fairly predictable: atoms, orbitals, the mole, valence electrons, Lewis structures, and the periodic table. Unless you have a wonderful new demonstration or a new analogy for covalent bonds, you probably do not need to spend another minute of class time teaching this concept. On the other hand, if you do have something new to say, why limit access to your students? Post it on YouTube. Either way, you no longer need to give lectures.

YouTube alone offers over 1,000 videos about ionic and covalent bonds, including animations, tutorials, and even a "Chemistry Music Video" (from the series by the prolific Mark Rosengarten www .youtube.com/watch?v=oNBzyM6TcK8). A two-minute "Ionic and Covalent Bonding Animation" by kosasihiskandarsjah (www.youtube .com/watch?v=QqjcCvzWwww) has been watched almost 500,000 times in three years. Some college students (like MyTutorBuddy, an undergraduate at Dartmouth) are prolific makers of video tutorials.

Search for "periodic table" or "chemistry" apps on your phone or iPad, and you will find multiple excellent free or inexpensive apps on the periodic table and chemical formulas and also a large iPad app/ book, *Elements: A Visual Exploration* ($13.99), which combines rich content and serious graphics. There is, of course, also a dynamic periodic table (www.ptable.com), and there are hundreds of articles about all things chemical at *Wikipedia*.

YouTube offers thousands of video demonstrations too. You may insist that students need to experience the live thrill of touching a feather to nitrogen triiodide (which is sensitive to touch when dry and explodes on contact), but the video from the National Science Digital Library (on iTunesU and one of hundreds on YouTube) makes the point pretty forcefully without dangerous iodine vapor in your classroom. Is there really no other use for those department funds than live demonstrations?

If you want to add relevance, connect students to the chemistry podcasts from *Nature* and other journals on iTunesU. For a bit of zing, try using a TED lecture (www.ted.com); these usually combine high-profile speakers with some fancy technology, all in a very short format. For basic content and consistent presentation, there are detailed blackboard mini-lectures from the Khan Academy with almost 100 videos and further exercises.

If you want to stick with university websites, there are plenty of animations, videos, and other materials. James K. Hardy at the University of Akron has a site with over 60 animations and a long list of topics summarized as part of a larger virtual classroom (www.ull .chemistry.uakron.edu/classroom.html). Carnegie Mellon's expanding

Open Learning Initiative offers three short courses on chemistry: (1) stoichiometry with a real-world problem; (2) chemical equilibrium and acid-base chemistry; and (3) a virtual chemistry lab course with over 35 lab assignments (www.oli.web.cmu.edu/openlearning/). The University of North Carolina at Chapel Hill has a text-based chemistry fundamentals website (www.shodor.org/UNChem/) with randomly generated tests. The Open University in England (www.openlearn.open.ac.uk) offers a 20-hour chemistry course called The Molecular World.

Several retired faculty continue to innovate in this area. Walt Volland, professor emeritus from Bellevue Community College in Washington, offers a complete Introduction to Chemistry course, complete with experiments that can be done at home using consumer products (www.800mainstreet.com/cl/101-online.html). Stephen Lower, a retired chemistry professor from Simon Frazier University, developed an extensive website (www.chem1.com/) that includes (1) a lengthy virtual chemistry textbook, (2) resources for chemistry teachers, (3) a detailed summary of online resources for students, and (4) a series of downloadable interactive tutorials.

Another general chemistry site is maintained by Fred Senese at Frostburg State University (www.antoine.frostburg.edu/chem/senese/101/index.shtml). An index to chemistry teaching websites is maintained at Morehead State (www.people.moreheadstate.edu/fs/h.hedgec/sciteach.html).

This is a small fraction of the available material from other college professors. It is all free. But if you don't want to piece together material from other sources or you want only Ivy League professors, several complete courses are available for free from major universities.

MIT offers Principles of Chemical Science on its MIT Open CourseWare website (one of many chemistry courses, including graduate courses) featuring a complete syllabus, all of the lectures as videos, lecture notes, all of the readings as pdfs, exams and exam solutions, and even resources for TAs.

Open Yale Courses offers Freshman Organic Chemistry (with many of the same topics as what most schools call General Chemistry) taught by Professor J. Michael McBride, winner of the Nobel Laureate Signature award in Graduate Education and the Catalyst Award of the Chemical Manufacturers Association for undergraduate education. It does not include all of the readings but has a video of every lecture and all of the exams. The University of California at Berkeley has recorded its Introduction to General Chemistry. Complete sets of video and audio lectures for every semester from fall 2007 are available at iTunes (or www.webcast .berkeley.edu). Video sets of lectures only (and not the other content) are duplicated in the chemistry section on Utubersity. Here you can also see ratings and the number of views for each video and compare them. Utubersity also includes chemistry courses from the University of California at Los Angeles, the University of California at Irvine, and the University of Houston. iTunesU has a long list of entire courses in chemistry, and the list is growing.

The Open CourseWare Consortium (www.ocwconsortium.org/), a growing list of universities from all over the world (although relatively few from the United States), has a searchable course list. A student looking for free science courses can choose from Tufts University, University of Toyko, University of Southern Queensland (Australia), Delft University of Technology (Netherlands), and many more.

Several sites offer a wide range of lecture courses for a very small fee. At Educator (www.educator.com), for example, the introductory lectures are free, and it costs a student $35 per month for unlimited access to all courses. Their Introductory Chemistry course includes over 25 hours of lectures taught by Dr. Harold Goldwhite, a University of Cambridge professor who taught at California State University at Los Angeles for over 40 years. Each lecture is accompanied by detailed notes and exercises.

There are websites that include chemistry quizzes, downloadable tests, and FAQs. There are online books at the Library of Congress and plenty of wikibooks on chemistry. A metasite (www.chem1.com/

chemed/#B7) contains bibliographies of online chemistry materials, with links to other sites that rank textbooks or materials. Perhaps the most useful site for chemistry education is a joint portal from both Merlot and the American Chemistry Society's *Journal for Chemical Education* (www.chemistry.merlot.org/beyond.html).

There will certainly be more and better video lectures to come, but already there are enough high-quality materials that most faculty in common undergraduate courses can use at least some existing material. Surely there is a lecture on covalent bonds out there that will meet your needs. Yes, it takes time to search, preview, and collate; however, your new course materials will be reusable and scalable, and you will have more time to spend interacting with your students.

Make Your Own Podcasts

Podcasts are easy to make, and you should make at least a few. Students like to hear the sound of your voice, and appearing on a podcast is a great opportunity to be a role model and offer support, even if you do not deliver most of the content. Good videos online, especially from Apple (www.Apple.com), explain exactly how, but hopefully your campus technology support people can provide you with additional help. If not, ask a student to spend an afternoon with you.

Podcasts allow us to do things we cannot do live. Early films were made by simply filming actors on a stage doing a stage play in the same way that our first video lectures were just recorded lectures. In both cases, the technology allows for much more than the early examples demonstrate, and we just have to allow the form to catch up with its capabilities. Movies have now advanced to where they can tell stories in new ways and in ways that cannot be done, or done easily, onstage. Tablets also allow newspapers to be more than just digital versions of paper. Podcasts and e-textbooks will also evolve into new forms.

I do not see the long-term advantage of lecture capture systems. They are expensive (you need systems in lots of different
classrooms), and after the first year they are redundant. If the
material changes, you can also make a new podcast (by adding to
your old podcast), but most of us reuse at least some material from
year to year, so why rerecord the entire lecture? A podcast makes
it easier to add or subtract material or fix mistakes. Mostly, however, lecture capture offers only a poor translation of what is often
just a mediocre pedagogy. So if you are going to record lectures,
make a podcast.

Implementation: Short Podcasts for Framing Material

Instead of spending five minutes at the beginning of class framing
the material in the way you want, try making a short podcast for
your students that asks them questions about the material and tells
them what you want to accomplish in class. They will prepare better when they know in advance what your goal is. Remember that
students can rewind and listen again, so you can put hard concepts
in short podcasts.

As already discussed, you can frame material in e-mail, but think
of a short podcast as you would a voicemail message. An e-mail
may be better when you need to spell something out in detail, but
a voice message is quick and easy and can also offer encouragement. The sound of your voice can motivate students and may also
allow for subtleties that are hard to convey in e-mail. Try posting a
short supportive video on Facebook or sending a voice file with an
introduction.

Learning Modules

Learning modules are collections of activities, resources, and
materials for teaching content, application, or a skill that (in best

practice) include learning objectives and an assessment. With the explosion of online content, corporate e-learning, and home-schooling, a wide range of learning modules is now available. While your entire course may not already be available, pieces of it surely are.

All faculty create learning modules. We break up our courses into topics and then determine which readings, lectures, assignments, and projects will best make the subject come alive to our students. Most of us are also willing to borrow a particularly good demonstration from our own college experience or a terrific handout from a conference presentation, and we integrate this approach into our teaching. Why not borrow online learning modules?

We already do this with textbooks. American primary education was introduced to textbooks by the McGuffey Readers, a series of progressively more challenging textbooks that were widely used from the mid-19th century until after World War II. College textbooks came later, and some higher-education faculty resisted the idea that a real professor could use materials created by someone else. (British resistance lasted longer: when I arrived in 1994 I was asked, kindly, to remove the textbooks from my syllabus.) Today, however, the vast majority of courses use textbooks authored by someone other than the professor who is standing at the front of the class, although few of us slavishly design our courses around existing textbooks. Textbooks offer more material than most of us can or want to cover, so we pick and choose. Recently, textbook publishers have made it substantially easier to mix and match materials from different textbooks to create unique books for each class, and the use of existing learning modules is simply a refinement of this technique. Instead of presenting readings (which most students will ignore) as the only option for first exposure, faculty could supply students with links to a variety of learning activities, videos, lectures, games, or demonstrations for each new topic. iBooks 2 (introduced in January 2012) does most of this and also allows students to underline, take notes and quizzes, and integrate different sort of first exposure techniques.

Online learning modules vary widely. Some learning modules are no more than a collection of text-based Web pages and an exam. Others might involve an interactive Web page, a 3-D model, or a game. Even a simple learning module can transform what you do in the classroom. Assigning learning modules for work outside of class creates other possibilities for your class time. If you can accomplish all of your learning outcomes with online learning modules, you either already have an online course or else you need to rethink what you want your students to learn in the classroom.

Implementation: Merlot

If you teach a common subject, you may never have to develop your own learning modules; a quick Google search or a visit to Merlot (www.merlot.org) will tell you what other faculty have already created. The best of them will inexorably attract your students' attention. Merlot offers free learning materials, personal collections of other faculty, and a huge catalog of learning exercises across all disciplines. There is even a virtual speakers' bureau where you can find guest experts for your class.

The role of the professor in the future will be less about creating new presentations of old content and increasingly about curating, assembling, and guiding students through existing materials. Most of us continue to use textbooks to help us cover the material, even when we radically disagree with the perspective or content chosen. Online learning modules give both faculty and students many more options and will also give you more class time to interact with your students.

Advance Preparation as a Learning Strategy

There is clearly an element of convenience in the use of podcasts: we could use podcasts to allow students to keep up with classes if they are sick or if we ever really need to deal with an H1N1 flu epidemic. Or we could use virtual classrooms to create more time for faculty research. What the abundance of information online mostly does for faculty, however, is give us an opportunity to enhance learning and increase real faculty–student interaction. With all of these lectures now available, we need to change our strategy.

One of the maxims of the new media is, "Do what you do best and link to the rest," coined by journalist Jeff Jarvis in a February 2007 blog posting on www.Buzzmachine.com). Jarvis was pointing out that there is a lot of duplication in journalism, with each outlet wanting its own version of the story. His question to journalists works equally well for academics: Can you do it better? If not, just link and spend your time doing something you can do better. Jarvis's observation that there is more value to thinking about the user than the content applies equally to the classroom.

With 2,000 students in General Chemistry and 50 TAs (at the University of California at Berkeley, for example), might we not skip the live lectures and just have the students watch the recorded lectures? Why not have the 50 TAs provide 24/7 live and online support or require students to attend problem sessions three times a week? What is the best use of face time? Perhaps small group meetings provide the best value. In other professions, the explosion of technology has resulted in radical experimentation, but higher education has resisted. Innovation and experimentation in how we deliver Chemistry 101 and other basic courses will lead to improvements we can all use to increase learning.

The abundance and variety of publicly available material mean that every student need not watch the same video or do the same problem sets in the same order. Technology offers many new ways for courses to be customized (see Chapter Seven). There is no longer a need to pick a single textbook: on the Web students will encounter a variety of different approaches, and courses should be designed with multiple modes of content delivery. Digital and customized textbooks are only one source of content. Try exposing students to alternative lectures, games, videos, animation, or interactive websites. Different options will allow content to reach students in different ways.

Podcasts save class time for more important activities, but they also allow students to time shift, doing a task in a new way or place due to mobile technology. I now use my phone to make bank deposits. I simply take a photo of each side of a check deposits at midnight from my bed. For me this is a convenience, but for the bank it tells a new generation of customers, your time is valuable and we want your business. (It also saves the bank money, of course.) Requiring students to come to lectures when there are plenty of other lectures online will eventually be an anachronism: students will just shop elsewhere. Providing podcasts or video lectures for students will save you time in the long run, but it also communicates that you understand and care.

The exploding array of lectures, interactive sites, phone apps, and games can be molded into better hybrid courses where both out-of-class and in-class activities are carefully coordinated. Picking a textbook and a list of topics was never a learning strategy, and ignoring that the world has changed will not impress your students. The first and easiest step, and the one with the most immediate impact, is in using existing materials for first exposure.

In today's world, preparation is everything, and face time is too valuable a commodity to waste. The most productive meetings are those where the goals (agenda) and any required background information have been circulated in advance. Most of us object to meetings with 40-minute PowerPoint presentations followed by 10 minutes for questions. What we really want is to see the presentation in advance with some time to ponder it. The point of meeting can then become the interaction and discussion.

The Web has changed the library, and it needs to change the classroom. The classroom used to be a place where information was revealed. Some students might go to the library between classes, but most students could (and still) get by with just the class notes and maybe a glance at the textbook. The Web has given every student access to the world's greatest library, but it has also made the oration of content in class completely redundant.

The best and most common way for students to receive first exposure is now online. Listening to a lecture and taking notes is no longer an important skill, but analyzing information from screens is. We elect presidents, make financial decisions, investigate new topics, discover medical conditions, and raise our children based upon what we learn on screens. Thinking and communication skills will remain critical, but these are hardly enhanced by sitting passively in lecture halls. We need to change how we deliver content and then teach students how to process that content.

Technology has provided both more content and more ways to deliver that content. Our challenge as 21st-century teachers is to leverage new content and new delivery systems into new course designs. We need to create courses that require and reward students who engage with material before and between classes. Starting with a strategy that uses technology to prepare students before class will fundamentally change the way you think about what is possible in class.

6

Technology for Engagement

Traditional teaching strategies allow undergraduate students to do very little meaningful work before class. Students might do some of the assigned reading (if the grading structure rewards this), but low motivation and the importance we traditionally have placed on our own introduction of the material result in students expecting the professor to provide first exposure in class. The most engagement with the material comes as students review before an exam.

On its own, providing first exposure to video or other forms of content before class (as in Chapter Five) is only a tiny extension of the traditional system. And most of the ideas for holding students accountable for classroom preparation (in Chapters Seven and Eight) apply equally to the current system of assigned readings. If you skip this chapter but give online tests before every class (Chapter Seven) and organize class so everyone has to participate (Chapter Eight), your students will prepare better for class. Your readings will get read and you can stop lecturing. While these strategies will activate your classroom as a better learning space, they still leave students on their own to absorb and process content during the hours they spend away from you.

To improve learning, we must force students into more substantive interaction with material outside of class. While faculty already ask students to take quizzes, organize notes, do assignments, play games, work together, and create communities outside of class, we can do all of these things better and more meaningfully with technology. The many new forms of e-communication and internet resources extend our ability to motivate and challenge students outside of the classroom and provide new opportunities to increase learning.

Technology has fundamentally altered access to information. With more raw data available, the need for more expert opinions to decode our content-rich world is greater, but its quality is more difficult to judge (see Chapter Seven). We need to focus on helping students build the skills that will be essential to navigate access to unlimited sources of data. We need to provide not only more content outside of class but also more and better ways to engage with that content. Asking students to read is not enough. Technology provides tools to motivate students for deeper critical exploration, application, and integration of the information now available to them, and e-communication provides strategies for building intellectual communities. Using both the search tools and the source data available on the Internet, we can engage students in much more significant learning and also advance their digital literacy.

Technology for Student Motivation

It might seem that motivating students should not be a part of the faculty job: should not students develop their own motivation? If we had wanted to be in the motivation business, we would be writing self-help books. We became faculty in part because we are intrinsically motivated by academic pursuits, and we cannot assume that our students, very few of whom are faculty in the making, have this in common. It used to be that motivation was communicated primarily by enthusiastic professors in front of large lecture halls. This approach can still work, but technology has created more and subtler ways to nudge student motivation.

Constantly demonstrating relevance, making connections to interesting ideas and information, and inspiring study remain some of the most important strategies a professor can adopt. In addition to providing students with resources, we need to guide students to the specifics of what we want them to learn during their preclass preparation and to combine preparation expectations with an assessment strategy that rewards that preparation. Fortunately, a number of simple technologies can help with all of these strategies. First, however, you need to understand what students are actually doing.

It is virtually impossible to prevent students from using sparknotes, Wikipedia, CliffsNotes, PinkMonkey, gradesaver, enotes, bibliomania, or any of the other thousands of what students (and many high school teachers) consider *study aids*. First, they are often excellent resources (bibliomania has a board of Oxford, Cambridge, and Ivy League professors, study guides by graduate students from these universities, and thousands of searchable books and references). Second, telling students that using these sites is cheating has little effect. Articulate, therefore, what students really need to do (with or without those aids) before class and why, and then hold them accountable.

If you ask students to read a book that is summarized online (virtually any standard text), most look only at the summary. Some might read a little bit of the book just to get the flavor of the experience, but they prioritize their time just as faculty do. If the dean sends a long report, most faculty will first look at the title and the executive summary and then decide if they really need to read the rest. And if you spend the entire class talking about the first line of the book, students may take away the message that they need to read only the first line the next time.

You must spell out the advantages of doing what you want students to do. You should try to convince them not to read the summary, even though it probably will not work. (It will work for some, though, so it is still worth doing.) It may be more effective to know the competition and to use it to guide student learning. Do what your students will do—Google the book or search the topic on Wikipedia. Look at the summary sites and see what shortcuts are available. When all else fails, find a student and ask what tricks she uses to prepare for class discussions. Then build all of this into an assignment that helps students think about both the text and the sources they are using to learn the text.

Implementation: Motivating Reading

Several of these techniques to motivate student preparation do not require technology, but the availability of technology in the form of online summaries makes their use more important.

- Convince students to read just a few chapters without knowing what will happen and then to look at the summary. (Most of them banned themselves from the Internet while they were finishing a new *Harry Potter* book to avoid spoilers.) Ask them to blog about how the experiences are different. What does the summary leave out? You can either pick a specific summary or allow students to choose any one they want. (This latter strategy has the tactical advantage of uncovering their favorite summary sites.) Let them argue among themselves.

- Reverse the process and ask students to read the summary first and then the chapters. How does doing this change your reading experience? Is it less or more enjoyable?

- Think carefully about the length of your reading assignments in relation to your learning outcomes. What do you want students to remember about this class in five years? Would you rather students skim a long reading or read twice a short and difficult passage and maybe be inspired to read the rest?

- If you want to do an extensive examination of the first line of a novel, do it before you assign the reading. Use it as a motivational device.

- Prepare students for reading by introducing the text in advance and explain why you have assigned it. You can do this using e-mail (see Chapter Five).

- Tell students in advance why the ending is important or how the parts fit together. Is there a way to motivate getting to the final chapter without giving away the climax?

- E-mail students between classes and point out to them a specific passage that you think they should consider; then make sure you ask them to demonstrate in class that they read it. Use the fact that students are always looking for ways to figure you out and learn what will be on your tests. If you tell them to make sure they read something and hint that doing so will be rewarded by a grade—and if you follow through—they will read.

- Encourage students along the way using Twitter or e-mail.

- Require students to reflect on the entire reading before returning to class (see Chapter Seven).

- Give a reading quiz before every class (see Chapter Seven).

- Structure class activities or assessment to reward those who did all of the reading. (If you can't, you have assigned too much reading.) Looking for shortcuts is a smart strategy used by productive people. Rather than blaming students for skimming or using sparknotes, think about your goals, design an assessment or activity that truly meets those goals, and then assign only the reading that you can demonstrate connects with the assessment.

- Avoid punitive measures like asking students who have not done the reading to leave or penalizing prepared students by canceling class.

- Coordinate courses across the curriculum. If it is essential for students in your major to understand the importance of Martin Heidegger or Michel Foucault, perhaps this understanding can (or needs to) be built over multiple classes. Maybe your introduction to one key concept can be done in 10 pages, and that will, in turn, serve as a motivation for a longer reading in another class.

Most of these strategies apply to simple textbook reading as well. If you want students to read for content or first exposure, create clear reasons to do so. The easiest way to do this is by connecting grade points and an assignment to the reading, listening, or watching, but more important is clarifying the connection with learning. Why are students learning this content, and what will they do with it? What will happen if they can't tell Gothic from Romanesque?

Motivating students is an essential part of teaching. As professors, we take our curiosity and our natural motivation for granted. It may not be discussed as much as critical thinking, but without some self-learning or the development of any passion for the subject students will not care enough to apply what they have learned in new situations.

It is equally easy to forget that professors are important role models and that our messages have power: encouraging your students works. Of course, not every student will accept everything we say (that would be too much power), but it seems like good ethics and good pedagogy to operate on the principle that everything you say could matter to someone. For example, the easiest and cheapest way to reduce cheating is to ask students not to cheat. While there are surely more expensive and more effective ways to reduce cheating, simply putting a strongly worded notice in the syllabus about what cheating is and that it is wrong will deter at least some student—this is also why honor codes have some effect on cheating (Franklyn-Stokes & Newstead, 1995; McCabe, Trevino, & Butterfield, 1999). The same is true for motivation. Students respond to teachers who are passionate about their subject and their students. The correlation between pure teacher enthusiasm and student ratings is fairly small, although it can't hurt (Ory, 2001; Perry, 1985). However, Fink (2003) and others (Svinicki, 1991) argue that students learn more when they recognize the information as important. New communication channels provide more ways for faculty to stimulate, encourage, and motivate students.

Implementation: The Syllabus as Motivational Tool

A syllabus can be many things (see, e.g., Grunert-O'Brien, Cohen, & Millis, 2008), but faculty should not neglect its power to communicate important messages and to motivate and set high standards. In addition to serving as a contract with students and a way to clarify the goals of the course, a syllabus is students' first contact with you and the course material. A long syllabus with lots of resources and options can be intimidating, but it also conveys your expectations.

Your first motivational opportunity is the learning outcomes. Most accrediting bodies require a syllabus for every class that includes learning outcomes. Articulating learning outcomes for each class and then discussing them at faculty meetings provide an excellent opportunity for departments to integrate learning in individual courses and to make sure that the four-year undergraduate experience adds up to more than the sum of its parts. However, learning outcomes are also important learning tools. Telling students what you want them to learn provides clarity and focus. Connecting class sessions back to course learning outcomes increases learning; just telling students that they are using critical thinking skills improves their critical thinking skills. Having and using learning outcomes also demonstrates that you care what students learn.

Your learning outcomes also set the height of the bar. Since we know that high expectations matter, your learning outcomes should convey what you expect. If you also convey that the class will be a supportive place for failure and learning, you can immediately establish the two most important learning strategies: high standards and a nurturing environment.

The syllabus is also an opportunity to demonstrate how and where students have control, another important aspect of motivation. Transparency provides some control, so be clear about grading systems and due dates. A syllabus quiz gives students control by providing an opportunity for everyone to do well, simply by reading their e-mail and making sure to do the work before class.

E-mail students the course syllabus or the website link in advance, and then provide a short online quiz on just the syllabus before the first class. If you really want students to know you are serious, also administer a short closed-book quiz on the syllabus in the first minute of class. If you can then make this first exposure relevant to what happens in that first class, you will have firmly established that coming to class prepared is important and useful: for example, spend a few minutes having students come up with ways mastering these learning outcomes will help them in some future task or life goal.

Technology for Application and Integration

Application and integration of knowledge are about making connections, and technology hands us a connecting tool. Students like to distinguish between the *classroom* and the *real world*, and if you interact with students only in the classroom you reinforce this false dichotomy. Even if you bring current events into the classroom, students can still walk out the door and not see the connection. By repeatedly connecting to students outside of the classroom and reminding them of classroom material while they are in the real world, you can help them apply their knowledge. (Students also say that the ideal professor spends much more time talking informally to students; Epting, Zinn, Buskist, & Buskist, 2004). For example, "Do a quick survey and calculate how many barrels of oil are needed to supply your friends with bottled water for the year," or "Collect an interesting dream from a friend and post an analysis on the course website today, or "Find out about today's Supreme Court decisions; which one might be relevant to our discussion yesterday?" You can use your messages or tweets to connect with your students in real time as things happen.

Chapter Five provided some ways to introduce students to foundational knowledge before they arrive in class. Before students can apply or integrate information, they need to recall it, and recall is easy to promote through social networking.

Implementation: Twitter or Text for Recall

Tweets and texts are immediate and short. Your short messages to students will arrive almost immediately on their cell phones, wherever they are and whatever they are doing. For longer or more comprehensive discussions, use e-mail or a discussion board. A Twitter question that a student should be able to answer without recourse to any sources, however, is a good way to test recall, to provide instant feedback, and to reinforce what you want students to know before class: "Name all the bones in the foot right now," or "Tell a friend the instruments in a typical bebop quartet."

Your text can stand alone—as simply a reminder of what you expect—or you can create a series of questions. The point is that you are asking students what they recall and not to search for the answer using their phone: "How many of the 56 signers of the Declaration of Independence can you name? You need to be able to list at least 10 off the top of your head before coming to class." Then the next day you might follow up with, "How many signers became president of the United States?" You could have students actually answer the questions via a Web pop quiz (send students a link in your tweet to a five-point quiz in your learning management system or on a website) or on an index card as class starts.

The combination of these activities has several benefits. Your students will quickly learn that you mean business and that they need to learn something before they come to class. Your texts or tweets can help guide them to what is most important. The growth of new brain cells is related to frequency and practice. Tweeting or texting is a great way to surprise students where they are and see if they are truly developing recall. Just don't overuse them (e.g., with several tweets a day or on Friday nights).

We also want students to see connections—Fink (2003) calls this integration—among people, ideas, and with other disciplines ("Can anyone tweet an example of how today's discussion of target markets might be useful in another class?"). Short messages can also remind students that the content from your course relates to other courses.

While we can't always agree on what thinking means, we are all trying to teach it or at least to stimulate it. Fink (2003, p. 41) borrows Sternberg's (1989) division of thinking into three subcategories: critical, creative, and practical. In psychology, for example, Sternberg gives the following examples: "Compare Freud's theory of dreaming to Crick's" (critical thinking), "Design an experiment to test a theory of dreaming" (creative thinking), and "What are the implications of Freud's theory of dreaming for your own life?" (practical thinking). Sending messages to students can be a way to get them to think about how to apply or integrate the content you are discussing in class. If you want to teach students a specific type of thinking, then communicate with them in a consistent way about that type of thinking. For example, if practical problem solving is a goal of the class, you might send a daily tweet or message with a new practical problem. You might also send a daily message to stimulate creative thinking in the safety of private space: ask students to come to class with wild ideas, and then the group might try to turn them into practical solutions. Labeling the type of thinking you want students to develop will help students connect your discussions in class to the type of thinking you want them to learn.

Most of these forms of short e-communication combine application, integration, and a demonstration that we care about our subject. "Why would a company want to make sure you got a receipt if you want one? Why would the law?" This frequent communication and constant demonstration of relevance and importance can motivate more learning at the same time as it integrates and applies classroom knowledge to the outside world. All of this technology allows your students to spend more time connected to you (probably a mixed blessing for most of us), but it also allows your students to be more connected to each other and to your subject.

Implementation: E-mail for Slow Thinking

E-mail is slower and less hip than Twitter and perhaps more useful for higher-order thinking skills that are crucial for engagement.

Integrate and Connect

Use e-mail to make connections between your class and other classes or disciplines. Students may be focused on other things during class (hopefully interactions with course content), and e-mail is a good way to summarize and connect the topic for students. For example, try sending a summary of the research that a colleague in another department is doing and how it uses some of the same assumptions or experimental methods that you just discussed in class. A humorous story may also have more impact outside of class.

Current Events

Regardless of your subject, it has some currency and relationship to the world. Helping your students see the connection will increase their motivation and their learning. E-mail a link to a current news story once a week and ask your students how it relates to class.

Reflection and Final Thoughts

E-mail is a great place to demonstrate how slow thinking can work. We've all had a surprise question in class or a terrific final thought after class ends. E-mail allows you to communicate your insight and also provides the space for your additional thinking. Suppose, for example, that a student in your accounting class asks if the fundamental basis of your work is unethical. Even if you have a prepared answer (and especially if you do not), try suggesting that this is a worthy question and you will think about it but that for now you want to make sure students can complete the homework due tomorrow. Then send a thoughtful e-mail later with your answer or, better, your acknowledgment that the student question has made you reconsider some aspect of accounting.

Another way to help students connect and apply knowledge is with an experiment or survey: "How many different types of literature can your roommate name? See who on your hall can come up with the most." Is there a way to run a virtual experiment in your class or have students respond in real time to an ongoing situation? This is how fantasy football works: you create a virtual team from players who play each week in real games, and the strength of your team varies in response to the actual results. Virtual pets (like the Japanese tamagochi) work this way too; they need periodic attention. Beyond playing the real stock market with virtual money, students might tend to virtual crops (using real-time weather data), manage a virtual business (using real-time sales data), or staff a virtual emergency room (using real-time police and medical data).

Implementation: Virtual Labs

Labs have traditionally been a key component only in science courses, but as students, parents, and employers seek more real-world experience (i.e., more immediately transferrable practical job skills), laboratories for practical application are becoming more common. In the business or engineering school this can mean an internship, a case study, or a real client, but can some of this be done virtually?

Investing real money in the stock market is risky, but software makes it easy to simulate and makes the results equally quantifiable. While there is no substitute for building the actual device and getting it to work, hardly a product exists that is built without a serious level of virtual construction and modeling. For example, virtual reality allows Procter & Gamble to test both the design of product containers and how they will look (or fit) on the shelf in different countries.

The *wet* science lab is not about to go away, but virtual labs have some advantages. Many science lab experiments depend on accurate micropipetting for their success. While advanced students will eventually need the physical skills to make sure their own experiments succeed, time could be saved and stakes could certainly be lowered by creating virtual experiments to learn how to use a digital micropipettor. Websites like the University of Virginia Virtual Lab (www.virlab.virginia.edu) demonstrate processes and setups, but why not create virtual experiments? Students would still be required to add enough heat or get the mirrors at the right angles, but there could be more and faster feedback, much greater safety, and, in the end, better data for student learning.

Time is an essential variable in most experiments, and, in fact, researchers use simulations that speed up time in many fields. Rather than grow four generations of plants or fruit flies (initially used for pedagogy and research precisely because of their short generation times), why not speed things up with a simulation? Being able repeatedly to run a 30-year experiment on how your investment choices will determine your retirement might also lower the stakes and allow for more trials, feedback, and learning. Jeschofnig and Jeschofnig (2011) argue that we have already reached a point where basic science labs can be taught 100% online.

Technology for Community

Application and integration are powerfully developed by working through new ideas with other students (Johnson, Johnson, & Smith, 1991a, 1991b, 1998). Many universities now engage students outside the classroom by establishing learning communities that integrate learning into residential life. Faculty can do this on a smaller scale by using virtual communities to promote student-to-student learning. Creating a discussion board for your class, for example, is an easy way for your students constantly to reengage with material and concepts while they are away from your classroom. It also makes them a community of learners and allows them to model for each other how to study and solve problems.

Creating a Facebook group puts your class right in the center of students' lives. Messages about course content will post next to the latest pictures of friends goofing off, but that is precisely the sort of integration that residential learning communities seek. "Is there a connection between Rousseau's theory of vanity and your current profile picture?" Be cautious—students often do not want you on their profile page—but this is a way to integrate living and learning. If your cyber presence motivates students to limit their drinking on a Friday night, it would be a miracle—but a good outcome. (See more on Facebook etiquette at www.teachingnaked.com.)

The best virtual classroom groups are those that mimic the best attributes of other integrated applications in the community. Successful service learning or internship programs (i.e., those that enhance learning) are designed to foster connection between the classroom and the real world. Picking up trash might be good for the community, but it does not enhance learning unless students understand why they are picking up trash and how doing so relates to a theoretical structure, classroom activities, or a larger project. Simply talking to your students on Facebook will not improve learning, but in the same way that successful service learning programs integrate the classroom and the service experience, the best uses of social networks are those that apply classroom content to students' lives.

In a course on gender, for example, you might create a Facebook group (or try www.pinterest.com, an online pinboard geared to images) for your class and ask students to post a video or photo example of a stereotype under discussion each week. In a math class, students could share real-world problems and then post different ways they might be solved. Students doing internships might benefit from a Facebook group where they could exchange stories about what they are learning in their internships. If you want students to pay attention to your social media group, then it needs to relate specifically to the class content and not just be another social circle, so use the group to foster a sense of shared mission.

Finally, we know that learning communities help students learn. Treisman's (1992) study of minority college students in math discovered that Black, Latino, and rural White students tended to study and do problem sets alone. Asian students, in contrast, formed study squads, and many White students also found social groups (including fraternities) that did peer checking and provided help and quizzing (Treisman, 1992). By creating small study groups and requiring peer checking among Black students, Treisman was able to eliminate the performance gap between Asian and Black students and reduced the rate of D's and F's among Black students from 60% to 4%. Treisman demonstrated that social isolation has academic consequences: forcing math students to share homework (even if only on the phone) increased learning. Technology now allows you easily to provide this advantage to every student. Networking technology can help students study together and learn how to learn.

Implementation: Virtual Study Groups

The hardest part of group projects or creating a study group used to be finding a meeting time. Now there are a host of ways to integrate calendars and request meetings automatically, but it is also easier to meet on cell phones or sequentially exchange information on a wiki or blog. Setting up virtual study groups in every class is easy.

Most learning management systems have a group function that allows the professor to create virtual groups with an e-mail list and a shared discussion space, but you can also use any number of social networking sites. Facebook allows groups large and small, and a group hashtag will allow its members to communicate on Twitter. In Ning, groups can form a homepage, and everything works like

Facebook but in a closed environment. (Ning is, unfortunately, no longer free and now requires all users to be members.) Google+ has circles that make it easy to divide up students (or friends) into isolated or overlapping groups.

You can chat almost anywhere. Facebook, AIM, Google Talk, Skype, and MSN Messenger all allow users to chat live. If you look at the bottom right-hand corner of your own Facebook page, you can click to see which of your friends are currently online and able to chat with you. When all else fails, there is always the phone and the conference call.

With cameras on almost every laptop and now on the iPad, video chat is becoming the norm. Skype, TinyChat, and Stickam all allow groups to have virtual conferences, essentially video chat rooms. These three are free, although limited in how many users can video chat at once (7 for Stickam and 12 for TinyChat in 2011), but a host of professional programs like AdobeConnect allow hundreds or even thousands of users to chat at once.

When setting up a virtual study group, create a shared purpose. Issue a problem set to each group and require each member to solve one problem and share it with the group. Ask the group collectively to check each other's work and then determine a shared grade for the group's wall. In other words, grade for answers, but also for supportive collaboration (if that is a learning outcome). Universities have not been good at teaching collaboration, but it is highly valued in the workplace.

Another common real-world assignment might be the production of a proposal for a new product or venture capital. Require students to work virtually and create shared documents (Google Docs, Tumblr, or Dropbox are perfect for this) and other online tools. Take it one step further and partner with universities in other locations (or even internationally) so that students get to work with students from diverse backgrounds whom they may never meet face-to-face.

Technology for Information Literacy

Our traditional goals are to provide students with both content and some practice in how to think critically about that content. The Web forces users to do both at once. As the Internet becomes our primary source of content, students need to sort, find, estimate, and discriminate what is the right content at the same time as they remember, comprehend, summarize, apply, and integrate that content. The way we learn on the Web mirrors the shift in pedagogy from teaching to learning in the last generation (Barr & Tagg, 1995). Instead of passively receiving and memorizing knowledge, actively learning and constructing knowledge—by simultaneously engaging in all of Fink's (2003) levels at once—are now the norm both inside and outside of the classroom.

The workforce of the future will always be connected to the Web, and learning how to triage information is a crucial professional skill. Life has always been an open-book exam, but life and work in the 21st century are all about who can find the right information quickly, analyze what it means, and then put it to use before anyone else can. This is a good time for skeptics. Fact checking now happens in real time during class, family meals, political debates, and tenure meetings.

More people now have access to more information than ever before in human history. Everyone recognizes that most of that information is opinion, advertising, incomplete, biased, too small a sample, or just plain wrong, but many people are still influenced if Bob in Middletown thinks a flu shot is dangerous or the new movie is terrible. If the Web is our new library, it is both exponentially larger and less reliable than the old library. Knowledge in the internet age is plentiful, but it is useful only if we can digest and evaluate simultaneously. Thus, the Web is the perfect training ground for any scholar.

Perversely, having invested in all-campus Wi-Fi, many universities have experimented with ways to deny access to the Internet in class, in the form of Wi-Fi jammers or by confiscating phones and other devices. The theme of this book is the need for more nontechnological face time, but it is unpractical and perhaps even foolish to think that we can design assignments for which students will simply choose not to use the greatest resource ever created for scholars. If you want students to learn to do something longhand that can be done in a fraction of the time on a computer or the Internet, you should have a good reason. However, for the most part you need to change the design of your assignments to account for both the normal behavior of the curious in the age of the Internet and the skills of the 21st-century workplace, which will help engage your students. Since students will automatically gravitate to the Internet to learn anything, you might as well understand what students will find when they go there. Even better, try building the inevitable Google search into your assignment.

Implementation: Googling Before Class

1. Describe: Have students read two very different summaries or views and describe the differences. Then have them read the original source material so that they have a basis for comparison: for example, find and compare two sites that have a character analysis for Charles Bingley in *Pride and Prejudice*. Since they will probably read one online summary anyway, assign them two and demonstrate how reading the novel will give them the power to form their own opinion about which summary is better.

2. Compile: Make a chart of the differences among a large body of summary sites to find the best one.

3. Compare: Give students an authored site that you know is good (perhaps an academic site) and have them compare it with a blogged source or one they find through Google. Give them a structure to help them make the comparison.

4. Evaluate: Find the best animation or tutorial on general relatively, Picasso, or the electoral college. Why is this definition/
   website/animation/lecture better? For a variation, assign half of
   your students to read the textbook and the other half to try to
   figure out the concept using the Internet.

5. Critique: Ask students to critique a popular online source. Is
   there a bias in the Wikipedia article on George Washington?
   Are there factual errors? What information is left out?

The traditional syllabus lists reading to be done as preparation
for each class. Instead, try establishing learning outcomes for each
class preparation. Start by articulating what you want students to
be able to do before every class. Then suggest some options for
how to achieve this preparation, providing different approaches
for different types of learners. Giving students the goal and showing them some paths gives them some control and helps them
learn how to learn on their own using the Web as a learning tool.

Providing learning outcomes both for preparation and class
will also help distinguish what you will accomplish in class.
Rather than simply listing pages of reading as preparation for each
class, present the preclass learning goal of defining phenotype,
genotype, and mutation and an in-class learning goal of identifying how mutations results in changes in genotype and phenotype.
Both faculty and students benefit from articulating the purpose of
preparation activities. Faculty can design assignments that accomplish desired outcomes. Students gain some choice and control
and an understanding of the relationship between the learning
that occurs outside and inside the classroom.

Much of this chapter consists of rendering traditional techniques more effective using technology. Close reading and critical thinking are important regardless of the source of the text;
using the Internet as a source increases the relevance for students

but does not constitute a fundamental change of strategy. The Internet, however, brings tremendous new repositories of texts, sources, and data to our fingertips, and at lightning speed. Many of us have been teaching for years with a resource-poor mind-set. Perhaps our library could not afford the materials or they were too far away. Certainly we did not expect our beginning students to have access to the same materials as our graduate students. The new information overload comes with both a blessing and a mandate.

The blessing is that the Internet provides source documents and primary data that were never available before. The mandate is that we simply must graduate students who understand how to do internet research. Our job is to create meaningful new types of assignments, even for first-year classes, that teach students how to find the information they need on the Internet, evaluate its reliability, apply it, integrate it, and construct knowledge with it.

Implementation: Primary Data Assignments

1. Controversy: Discover the controversy about an issue. Assign two different readings or sites and ask students to categorize what the two sides agree upon and what they disagree about. Is the difference one of evidence or interpretation?

2. Error regression: One of the great problems of the Web (and also of scholarship) is the repetition of errors. If an encyclopedia misprints a date of birth, most later sources will simply replicate the mistake; it takes some serious cynicism to request a birth certificate for a well-known historical figure. If you can find an error about your field on a popular website, it is most likely also repeated on hundreds of other sites. See if students can discover the source of this error and correct it.

3. How does it work?: For most processes or systems there are at least two levels to how something works: the theoretical

level (think about how a bill becomes a law, for example); and the practical level (from lost paperwork and typos to the applications of power and politics). Ask students to use source data to compare the theory with the reality of a process.

4. Needle in the haystack: Most primary data sets are huge (the Human Genome Project or the Congressional Record, for example). Asking students to find a detail (what gene is overexpressed in breast cancer, for example) generally requires some understanding of the conceptual framework and the organizational principles of the data. With the right question, students will independently learn the structure to get to the detail.

5. The creative process: From Bach to the Constitution and from Watson and Crick to Mark Twain, the drafts, papers, letters, and sources of important work abound on the Web. Comparing differences between drafts leads to substantial questions and creates a sense of urgency. I provide music performance majors with two different manuscript versions of a flute part from a Bach cantata (www.bach-digital.de) and ask them if the differences represent mistakes or have some other explanation. By providing information on the performance conditions, locations, dates, and pitch of the organs (the standardization of the note A as 440 Hz did not occur until the 20th century), students have to figure out on their own which information is important and which questions to ask. (I am grateful to Joshua Rifkin, who created the original version of this assignment.)

Never before have such tremendous sources of primary data been available for teachers. Even before WiKiLeaks (www.wikileaks .com), governments created extraordinary access to their inner workings and records. Everyone with a computer now has access to the Congressional Record, complete texts of every bill, and even the internal letters, memos, and e-mails of our government. Students of the past were limited by what was in their textbook and the school library. Now every branch of government has an extensive website filled with videos, podcasts, and documents. Government officials and cabinet ministers conduct live chat sessions, and speeches are captured on video. The Department of the Interior has a massive website with information on every bureau, webcams at national parks, safety reports, organizational charts, information on climate change, and all 582 pages of the complete BP Gulf Restoration Plan. Students can now discover directly how a government department works and get access to huge amounts of original source material.

Historical documents are also abundant. The National Archives has high-definition photos of everything from the Bill of Rights to the Apollo 11 flight plan. The British Library has maps, drawings, photos, manuscripts, bibles, rare books, and documents, including the Magna Carta, all searchable online—150 million items in all. The Library of Congress provides audio and video of famous recordings and speeches and a mountain of source documents. The websites of the presidential libraries and the National Center for Biotechnology Information (www.ncbi.nlm.nih.gov) have tremendously large data bases. There are official and unofficial websites for lots of people (from Christopher Columbus to Michael Jackson) and major historical events (e.g., the Wounded Knee Museum, http://woundedkneemuseum.org). Students can now use the Web to read Marie Curie's description of her discovery of radium, attend the annual meeting of a Fortune 500 company, learn Sanskrit, browse the entire human genome, or study the original Beethoven sketchbooks and manuscripts online (at the Digital Beethoven House in English, German, and Japanese, www.beethoven-haus-bonn.de). From cave paintings to nuclear bombs, there is abundant source material online. Whatever your field, you need to identify some primary sources where you can engage your students in real exploration using real problems and real data.

Anatomy, for example, is largely about memorizing details. One way or another, students must learn a lot of names and functions. Anatomy courses used to be taught with lectures and slides. Bain (2004), however, tells the story of two anatomy classes at Harvard Medical School. One is taught the traditional way, whereas another professor turns the class into an episode of the television show *CSI*. Students still need to memorize the basic content, but there is now a mystery and the possibility of a real patient to motivate that learning. So instead of asking students to learn the names of all of the foot bones, the professor might present a patient with an unusual wound in his foot. With carefully chosen cases, students need to learn the name of the bones to solve the problem. The *CSI* students did better on their medical boards.

In other words, students actually learn better when they learn both content and theoretical frameworks simultaneously (Bain, 2004). Complex problems provide motivation, but the challenge of having to sort data by relevance as you are learning it is a lifelong skill. The Internet requires exactly this combination of learning in context: everything you need to know is there, but you need to digest and evaluate at the same time.

Today's employer now expects anyone coming for an interview to have studied the organization's website carefully. Everyone now expects the opening interview question, "What makes you interested in coming to work for us," and the final wrap-up of, "What further questions do you have for us?" In the old days, an interviewee needed to ask for information to be sent and hopefully had a few friends to ask. Now the question is which information is relevant. Should I watch the video of the annual meeting? Has the mission statement changed? Should I memorize the faces and names of people in the department? Does the org chart match the list of personnel? Which other positions are open? Are salaries available publicly? Learning about an organization through its website and determining what is relevant for different research agendas is an assignment that will be relevant for students in any possible career. It does not require an expensive textbook and should also be a fun way to learn.

Crafting assignments and learning modules that have the right entry point and then motivating students to do their best work as they navigate a pathway through difficult material is an enormous challenge, but it is the holy grail of teaching and learning. New technology provides faculty with many more opportunities to motivate and engage students outside of the classroom and to create new scenarios for learning. The same tools, of course, also provide more opportunities for faculty error and student distraction, making clarity of learning outcomes, course design, and accountability even more important. Fortunately, technology also provides new strategies and models for student assessment.

7

Technology for Assessment

In Fink's (2003) model of integrated course design, our reward structure needs to reflect our course goals and activities. The activities, assignments, and exams we offer carry a message. When we connect content, homework, preparation, and assessment with student learning outcomes that matter, then students are intrinsically motivated and assessment becomes another learning tool. If we consistently connect the right assignments before class to the right activities during class (Chapter Eight) and then reward students for achieving the goals we have identified, we have a powerful tool to increase student motivation.

Posting readings, lectures, podcasts, or videos online before class enables us to give students options for first exposure (Chapter Five). Thoughtful use of e-communication, social media, and Web resources enables us to demonstrate relevance and stimulate recall, application, and integration (Chapter Six). As with content and communication, technology in the form of well-designed assessments can increase opportunities for thinking, reflection, risk, and reward and free up more class time for other things. The first half of this chapter focuses on digital opportunities for conducting traditional assignments (like exams and writing). The second half explores how technology is fundamentally changing the nature of assessment, authority, and collaboration.

Multiple-Choice Tests Before Class

Technology has provided lots of new ways to prepare for face-to-face discussion. Brainshark (www.brainshark.com) is a corporate software package and service that allows users to turn PowerPoint presentations into videos with voiceover. (Lots of programs can do this.) Brainshark then moves the presentations into a cloud and lets employees access the presentations from computers or mobile devices any time they want. (This can also be done on YouTube.) What Brainshark really offers, though, is the ability to track exactly what everyone has actually watched—before the meeting. It holds employees accountable for being prepared, and Brainshark claims that a third of Fortune 500 companies are already using this technique. This sort of tracking is also a feature of most college learning management systems (LMS). The combination of available Internet content and a preclass exam offers some of the same, and maybe more, benefits for both students and teachers.

Multiple-choice tests often focus on only a limited type of learning, and they tend not to stimulate creativity or original thought but are easy to make, reusable, and scalable for large classes: both the grading and posting to a grade book can be automated in most LMS. They are an essential part of the assessment arsenal. A test before every class is a simple but effective way to encourage better preparation for class.

For information that really needs to be at hand, like multiplication tables, verb conjugation, identification of plants, or recognition of musical chords, timed tests are appropriate and also prevent internet use. LMS enable timed multiple-choice tests, and if the time allotted is short enough, students have to memorize to do well. It should be clear why no one wants a doctor who needs to Google the signs of an impending heart attack, but be prepared to demonstrate why memorization and speed are essential. If timing is critical, then perhaps a game where the patient has realistic consequences can drive the point home. Especially in large classes, multiple-choice exams before every class can be a cost- and time-effective way of simultaneously motivating and assessing the acquisition of foundational knowledge.

While multiple-choice tests appear most useful for assessing foundational knowledge, they are also a reliable starting point for more advanced learning. Even for an in-class essay, students still have more information available from their mobile phone than any of us had in a college library. It now requires serious thought to craft a test or assignment that prevents the use of the Internet. Why bother? The real world is "open book." Instead of asking directly for the information—what is the difference between British parliamentary democracy and American republican democracy, which can easily be Googled—ask instead why the information matters. How and why did the difference in British and American styles of democracy affect the tactics of women trying to get the vote in the 19th century? Instead of asking students for the steps of the Krebs cycle, ask what consequences arise from the reuse of oxaloacetate as a starting material in the citric acid cycle? Ask students the second question, and allow them to Google the first one.

Account for the fact that the Internet will easily be at hand, and design questions to make use of or analyze something that might be found there. More and better testing can be part of a strategy for improving student learning.

Implementation: Better Multiple-Choice Questions

Suskie's (2009, Chapter Eleven) advice for writing better test questions is generally good: unless you are testing vocabulary, use the simplest possible language. Distractor answers based on common student misconceptions can help identify where a student has gone wrong. She also points out that creating a good test will take several cycles of testing, analysis of the results, editing, and retesting. Following her advice, you can create multiple-choice tests that give you good data on student content learning. Suskie's (2009) Exhibit 11.2 is an excellent example:

> Which statement refers to measurement as opposed to evaluation?
> A. Emily got 90 percent correct on the math test.
> B. Lin's test scores have increased satisfactorily this year.
> C. Justin's score of 20 on this test indicates that his study habits are ineffective.
> D. Keesha got straight A's in her history courses this year.
> {A is correct}

The answers are plausible and of the same length, the question is phrased in the positive, and neither *all* nor *none of the above* is an option. Most importantly, the answers cannot be found on Google. Such questions will help you assess basic understanding of content and can be very useful as a measure of student progress.

However, tests on content send an implicit message that knowing content is sufficient, that knowledge comes in discrete units, and that the important (or at least measurable) things are black and white. If you want to emphasize that knowledge is a starting point and that argument, insight, and persuasion are where the added value is, write multiple-choice questions that emphasize the message that the important things in life are messy.

Each week I teach both new content and a new writing or critical thinking technique. As the semester progresses, so does the format of the preclass multiple-choice questions. Early in the semester, I want students to learn about evidence and to practice identifying which facts are the most important, so for the first weeks all of the questions before class are in the same format:

Question 1

The following are all true statements about Jimmie Lunceford and Duke Ellington. Which of them are most relevant to why each (or both) band leaders are important to the history of jazz? (Check all that apply. Partial credit is available.)

Answer (and percent of students who answered each correctly) Average score = 0.9 out of 2 points.

Y—Lunceford and Ellington both treated jazz as a serious art form. (69.7%)

N—Lunceford was famous for his slightly old-fashioned two-beat swing feel (instead of the increasingly common four-beat swing feel). (45.9%)

Y—The Lunceford band was extremely well rehearsed and could play together very precisely. (55.0%)

Y—Ellington was interested in the unique and individual timbres (sound and way of playing) of each member of his band and mixed these particular textures rather than just using the entire section as a similar-sounding unit. (95.4%)

Y—Duke Ellington performed for floor shows for a white audience at the Cotton Club from 1927 to 1932. (53.2%)

N—Lunceford band performances often included hand motions and stage antics like throwing trumpets up in the air. (59.6%)

Y—Ellington's most famous soloists included Johnny Hodges, Cootie Williams, Tricky Sam Nanton, and Ben Webster. (42.2%)

Suskie (2009) suggests avoiding *select all that apply* questions as they can penalize slow readers. However, I want to reinforce the importance of careful and slow reading and thinking: that seems to me the entire point of a liberal arts education (and ironically, something that is hard to teach in class). The point of these questions is to teach students how to consider all of the evidence before they determine which is most important.

Since the point here is not speed, but judgment, none of these exams have much time pressure. I do not want to give students so much time that they try to beat the system with endless searching, and I try to ask questions for which such searching will be fruitless anyway—all of the answers are true. The emphasis here is on judging for themselves how the facts fit together. This question format makes every student a historian; they now need to assess the facts and decide which are relevant.

Most LMS also allow faculty to give feedback on individual questions, so students can learn from their mistakes. With most online testing tools, feedback and subsequent questions can be linked, so it is possible that the answer to one question can determine the next question. A student who is doing poorly can get the same type of question again (this is, of course, how computer games respond). The point is that feedback is a part of the learning cycle and that it also needs to be a part of the assessment strategy.

Allowing students to write their own feedback to questions can increase engagement and also help clarify both their thinking. A discussion board on this question might start with your feedback and invite argument or simply ask the students why each answer is relevant.

A few weeks later in the semester, students start pulling together evidence into arguments and rebuttals, so the question format changes slightly.

Question 2

Which of the following statements about the music on the ECM label (all of which are true) would be the best evidence for supporting the argument that music on the ECM label is jazz?

Answer (and percent correct for each answer) Average score = 1.6 out of 2 points.

Y—This music includes soloists over a rhythm section. (95.3%)

Y—This music features melodic improvisation over a modal groove. (91.6%)

Y—This music is a fusion of jazz process with the native musics of the players. (88.8%)

Y—The musicians are encouraged to find a unique personal sound. (92.6%)

N—This music does not relate to the cultural heritage of African Americans. (96.2%)

N—There is a house sound. (86.0%)

N—There are American musicians in some of the bands. (78.6%)

N—This music does not swing. (96.3%)

N—The blues are not essential in this music. (91.6%)

Suskie (2009) suggests avoiding negative statements, but in more sophisticated argumentation the absence of something can be significant. As the semester progresses, both the language and the concepts increase in complexity. By the end of the semester, students should be able to analyze the same data set (the same set of true statements listed in Question 2) to gather evidence either for the positive argument or its rebuttal. This is not just a skill for trial lawyers.

Question 3

Which of the following statements about the music on the ECM label (all true) would be the best evidence for refuting the argument that music on the ECM label is jazz?
Answer (same data set as above) (Ave. = 1.3 out of 2):

The evidence that rebuttal questions are harder appears in the lower average class scores (1.3 points out of 2 instead of 1.6 for the positive argument). These questions send a constant message that what you do with the data (or what you find on the Internet) is critical. Students learn that prosecutors and defense counsels, scientists and theologians, historians and anthropologists have access to the same sets of data and that relevance depends on which story you want to tell.

Asking questions that have debatable answers sounds like a recipe for trouble, but there are two ways to manage the resulting controversy. First, arguments about the correct answer can be important teachable moments. Students' motivation to collect evidence to support why their answer is right is motivation you can harness for learning. Second, by asking lots of questions and awarding partial credit (the previous questions use the multianswer format in Blackboard with partial credit turned on), you decrease the stakes for each question, and students will soon realize that no single answer will affect their grade.

Encouraging students to argue requires the loss of some faculty control. (I tell students we can argue about every question, but I do not change the acceptable answers until the following year.) Argument is messy, but students will be there in the mess with you and will be engaged. Bain (2004, p. 59) found that professors who helped students understand that the right answers change over time had greater impact than those who presented truth as static. Changing the format of your questions to reflect your values and learning outcomes will help students see tests as more than just measurements but rather as part of the learning process.

Learning facts while learning to use, doubt, or apply them is a pedagogy of the best teachers. Michael Sandel, a political theorist at Harvard, compares two methods of teaching a child to swing a baseball bat: you can provide detailed lectures, or you can hand the child a bat, allow him to take a few swings, and make one adjustment at a time (Bain, 2004, p.110). The Internet is the new baseball bat, and everyone is already taking swings. Teaching facts and analysis together requires both teachers and students to grapple with the fundamental shift in how we now relate to information: the collection and analysis of data are now simultaneous.

Just-in-Time Teaching

Just-in-time teaching (JiTT: Novak, Gavrin, Christian, & Patterson, 1999) was developed in the physics department at Indiana University-Purdue University Indianapolis to prepare students for more active classroom participation. Students respond to online assignments that are due just in time before class so the professor can adjust what happens in the classroom in response to student needs. The initial assignment in JiTT is designed to motivate students in accordance with desired learning objectives. Rather than quizzes, JiTT uses warm-up questions. Students are sent three questions before each class: two on key principles and a third, open-ended question. Responses are due two hours before class.

Implementation: JiTT Example

Here is a JiTT biology example from Kathy Marrs (www.webphysics .iupui.edu/jitt/jitt.htm).

Warm-Up 5: Mitosis/Chemotherapy

QUESTION 1: Each minute, 300 million of your body cells die!!! However, some of the body's cells last for years, and some divide every day. List three types of cells in your body you would think would be replaced frequently. List 2 types of cells you think would be replaced slowly, if at all.

QUESTION 2: A protein called "p53" normally functions to find damaged DNA in the nucleus. p53 prevents cells from going through mitosis until the DNA damage can be repaired. However, smoking cigarettes frequently causes mutations in p53 in lung cells. How do think this might play a factor in the development of lung cancer?

QUESTION 3: Why do you think chemotherapy drugs, which are given to fight cancer, cause a person's hair to fall out?

The point is for students to go beyond simply reading the material to thinking about it before class. JiTT warm-ups often ask students to estimate, explain in your own words, or ponder what might happen if. . . . Creating pointed, but not overly open-ended, questions leads to student engagement both before and during class, when a student-raised controversy can become the center of discussion.

JiTT professors initially used e-mail and websites to both propose questions and get feedback. Now such functionality is built into most LMS. In the previous Implementation box about multiple-choice questions, each answer is followed by the percentage of students who correctly identified that answer and an average score, both provided by the LMS software. Such data may not give faculty as much feedback as written responses, but it is fast and easy to analyze. For example, we can learn from Question 1 that students did not understand why unique soloists were especially important for Duke Ellington: such feedback can help in the design of classroom activities. I might, for example, now play an Ellington piece in class and give students the opportunity to analyze how the musical composition is built around the qualities of a unique soloist. Data mining is already an important tool for advertisers, but such instant feedback about who understands what can also be used to improve teaching.

Writing

Writing and reflection are critical steps in synthesizing new knowledge. Writing, in addition to helping students reflect on new knowledge, integrate it into their own conceptual framework, and practicing honing the skill, is a critical assessment tool, excellent preparation for class, and a way to evaluate our own teaching. While technology has changed writing in many ways (surely most profoundly in the ability to edit our words easily using word processing software), it also makes it easy to share and evaluate writing.

Students are already blogging and posting on discussion boards, so why not force them to use the same tools for class writing?

Asking students to write outside of class has a long tradition. We assign journals and papers, and we know they improve not only writing but also preparation, thinking, and assessment (Bean, 2011). We can improve learning, however, by improving the instructions. Instructions should include more than an expected page length and a topic. Make it clear that the writing assignment requires thinking. Be explicit that *critique* means more than just criticize; be specific about what it means to argue for a position. Suggest how the paper should be organized, and be clear about the customs of your discipline. Include a rubric as part of the instructions: by providing students with your goals and priorities in advance, they will better be able to work to meet your standards.

Implementation: Rubrics

Rubrics are usually discussed as an evaluation tool. Using what Walvoord and Anderson (1998) call primary trait analysis (PTA, what we now call *rubrics*; see Levi & Stevens, 2005) will move you from unstated criteria ("It feels like a B") to more explicit criteria and from norm-referenced (grading on a curve) to criterion-referenced (grading based on defined standards and characteristics) scoring (p. 67). Clarifying standards and expectations will save you time during the grading (and complaining) process, but it is also an important way to enhance learning.

When a rubric is made part of the instructions for an assignment, it provides a guide to the student. A good rubric should show your students both your criteria and your standards, and putting them into a table ensures that you provide both. Note that with a detailed and specific rubric, the assignment is apparent almost without further instructions:

Your criteria (the first column on the left) should indicate your priorities and weights. If a creative thesis is more important than a

Table 7.1 College Writing Rubric

	Absent (0%)	Poor (40%)	Average (70%)	Good (90%)	Great (100%)
Thesis, Ideas, and Analysis (20%)	There is no thesis or focus.	The thesis is split or unclear; the paper wanders off-topic.	The essay is focused around a single thesis or idea.	The thesis is interesting, and there is at least one original perspective in one of the points.	The thesis is original, and there are compelling ideas throughout.
Evidence (30%)	There is almost no detailed evidence to support the thesis.	There is some evidence, but in key places evidence is vague or missing.	There is supporting evidence for most of the claims, but some evidence may be unrelated or vague.	There is supporting evidence for all claims, but it is not as strong or complete in some areas.	There is a variety of support for every claim, and it is strong, concrete and appropriate.
Organization (20%)	There is little or no organization.	There is some organization, but the paper is "jumpy" without a clear introduction and conclusion and paragraphs are not focused or out of order.	There is a clear introduction, body, and conclusion, but some paragraphs may need to be focused or moved.	Each part of the paper is engaging, but better transitions, more/fewer paragraphs, stronger conclusion are needed.	Each paragraph is focused and in the proper order. Introduction and conclusion are complementary, and there are excellent transitions.

Language Maturity (10%)	Frequent and serious grammatical mistakes make the meaning unclear.	Grammatical mistakes slightly interfere with the meaning of the paper.	Writing is clear, but sentence structures are simple or repetitive; there are repeated grammar errors.	The language is clear with complex sentence structure but contains minor grammatical errors.	Creative word choice and sentence structure enhance the meaning and focus of the paper.
Style/Voice (10%)	Writing is very general with no sense of either the writer or audience.	Writing is general with little sense of the audience or communication of the writer's voice or passion.	Essay addresses the audience appropriately with some examples of creative expression.	The essay addresses the audience appropriately and is engaging with a strong sense of voice.	There is a keen sense of the intended audience, the author's voice, and the writing conveys passion.
Citations (10%)	Material is presented almost entirely without citations.	There are some citations but either incomplete or inappropriate.	There are good citations but not enough of them.	All evidence is cited, but with minor format errors.	All evidence is well cited in appropriate format.

bibliography, then it should be worth more points. If you do not care about voice, eliminate it from the rubric. Across the top are the standards for each criterion: these could be A, B, C, D, and F, descriptive levels, or percentages. Start by writing standards for the highest level of performance and keep them high: that gives students a target.

Rubrics are highly personal; they will get better as you use and adjust them, but they will immediately improve the quality of your instructions to students. Students often complain that it takes half the semester to discover what individual faculty want. One of the most common complaints is that a student will use the format, style, or type of writing they learned in an earlier class and then will get a poor grade on the first paper for doing what they thought was rewarded previously. A rubric can give students guidance for the first writing assignment, without having to wait for the grade.

You can find thousands of rubric templates and examples online. You will want to customize whatever you find, but start with a search for disciplinary rubrics or with the Association of American Colleges and Universities (AACU) Valid Assessment of Learning in Undergraduate Education (VALUE) rubrics: (www.aacu.org/value/abouttherubrics.cfm). A very good tool is iRubric (www.rcampus.com/indexrubric.cfm). You can probably create a rubric in your LMS, and maybe even use it for speedy online grading.

We can also improve the design of the standard term paper assignment. Based on the research from Chapter Four, we know that breaking a task into shorter segments (e.g., outline, annotated bibliography, first draft, final draft) lowers the stakes for each submission and improves learning. If you provide more chances for feedback, more guidance about topics and materials, and sample papers, students will be able to try out ideas and aim higher.

If we want our students to focus more on risk, style, creativity, or argument, then we need to provide assignments that inspire more than adherence to citation style, and margin width.

We need to give students context for writing assignments. Explaining is the cheapest tool we have, and it is often very effective. How will writing help me learn to think? What is the purpose of this paper? A good assignment engages the student as an important project and not just as a task for a grade.

Implementations: Better Writing Prompts

Whether trying to stimulate thoughtful papers or good discussions, faculty need to ask questions that are open-ended but neither too broad nor too narrow. Writing is a wonderful way to clarify and organize thought, so it should be connected with the new ways of thinking we expect in college: the more assignments and class discussion can reinforce each other, the better. Requiring that students bring a short essay to share can ensure that everyone is prepared for class discussion.

- What does the text say? Students will be comfortable with paraphrasing the basic facts, but doing so is nevertheless an excellent way to both check and deepen understanding. For a variation, ask students to explain or translate a concept into a new context: "explain this to a person who has never seen a wheel," or "What might a Martian not understand about this?"

- How do you or others interpret this text? This task is much harder and students will need guidance. Start by giving students a specific context: what did the author mean by this? How might a Christian and a Buddhist interpret this text differently? How might this text appear to a person from a different time period, geography, or scientific discipline?

- How do you understand this text? Be specific and clear about the difference between student judgments and opinions. Ask *why* and *what* questions. "Did you like Hamlet?" is too open-ended to generate either much quality or quantity of discussion. "What did you like about Hamlet?" or "Why did you like

Hamlet?" are better, but even more specific questions that allow for opinion but require evidence will increase the focus of discussion or papers. "When is Hamlet most sympathetic and why?"

- Why is this text important? Here again, make the context clear. Why was this an important text for its audience at the time it was written? More importantly, why is this text still important today or for you? Beware that if you do not have a convincing answer to this question, you might not want to assign this reading.

- How does this text do a good or poor job of conveying its message? How does the form match (or not match) the content? This question reinforces the importance of style in students' writing.

- Why is this passage important? If you want students to learn to take better notes, then require students to explain why they identified something as important and how it relates to the main thesis of the chapter, article, lecture, or video.

- Why is this passage disturbing? Require students to take a side and argue against the reading. What did the author not anticipate? The best debates and papers come from rich and complex questions.

Writing can serve as vehicle for processing the tremendous amount of reading, podcasts, and videos students encounter. Clear instructions, good prompts, and an explicit rubric improve motivation, thinking, and learning.

Once students have created a written response to the material, there are many different ways to share and use it. Have students copy out a favorite passage on one side of an index card and then explain on the reverse why it is important, funny, unintelligible, or meaningful. Bring the cards to class and share.

Technology, of course, greatly expands the possibilities: writing can now be posted on a discussion board, blogged, or sent to you in a file. Sharing writing before class can provide an excellent springboard for in-class discussion (see Chapter Eight), but the exponential leap is in the frequency and quality of feedback that can now be provided to students from all directions.

Peer Feedback on Writing

Students in the 21st century probably write more outside of class than faculty ever did; they e-mail, tweet, text, and post on Facebook constantly. The conventions of expression are different, but the content probably bears some relationship to a few faculty adolescent diaries. A key difference is that students today are used to others reading what they write; public written expression has become a major part of modern teenage life. You still need to teach your students how to use commas and the inappropriateness of emoticons in professional writing, but you do not need to teach that writing is meant to be read.

Evaluating writing takes time and is one of the least scalable tasks in teaching. Therefore, large classes need special strategies for the assessment of writing. We can improve the speed and quality of the feedback we provide to students using rubrics and computers, but we can still read only one paper at a time. Students want our feedback and grades, and we have too many students to grade papers for every student in every class every week. Technology offers at least some help.

Students will spend more time editing and polishing their writing if they know that rather than being read only by the professor it will be read by other students. In other words, even if you do not change anything in your method of teaching or assessing, just telling students that other students may read their writing improves both the motivation and the product.

The easiest way to get students writing and reading each other's work is on a wiki, blog, or discussion board. All of these technologies are easily adaptable to a college writing assignment, but someone needs to nudge things along. Moderating an online discussion is much like keeping a good discussion going in class: you want to encourage good ideas, ask for clarification, and pose a new question when things get off track. Your standards for discussion should be higher in the online world than in the classroom. With time for reflection and the ability to stop and find and references sources and complementary ideas, discussion should be richer.

Alternatively, have students write something that can be sent as an e-mail to a friend or relative. Require that they send it and get a reply. While I caution against invading students' personal Web space too often, asking students to post a Facebook status update about what their friends need to know about Plato or the North Atlantic Treaty Organization (NATO) gets their attention: tell them their posting needs to stay up until they get four Facebook likes (and have them save their profile page if you want to give credit). Viewing the Facebook interaction allows you to see what students understand and what they think is important and can serve as a starting place for further class discussion. The real goal is to get students writing about and discussing the reading with each other.

Creating a robust peer review process improves reading, writing, and feedback. Just as rubrics improve your own assessment and feedback, they can improve student feedback. Students may need a different and more explicit rubric than the one you use (Nilson, 2003). You can find some basic forms and a rubric for peer review of writing at the Writing Center at the University of Washington (www.depts.washington.edu/pswrite/peerrev.html) or the University of Hawaii Manoa Writing Program (www.mwp .hawaii.edu/resources/wm7.htm). There is an excellent guide to peer review of writing at the Teaching Center at Washington University in St. Louis (www.teachingcenter.wustl.edu/node/425).

A good crowd-sourced peer-review writing site does not exist yet, but when it emerges it will provide students with an easy way to get multiple responses using the same rubric. Using peer review will reduce your workload, and both evaluating and being evaluated improve student writing.

If you want to take peer review one step further, try the Calibrated Peer Review (CPR) process developed at the University of California at Los Angeles and used by hundreds of universities (www.cpr.molsci.ucla.edu/). CPR involves some work to set up: you have to write bad, good, and excellent sample essays as models. Students start by submitting their own essay. Students then grade the model essays and become calibrated as graders based on how closely their grades correspond to your standards. If a student correctly identifies the bad, good, and excellent essays, then her grades carry more weight. Once the essays are calibrated, students then grade their own and others' work. When everyone is finished, students get a peer-review grade for their essay. Thus, students learn both by writing and reviewing. This system works especially well in large classes as a way to get students to write essays and get feedback, without faculty having to do any of the grading.

Another technique for peer review is Inkshedding (www .stthomasu.ca/~hunt/dialogic/inkshed.htm), developed by Russell Hunt and Jim Reither as an adaptation of freewriting well before the computer was standard equipment. Inkshedding was initially a classroom technique in which students would write in response to a question, news event, class discussion, or other shared experience. Students would then pass their text to another student who would mark any striking passages (something that changes their thoughts on the subject) with a mark in the margin. Passages that accumulated lots of marks would then be transcribed and circulated in the next class for further discussion. The point is to make space for more voices than could happen in a class discussion where only one person gets to talk at once and to allow an idea to be shaped and developed before being subject to potentially negative assessment. Inkshedding—like any writing—has the potential to allow all students to pursue multiple ideas at once.

Inkshedding can easily be adapted to an online environment. Google Docs, Tumblr, Dropbox, or even e-mail can be used to pass papers for multiple students to highlight and comment. A peer or the instructor can then extract the ideas with the most traffic. This could be done more publicly and online as a wiki or as a discussion board. Like JiTT, CPR, or any peer-review process, the primary benefit is to get every student writing and processing individually before group dynamics enter the mix.

All of these peer-review techniques force students to value writing as a form of expression and to interact deeply with the material. Peer review offers a way for even large classes to require some student writing and give feedback on that writing without requiring an army of teaching assistants.

Games for Assessment

Like any good assessment, computer games promote motivation and learning. Since games are often structured in levels or challenges, they are also useful as assessment tools. While it is possible to elect to return to a lower level, games motivate players to get to higher and harder levels. At the first level or challenge, you might need to master skill or knowledge A to degree Y. The next challenge will seamlessly ratchet up the use of skill A while introducing a little of skill or knowledge B. A higher level might introduce an entirely new skill. In teaching, you can use games for assessment by assigning grades or points to each level.

You can either use an existing game or create a new game. In either case, you begin with a grading rubric, a table of both the criteria and the standards of achievement that will convert to grades. Then determine which of these criteria might be measured by a game. If you are mapping onto an existing game, the number and levels of standards need to be adjusted to match the levels in the game.

Chapter Four in Walvoord and Anderson (1998) is titled "Fostering Motivation and Learning in the Grading Process." As I considered the connection between motivation and learning in my grading process, I realized that my *drop-the-needle* exams (in which students are tested on their ability to recognize musical styles by identifying random audio clips) were encouraging students to be *grade oriented* rather than *learning oriented*. So I created practice exams that students could take online. Eventually, I decided that once students had mastered the practice exams, in-class tests were redundant. When a technical support person cautioned that a student could cheat by memorizing all of the 150 music examples, I realized that memorizing was not cheating but was actually promoting the learning that I hoped they would achieve. That insight led me to move my online identification exams (*click on the file*) into a gaming format where students move up levels as they master genres, composers, or performers.

What distinguishes the game from a multiple-choice exam is, in part, a more playful interface (students use an arrow button or drag musicians onto a virtual stage). But the most powerful motivator is that games are challenges whereas exams are just scary. The game *level* converts to a grade in the LMS. Therefore, students know at the beginning of the semester that they need to get to Level 9 to get an A on this assignment, and grading becomes both part of the motivation and something they can control. Instead of an exam every week for 10 weeks, there are 10 levels of the game. Students can repeat a level as many times as they wish, control their own progress and learning, and accumulate points toward the final grade (one for each level). Students must master each level before moving up (Bowen, 2006).

In the exam model, you can force mastery only in a punitive model: learn or fail. With a game, mastery of increasing difficult challenges is built-in. In fact, one of the greatest reasons for starting work on a game is that it will force you to clarify exactly what you want students to learn and when.

Implementations: Creating Games

Many of us are very creative when it comes to pushing the boundaries of our discipline, and pushing paradigms for learning is equally creative and perhaps even more important work. Almost every campus now offers some assistance with educational technology. While there are good Web tutorials on how to program in Java or build an iPhone app, most faculty would be well advised to create games by finding the right partners and support on the campus.

Start with a small unit of content or skill that sounds like it will work well as a game:

- Balancing chemical or mathematical equations
- Doing stock evaluations
- Prepping for surgery
- Tuning your guitar
- Identifying an autistic child
- Classifying species, cars, food groups, or gender roles
- Managing a crisis
- Designing a business card
- Identifying works of art or molecular orbitals
- Putting together a band in 1910 New Orleans
- Reading maps
- Understanding foreign languages
- Building a microphone

The most important part of creating a game is creating the rubric. What do you want students to learn at each level, and how might the levels correspond to grades? Then consider how the game will teach the new content. How will experimentation be rewarded? What kinds of mistakes are students likely to make, and how will the game correct them?

All of these small games were developed by faculty working with the Miami University technology group. Links to games and more detailed explanations can be found online (www.teachingnaked.com):

- Violence counter: Students watch a first-person shooter game demo or trailer and press a button every time they think they see a violent act or encounter. At the end of the activity the player's score is compared with the actual number of violent acts.

- Morphology of the folktale: Students select from 160 narrative elements in a storybook interface using generic graphics and make a movie telling a story in their own words. Other students view the movies and analyze which elements are being used to tell the story.

- Stage makeup: Students apply virtual stage makeup to a photo to make themselves look older.

- Simple and complex matrices: Students interact with a series of animations designed to help students visualize patterns in a finite mathematics course.

- World history timeline: Students view a series of interactive maps that show changing political boundaries and cultural artifacts.

Think also about making the creation of a game a class project. You may have students with skills in game development, and this will allow them to integrate what they are learning in your class with what they know from another.

Rethinking the Test: Authority and Collaboration

An interesting paradox about the Millennial generation is that students are used to e-mailing experts at their desks but also value the collective opinion of strangers. They are used to checking the advice of peers before they buy a book, download an app, see a movie, or choose a professor. Luckily, at least for music professors, we have American Idol. Say what you will about the panel of judges, but for a generation raised on self-esteem and "you can be anything you want to be," it was enlightening for teenagers to see ridiculous Idol wannabes claim that they knew in their heart that they could sing when they obviously couldn't. There were times when the popular vote went to someone who sang less well, but the blogosphere made it clear that in those cases popularity had trumped singing talent. American Idol taught our students that, sometimes, expert opinion really is better than popular opinion.

Understanding the reliability of information is a traditional part of many college courses. Because the Web allows anyone to publish, and because the blurring of the divide between journalism and infotainment has equally blurred the lines between fact and opinion, students need to know how to evaluate the credibility of sources. Are you more likely to get accurate information on Wikipedia or a company website? The Internet has created more access to experts and more confusion about who they are and why and thus both reinforces and undermines the authority of experts.

Google, with its secret search algorithm, the crowdsourced Wikipedia or Yelp, and Wolfram|Alpha, which aims to "collect and curate all objective data," are the new virtual experts, but they work in radically different ways. Googlebots search the Web and create a database of every word and every link on every page. Google then uses an algorithm to determine reliability or authority, what Google calls PageRank. PageRank is calculated from over 200 signals, but the most significant are the quality and quantity of the pages that link to the page being ranked. The higher the PageRank, the higher the link appears in response to a user search. Wikipedia provides articles written by users; its reliability is based upon other users who spot errors and correct them. Wolfram|Alpha is a computational knowledge engine that does not search the Web. It uses built-in knowledge curated by human experts to compute answers based upon its own database. Google responds with links and Wikipedia provides articles written and edited by users, whereas Yelp provides individual reviews and rankings and Wolfram | Alpha computes an answer based upon its own database.

The most interesting new expert is Siri, the all-knowing intelligent personal assistant of the iPhone 4S, introduced in 2011. You can ask Siri if you need to wear a sweater tomorrow or to remind you to brush your teeth, but you can also ask Siri for the gross domestic product (GDP) of Sweden or where to hide a body. Siri knows when to use each of the aforementioned experts, so if you ask her "What is my heart attack risk?" she starts with the information in your phone. She can determine from your calendar or your Facebook page that you are a 49-year-old male and maybe even a nonsmoker. She knows that neither Google nor Wikipedia will return useful data but that Wolfram | Alpha will calculate 5.1% (assuming average cholesterol and blood pressure).

In November 2011, Siri was accused of being prolife when a blogger discovered that Siri had trouble locating abortion clinics. The unverified and opposing explanations focused on how Siri uses crowdsourced databases (like Yelp) to find places and computational sources (like Wolfram | Alpha) to find data but avoids Google (which is an Apple competitor but also less reliable for data). Some even suggested a prolife manipulation of the underlying internet database. The point is that Siri, Google, Yelp, Wolfram | Alpha, and any of the other interfaces we now use to navigate this mountain of new data have become a new sort of expert, and, as with any other expert, we need to analyze and understand the bias inherent in any editing of data. The card catalog and your family doctor had biases too; however, we've become dependent on a new category of virtual experts, and it has changed how we determine authority. Just as we used to show students around the library and explain the different sorts of sources, students (and faculty) need to understand both how to get information from your phone and also how to judge its reliability.

The Internet is also redefining cheating. With so much information available, both good and bad, why is it cheating to use the Internet to find information you need on a test? In the workplace, the ability to evaluate the reliability of information and know how to use it is more important than where the information came from. Is it cheating if your doctor uses a computer to establish the right dosage for your medication? The *Physician's Desk Reference* (PDR) contains, among other things, correct dosages of prescription drugs. The online version enables more accurate dispensing and more extensive tracking of drug interactions, and it is certainly more comprehensive and current than any human doctor could be. The PDR will not replace doctors; it is a tool, like a stethoscope, and it still needs expertise to be used to advantage. Long division by hand used to be an important part of finding the right dosage, but now it's more important for a doctor to know how to ask the right question to access the best data and dispense the right prescription. Do you want a doctor who can do the math or knows what questions to ask? Do you want students who can memorize right answers or analyze input quickly and determine which answer is correct?

Whether we are educating citizens, job seekers, or scholars, it makes sense to ask students to memorize less and analyze more. Whether we call it digital literacy or critical thinking, future students must be able simultaneously to find information and evaluate it. Making tests open book and open Internet creates a situation that is much more like the real world, but it also requires a radical rethinking of the notion of testing. We can still use multiple-choice questions, but rather than ask questions that are about only pieces of information we need to design questions that test thinking skills.

As Bain (2004, p. 44) makes clear, even before the Internet, teaching the debates of our disciplines had an enormous impact on students. Textbooks had their biases too, but most students got to read only one at a time; unless faculty did considerable work to collate alternative versions, students had to take our word for what else was being said. Now it is easy to find disagreement about almost anything. Colleges and universities talk about teaching critical thinking, but we need to work much harder if we are really to change our focus from content to analysis and integration.

Implementation: 2009 Mammogram Controversy

Helping students sort out competing expert opinions has never been more important, and the Internet has made it easy to give students an incentive to build an argument outside of class. The mammogram controversy demonstrates both the difficulty of getting detailed information and the blurring of the lines between expert and amateur.

In November 2009, the U.S. Preventive Services Task Force released new recommendations for breast cancer screening, suggesting that screenings be optional until age 50. The American Cancer Society, however, continued to recommend annual screenings beginning at age 40. The new recommendations were intended to improve the efficacy of screening and to lower unnecessary biopsies and distress for women at average risk for breast cancer; instead, they created enormous controversy. The mathematical models and statistics demonstrated that lives would still be saved by starting the screening at 40, but with increased costs that included many more false positive results. (A mammogram becomes more accurate as women age.) Both sides used some of the same math but emphasized different facts: one to argue that for women under 50 the cost was too high (anxiety and unwarranted surgery) and the other that the benefit was too great (a live saved is a life saved).

Here is an opportunity to teach about science, statistics, public policy, journalism, or all of these. You might ask one group to make the case for why the recommendations are for the public good and another group to argue the opposite. Maybe the groups switch for the second class? Another group might be assigned to write a fair news story or understand the science or math—are the primary data available? Maybe another group tries to find the best websites and assemble a metasite that diagrams the controversy with links.

Such a public controversy is also a demonstration of the difficulty of finding an expert and understanding the basis for expert disagreement. Students will ask Siri, but they could also look at news stories and e-mail experts directly. Are there different sorts of experts? Do they have different missions or outlooks? Students could conduct a survey and create new data. Which data are most relevant? What role does or should emotion play? Such an assignment can be largely managed online. The classroom then becomes the place where fact is sorted from fiction and students learn the importance of analyzing the data they have collected.

Complicated and messy problems make great teaching tools. Virtually all students know a woman between 40 and 50, so this controversy will also be personal: in the end each of them will need to make a decision and give advice.

Online collaboration presents another challenge to traditional definitions of both authority and cheating. A confused student is much more likely to post his confusion on Facebook than raise his hand to ask you. Unbeknownst to you, students have probably already created websites and wikis for your class, and if you teach a class routinely some fraternity or sorority has a website that includes your last exam (captured on a cell phone). Students capture video and audio of your lectures and photos of your slides or whiteboard examples. The app Notability allows students to do all of this simultaneously and then e-mail or post notes, audio, video, or images immediately from a phone or iPad.

Students post questions on Facebook during class or send a picture of a homework problem to a friend because it works. Students are used to collaborating—the whole point of social media or crowdsourcing is that the collective will figure out if the movie is good or not and no one needs to read the expert review (although Fandango and other movie sites present the metascore from critics and fans side by side). Then faculty try to tell them such collaboration is wrong.

You can fight or use this trend. Rather than trying to turn off the Internet during exams, perhaps we simply need to rethink what we put on exams. If faculty believe collaboration is wrong, then we must design courses and assignments that demonstrate both the power and the pitfalls of collaborative information. Determining who is an expert, what skills will be most useful in the future, which information is relevant, and if and when collaboration is better than expertise needs to become a central part of course design and assessment. The types of questions we ask our doctor or banker have changed forever, and the types of questions we ask our students should change as well.

Implementation: Open-Book Assessment

Exams are rare in the workplace, but assessment is commonplace. If you must have exams:

- Design open-book exams for writing and analysis—then don't turn off the Internet.

- Build the use of the Internet into exams. Ask questions that require students quickly to find and analyze information.

- Test your questions against Google or Siri. You should know what happens if the exam is open book, even if you want closed book.

- Use timed tests for information that is indeed time dependent. Where possible, try to lower the stress and duplicate workplace conditions. If urgency is a part of the stress (because you are teaching crisis management) you still need to consider that exams are a different and additional source of stress. A three-hour test is still timed and adds stress. Match the amount of time to the task.

Consider how you can evaluate learning without exams:

- Use peer review of writing. Students work harder for each other.

- Increase the number of assessment events. More and shorter low-stakes routine assessment gives students control and reduces cheating.

- Use games. An ongoing fantasy version of your crisis management scenarios may be more realistic and provide better training.

- Use projects. Final papers have a long tradition in college, but try giving students case studies and creative, relevant topics.

- Get beyond paper and allow students to create a website or make a movie.

- Grade process. Instead of just grading the final result, create steps along the way so you can assess progress and how students are thinking.

- Make collaboration more like the workplace. Students dislike group projects; then they graduate, and few work alone. Create projects that have assigned roles and grade the process as well as the final result.

- Think like a teacher in an art or design school. What could you have students do to demonstrate mastery?

Aligning Classroom Activities and Assessment

Classroom activities and assessment methods should align to create conditions that foster motivation to achieve the high standards of the learning outcomes. Motivation, however, is related to relevance, and traditional assessment fails on that score. When content was more rare and valuable, it was easier to see the straight line from good testing to success in life. Today, it is hard to argue that doing well on closed-book tests prepares you for anything except more testing: college remains one of the last places where the ability to take tests matters both to get in and to get out. We should either change our mode of assessment or find new ways to demonstrate its relevance.

Professional schools use different teaching and assessment strategies than do colleges. In medical school, students do bedside rounds in small groups. In architecture school, students design and build. In theater school, they act and direct. In each, the motivation is built into the activity and the assessment: acting students don't take tests; they act. Medical students have to pass exams, but mostly they observe lots of operations, eventually hold a few clamps, and finally operate on their own. Lee Shulman (2005) calls these authentic activities the *signature pedagogies of the discipline*. Law school requires plenty of tedious memorization, but Shulman demonstrates how key ways of disciplinary thinking are embedded in every classroom. Law school classes may be large, but students are accountable both for preparation of cases in advance and for being able to analyze the arguments of fellow classmates in real time during class. Law classrooms are curved so students can see each other. Student A presents the case, and then student B is called upon to restate the arguments of student A or disagree. Students are highly motivated to prepare and pay attention in class: once they have been embarrassed once, they improve their preparation.

Law school assessment methods are also designed to reinforce the strategies of the profession. Some tests are closed book because some pieces of information must be instantly available. However, plenty of open-book exams, designed to see if you can think like a lawyer, are also given. In either case, what law professors really want is an exam answer that does more than just repeat the law. A good law answer evaluates which arguments are strong and which are weak, applies the law to the specific facts, identifies the key issues in the case, and demonstrates insight and judgment.

Every profession is becoming more like law and medicine: there is now more information than anyone can memorize and more need for analysis. The closed-book exam is becoming obsolete. Technology has given us new types of assessments and new ways to give students more and better feedback and increase motivation. Putting into practice what you have just learned and seeing the benefit of your hard work both motivates and reinforces learning.

For assessment to be motivating and relevant in the 21st century it needs to consider the changing importance of knowledge, analysis, customization, authority, and collaboration. We need to structure assignments so that preclass preparation and in-class activities align. When classroom discussions or activities make it clear that success occurs only by doing the preparatory activity, students prepare. Using technology to shift some assessment outside of the classroom can also improve both the quantity and quality of the classroom experience. With more prepared students and fewer exams in class, we have more time for interaction. The next step is to rethink what we do inside the classroom.

8

The Naked Classroom

We have a national problem: college is boring, and students are not graduating. Even for students from the top half of income distribution and with at least one parent with a college degree, a third quit before graduation (Bowen, Chingos, & McPherson, 2009). Administrators across the country have been willing to talk openly about the failings of our traditional lecture courses and the need for reform. You don't need a PBS special (*Declining by Degrees*, 2005) to show you students sleeping in class. If you see them dozing (or absent), it may be time to try a new pedagogy.

Technology gives us access to more and better content, communication, and assessment, but technology by itself does not create engagement. Traditional lecture courses can be improved by the judicious use of technology, but the primary benefit of technology-mediated content delivery, communication, and assessment outside of class is the additional time it creates for more active and engaged learning with prepared students inside the classroom. Nothing has more potential to eliminate boredom and create an incentive for students to come to class than a complete rethinking of the use of class time, overhauling it from a passive listening experience into a transformative learning environment.

There are things to be gained from a magnificent lecture, but the extra time that technology creates will not increase student learning if it is used to deliver more lectures. Think instead of the deep learning that might happen when students arrive to class prepared, giving us a chance to use that time with them to process information. Faculty have spent years refining their lectures and PowerPoint presentations, but all that content is available on the Internet and is now redundant. Face time with students was never very good at delivering content, but those same hours can be essential for:

- Interactive classes that find the right entry point, motivate change, or enhance intellectual curiosity
- Active learning and problem solving that deepen perspectives and investment in the material
- Writing and feedback on that writing that improves communication skills, personal expression, and reflection on the significance of material
- Discussions that challenge beliefs, connect information across disciplines, and develop high-level cognitive processing
- Lab and studio experiences, where new knowledge is constructed and new meanings are negotiated with faculty and peers
- Internships, work experience, and study-abroad and service-learning projects that demonstrate the human dimension, apply the material to new contexts, or create real-world contexts
- The appropriate use of technology in mentored or group activities

All of these activities are hard to do remotely, but in a naked active learning classroom where students are discussing, doing, and cooperating, the interaction between students and faculty can stimulate significant learning. Traditional college classroom sessions have generally focused on introducing content and assume that analyzing, reflecting, synthesizing, and caring will happen when students are alone and away from the professor. Technology offers us the chance to invert this model: naked pedagogy aligns the most critical aspects of learning with our most precious asset of nontechnological faculty–student face time with faculty in the classroom.

The Place of Lecture

Search committees and professional societies have pleaded with graduate programs to include more training in teaching for new PhDs, and for the most part our newly minted colleagues arrive with more teaching experience than more established faculty had when they first started out. Still, most new faculty spend enormous amounts of time creating what will ultimately be average lectures that offer nothing substantially different from those of their colleagues. The widespread availability of Web-based content means that those hours could be better spent improving learning rather than reinventing mediocre or even great content lectures.

Students want both convenience and quality. If I know that you are going to stand and deliver PowerPoint content for 50 minutes, I have many better options without getting out of bed. If I am deciding whether to go to your lecture on p-orbitals, I might first type the topic into iTunesU. I have my choice of audio or video and of 12- or 90-minute versions of the lecture. I can listen to another student or a professor from Columbia or the Khan Academy. If internet sources fail, I can have another student in class record or stream your lecture for me. Technical quality might motivate me to expend extra effort, but I will do the cost–benefit analysis. There are times when I just want to see my favorite clip from *Harry Potter* and the grainy YouTube video will do. Other times, I want the widescreen Blu-ray disk and will take the extra time to go rent it. In fact, many recorded lectures are far superior to those delivered by the average professor. Students will come to your lectures if they truly provide something that cannot be found in a more readily available format. Here are some ways to add value to your lectures:

• Lectures are good at showing students the right entry point into the content. The details of the American Revolution may be better explained by expert lecturers, in a book, or even by you on iTunesU, but you are in the best position to identify exactly what your students already know and which analogies and examples will resonate. Senior history majors in Virginia and freshmen at a community college in Oklahoma have different sets of assumptions and experiences. The Virginia freshmen will be more likely to have visited Mount Vernon or other local sites. Ignoring connection with our students can be catastrophic. As faculty with too much to cover, we sometimes do not spend the necessary time to find the aspect of our subject that will excite our students, and then we complain when students are disengaged. It is easy to dismiss the typical student complaint that "I don't know what the professor wants" but it contains a fundamental truth. If I push a student off the piano bench and say, "Play it like this," I better explain what *this* is. Do I mean louder, faster, or with my foot tapping? Students want to understand what and why we want them to learn. It is worth the time to find the best entry point.

• Lectures are excellent at motivation, so the world is full of live preachers and motivational speakers who have a book to sell. Books are better than lectures at delivering content, but a motivational speech can deliver a few new ideas and inspire you to think more deeply about a subject. A large part of motivation is style. Charisma helps, but visceral passion for the subject is essential. Even if (or maybe especially if) you think you are a poor lecturer, your chances of success are better if you reduce the content and aim to inspire.

• College students are looking for role models, and lectures are one place where we model our own intellectual, personal, and moral values (Bask & Bailey, 2002). With the paucity of good role models in sports or the media, this is your chance to be a role model for young people. Do you admit mistakes readily, consider both sides of each issue, and treat uninformed students with respect? Do you model caring for your students and the critical eye of scholarship even in your introductory classes? *Who you are in the lecture hall is as important as anything you say.*

• Lectures can be good at making connections and creating better questions. Lectures can be a place to question, identify, and undermine assumptions from the readings or that students bring to class. We often get so focused on content that we reduce or even delete the thinking parts of our lectures: it is hardly a surprise that most lectures rarely convey what we really want them to. Getting good responses to questions raised in lectures requires silence and time for contemplation. All of us have made the mistake of becoming nervous in the silence and answering our own question before students have a chance to think. Repairing this pattern of interaction models what inquiry is really about: in life we attend much less to the person who raises her hand first and much more to the person who gives us a thoughtful and interesting response. Model that approach in class.

So lectures can still be an inspiring and motivating force that can give us insight and open new doors. Rather than default to lectures because they are easy or because we don't know how to do anything else, however, we should lecture only when doing so meets the same criteria that we expect of any other pedagogical technique (Nelson, 2010). Is a lecture at this time best suited to the particular students in this class? Does it give students a sense of control, enhance motivation, and require high standards? Does it lead to higher-order thinking? Can you demonstrate that it will promote the learning outcomes you desire? Do you have something unique to say? And, perhaps most importantly, can you convert students to your discipline and make them shout hallelujah?

Implementation: Picking the Right Pedagogy

That lectures work is one of our common-sense academic assumptions. (Our bias, of course, is that as faculty we were a part of the small subset who enjoyed and flourished in that academic environment.) Craig Nelson (2010) argues that the evidence that *alternative* pedagogies (like those discussed in this book) are more effective is now so compelling that the burden of proof has shifted. His revealing list of *Dysfunctional Illusions of Rigor* should be nailed on the door of every classroom:

1. "Hard courses weed out weak students. When students fail it is primarily due to inability, weak preparation, or lack of effort." (p. 179)

2. "Traditional methods of instruction offer effective ways of teaching content to undergraduates. Modes that pamper students teach less." (p. 180)

3. "Massive grade inflation is a corruption of standards. Unusually high average grades are the result of faculty giving unjustified grades." (p. 180)

4. "Students should come to us knowing how to read, write, and do essay and multiple-choice questions." (p. 182)

5. "Traditional methods of instruction are unbiased and equally fair to a range of diverse students of good ability." (p. 182)

6. "It is essential that students hand in papers on time and take exams on time. Giving them flexibility and a second chance is pampering students." (p. 183)

7. "If we cover more content, the students will learn more content." (p. 184)

8. "A good, clear argument in plain English can be understood by any bright student who applies herself." (p. 187)

9. "Without further study, faculty know enough to revise their courses and departments know enough to revise their curricula.

> Course and curricular revision are primarily about what content to cover in what courses." (p. 188)
>
> Nelson (2010) methodically reveals the research that refutes each of these traditional views. As academics, we understand the value of research, yet we hesitate to reject our own assumptions, even in the face of overwhelming research that tells us how we can improve learning and retention. Institutions must demand that our teaching methods meet the same standards of evidence as the content we teach.

You should ask the same questions of your lecture that you might ask of a student who wants to put on a play in your class. Clearly, performing *Tartuffe* will enhance the student's learning of French, but will it also be the best technique for *this* class? Will it be worth the investment of class time and resources? The answer depends entirely on your learning outcomes. Watching fellow students might increase student engagement, but not always. We have all sat through too many hours of bad student presentations. Consider the level and abilities of the students: French 1 students might not be ready for *Tartuffe*, but it might be an excellent project for French 4, if many students participate. If you want to convince your students that Tartuffe is a character of great depth, would a student stage play or one of the great films be better? Likewise, does your lecture reach the heights of the best *Tartuffe*, or is it simply a restaging of content you learned in graduate school?

The key to any good class (or other) meeting is to make sure you really need people together in that place before you assemble them and then have clear goals for your time together. You can require attendance, but that works about as well for students as it does for faculty. The next time you fall asleep during a boring meeting, remember your own students. If students are in class, be clear about what the lecture needs to deliver beyond content.

Lectures do their best work when students do not take notes. Connection comes from attention, and note-taking inherently divides attention. Technology has already afforded us lots of ways to avoid the furious scribbling of our college days. Faculty can hand out the PowerPoint slides or put detailed notes in an LMS or a course notebook. We used to have paid note-takers, and now we have video capture. All of these methods, however, are still focused on the old technology of the audible transfer of content. If class were more like a well-run meeting, where ideas were exchanged and a defined outcome were achieved, students would still need to take a few notes, but mostly as a list of things to do.

Active Learning for Classroom Engagement

Students learn by doing. The term *active learning* includes a wide range of pedagogies from class writing and discussion to role-playing and lab work as well as collaborative, cooperative, and problem-based learning. Many of these labels and techniques overlap: all collaborative learning is done in a group, but it is also almost always active learning. What unifies these pedagogies is that students do much more than simply listen passively or take notes, and they are rarely bored.

Mark C. Carnes at Barnard College, for example, created a set of elaborate history games from a wide variety of periods and cultures from Athens in 403 to India in 1945 called Reacting to the Past (RTTP, http://reacting.barnard.edu/). Students are assigned roles informed by classic texts, and class sessions are run entirely by students. Consistent with Bain's (2004) research on effective learning, Carnes focuses these games on key moments or controversies, like the trials of Galileo or Anne Hutchinson. Professors advise and grade oral and written work. RTTP has been implemented at over 300 colleges and universities with overwhelming response. For example, at Dordt College in Iowa, students in Professor Paul Fessler's class spent a month on a French

Revolution game. When students needed more time to complete the game before the end of the semester, they volunteered to come 30 minutes earlier to every remaining class, a class that met at 8 a.m. One student explained, "Every student felt a strong investment in their roles. We read more in the weeks of the game than we had at any time before in the class. We plowed through the game manual, our history texts, Rousseau, you name it. We spent hours writing articles. I spent several all-nighters editing my faction's newspapers, and the other editors did, too. It had become more than a class to us by that point. The early-morning sessions were the only way to honor the sacrifices everybody had made" (Carnes, 2011).

Students learn from each other. There is good research to show that cooperative activities improve learning in higher education, even in science, technology, engineering, and math (STEM) fields (Hulleman & Harackiewicz, 2009.) One reason may be the curious discovery that direct instruction limits spontaneous exploration: students tend to assume that teachers have all the answers, so once a teacher has given the answer they stop trying and stop asking their own questions (Bonawitz et al., 2011). Prince (2004) found that the use of class time for active, cooperative, or problem-based learning resulted in improved retention, greater facility in application, and deeper understanding of content in a wide variety of disciplines.

The evidence that student attention and retention decreases dramatically after 15 minutes—regardless of the quality of the lecture—is long-standing (Wankat, 2002). Hartley and Davies (1978) found that even immediately after a lecture, students remember 70% of the content from the first 10 minutes and only 20% from the last 10 minutes. Even small adjustments can have large effects, though. Ruhl, Hughes, and Schloss (1987), for example, found that just pausing for two minutes three times during a 45-minute lecture to allow students to compare and clarify their notes significantly improved both short- and long-term content retention (immediately after class and five weeks later, respectively).

More engaging techniques provide even bigger benefits. Hake (1998) studied over 6,000 students in introductory physics courses and found that those using interactive pedagogies scored nearly twice as high (an improvement of two standard deviations) as those in traditional lectures on tests of conceptual understanding. Laws, Sokoloff, and Thornton (1999) confirmed the magnitude of this effect, whereas Redish, Saul, and Steinberg (1997) demonstrated that the improved learning was due not to additional time on task but to the nature of the learning activities.

Not all activities are equally effective, of course: the best activities foster thinking and develop conceptual understanding. Much of the research is discipline specific, and implementation and results vary. The same methods are unlikely to work on every type of student. Looking only at STEM fields, Springer, Stanne, and Donovan (1999) found that group work produced substantial gains in learning but that the magnitude of the benefit of group work eventually tapered off: in other words, it was possible to spend too much time in groups.

Restructuring your class with active learning exercises requires a different sort of preparation than preparing another PowerPoint lecture. The good news is there are plenty of options and huge banks of ideas to stimulate experimentation, spanning the spectrum from lecturing with pauses to turning your classroom into a historical game. *Active Learning: Creating Excitement in the Classroom* (Bonwell & Eison, 1991) is a short, easy read that works its way from modified lectures to debates, role-playing, and peer teaching. There is probably already a list of good activities designed and proven to be effective in your discipline. Barbara Millis's (2010) *Cooperative Learning in Higher Education* includes examples from a wide variety of fields from accounting and literature to STEM, but many of the techniques and examples can be applied to any discipline. Barkley (2010) sees student engagement as the intersection between student motivation and active learning. In her excellent catalog of 50 student engagement techniques, she emphasizes that both motivation and structured activity are required. Her techniques—largely structured activities—come with clear instructions and examples across all disciplines and class sizes.

Implementation: Barkley Student Engagement Technique No. 24 Think Again!

Barkley (2010) proposes that the teacher should present a common misconception and poll students on whether the statement is true. A following activity then provides students the opportunity to prove they are wrong. It almost does not matter what the subject is: imagine the intellectual benefit if undergraduates were constantly being forced to reevaluate their beliefs in every class they took. She provides an example from algebra, a subject known for its content-heavy *chalk-and-talk* classrooms:

Professor Polly Nomeal presented students with the following statement: "The maximum speed of a sailboat occurs when the boat is sailing in the same direction as the wind." She took a quick poll, and 80 percent of the students agreed. She then explained that their intuitive answer was wrong. She formed groups of three and told students, "Sailboats can actually go much faster when they sail across the wind. How so? Using what you have been learning in vector algebra, explain why sailboats can sail faster when the wind blows sideways to their direction of travel rather than from directly behind them. Make your explanation clear enough for the general public to understand. You can use diagrams if that helps." (Adapted from Bean, 1996, p. 27)

While *opening minds* is supposed to be a principal goal of a liberal arts education, the data consistently tell us that challenging student beliefs and preconceptions remains one of our most difficult and unsuccessful tasks. While the classroom seems an ideal place for challenging and exploring new ideas, furiously transcribing oral content is clearly not the ideal learning activity for teaching critical thinking. Active learning has been demonstrated to improve retention of content, but it can also stimulate critical thinking, as in the previous Implementation box.

For faculty with years of ready-to-deliver lectures, shifting to active learning is monumental. Start small: making minor modifications to create interactive lectures or breaking up lectures with demonstrations, buzz groups, mini-writing assignments, or other engagement techniques is relatively low risk and still pays dividends.

For new faculty, the conceptual leap to untried teaching styles is equally great as for seasoned faculty, and the fear of starting a new teaching career with new teaching techniques is even more daunting. Younger faculty need support in the form of mentorship and encouragement from colleagues to support their risk-taking in the classroom. New faculty should know that designing new courses that use class time for learning activities might take less time than preparing 45 PowerPoint presentations a semester.

Structuring Good Discussion

Discussion is an outstanding way to make the most of face time with students and to promote higher-order learning, but leading a good discussion that results in the learning outcomes you want can be much harder than delivering a competent lecture. A small group of prepared, talkative, and comfortable students and an engaging topic can make preparation easier, but striking a balance between guiding the discussion and letting students discover their own connections is difficult. Knowing when and how to intervene and cultivating patience and the ability to tolerate classroom silence takes practice, but there are some ways to foster productive student discussion.

Christensen (in Christensen, Garvin, & Sweet, 1992, pp. 153–172) frame the roles of discussion learning into questioning, listening, and response. Start by preparing a few good questions in advance (but not organized sequentially, as discussions are never linear). Different types of questions lead to different types of discussions, and one of the first tasks of the professor is to assess student needs and interests and connect them with the instructor's goals.

There is a crucial difference between the quantity and quality of classroom discussion. You can generate quantity by asking students what they think about the food in the cafeteria, but a high-quality discussion that fulfills your learning outcomes also requires student preparation. Many of the techniques in Chapters Five through Seven on how to prepare students for class can also be used to stimulate class discussion.

Faculty commonly assign reading as preparation for discussion. It is essential, however, to make sure that whatever preparation you require is directly relevant for the discussion. Do not assign a reading as background that won't somehow be discussed in class. Students will rarely make the connection on their own between the reading and the discussion. And once students discover that they can participate in class without reading the background, they will do so. A typical faculty mistake is to forget to refer directly to each specific reading in the class after the reading is due. Take five minutes (or find some other assessment) to make sure that students can articulate the basics of each reading: what it said, what it means, why it is important (see Chapter Six). If you can't afford the time to do this, then the reading is probably not essential.

Since writing is a skill that we want to cultivate and grading writing is time-consuming, using writing as a springboard for class discussion solves two problems at once. In a large class, you might start by asking pairs to discuss ideas written on index cards or in short papers. For a smaller class, Walvoord and Anderson (1998) includes a set of guidelines for group responses to draft writing. While their focus is on using this process to improve writing without more grading, it also provides a framework for class discussion (see Walvoord & Anderson, 1998, p. 114).

Running a good discussion is an art and takes flexibility, practice, and preparation. Christensen (in Christensen, Garvin, & Sweet, p. 159) recommends preparing with a very short typology of questions, including diagnostic, hypothetical, implication, and action. During the discussion, Christensen describes what amounts to a dance of alternating listening and responding, with ongoing choices between attending to content and to process. Students also need guidance in how to conduct themselves during a discussion.

Implementation: Teaching Discussion Behaviors

Faculty need to be transparent about what discussion behaviors will be rewarded and how.

Ask students to focus on making two types of comments (from Harnish, 2008):

1. Comments introducing substantive points that are "clearly a result of thoughtful reading and thinking about the assigned text and become . . . the focus for group exploration lasting several minutes." Examples include:

   a. Identify essential issues or questions the text is discussing.

   b. Point to the author's main hypotheses, claims, and supporting arguments and evidence.

   c. Point to important passages that need to be understood.

   d. Explain the complexities faced in exploring this text.

   e. Describe passages that are personally meaningful or connected to some shared experience.

2. Comments that deepen the discussion, such as:

   a. Provide additional supportive quotes; explain relevance; ask clarifying questions.

b. Share the thought process that was personally used in developing an idea.

c. Paraphrase what the author means in a specific passage.

d. Summarize the arguments being presented.

e. Identify similarities and differences in positions being argued.

f. Challenge an idea or present an alternative interpretation.

g. Connect ideas from several participants or from other texts the group has read.

h. Formulate insightful questions that spark group response.

i. Introduce personal experiences that illuminate the text for others.

Faculty should help prepare students for group discussion by providing in advance (1) guidelines for good behavior (like those previously outlined), (2) learning outcomes for the discussion (that might include learning how to make quality contributions to discussion), and (3) an entry point for the reading (see Chapter Six). Faculty should also clarify that discussion is a group exploration and that, like faculty, students should weigh the individual importance of what they want to say against how it will help the group progress.

Such behaviors can be reinforced if students understand the grading system for class discussion. Students are conditioned to think that talking more in class is a good thing. Grading participation will encourage students to talk, but if you just want to encourage talking you can probably get the same results by handing out pieces of chocolate for every comment. (I use about two bags of chocolate kisses every semester.) Creating a system that rewards quality over quantity will improve the substance and depth of your discussions. For example, after each class send out an e-mail (or post on the class discussion board) the best examples of good seminar behaviors. Alternatively, post what contributions were most useful in discovering new insights or including new members. Such contributions could be an extra credit or required part of the grading scheme: for example, each student must make two substantive contributions to class discussion during every week.

The way you conduct the discussion also matters. You can model good discussion behavior for students by providing compliments, defusing tense moments, and creating the right environment. Do what you can to create the best physical environment. Rearrange the rows of chairs into a big circle. Call on students by name. If you can tell a student is having trouble getting a word in, then hold off the others and call on that student. You might start by allowing students to introduce themselves by completing the statement, "Hi, I'm Joe, and in discussion sessions I usually . . ." Explain and model good active listening with eye contact, smiles, nods, and supportive body language.

It is also the responsibility of faculty to manage the discussion in real time by keeping the group focused on the topic or text. If there is a lull, you can summarize the discussion so far and either (1) ask for a clarification or deepening insight on the current topic (perhaps from a new voice) or (2) introduce or ask for a transition to a new topic. Providing potential questions in advance will also help guide the discussion.

Another method is to have students monitor the discussion themselves. Ask them to sit in two concentric circles: the inner circle participates in the discussion; the outer circle (where faculty sit) observes and then (after 10 minutes) analyzes the quality of the inner-circle discussion. For example, did the question get resolved? Was participation spread adequately? Did anyone monopolize or make negative attacks? Did the group introduce new questions or insights? Then have the groups switch and pose a new question. If you want, you can put an empty chair in the inner circle and allow outer-circle students who simply must make a comment to briefly use the empty chair.

As with a good lecture, discussion or seminar classes need to be structured into clearly defined sections to help students understand the purpose of the discussion. You might not want to tell students the exact aims of a discussion, but hoping students will stumble upon the key passage in a text is not a sound pedagogical strategy. Try telling students that you want to talk about a particular topic for 15 minutes and why. Then at the end of the section you can tell them what you hope they discovered through their discussion. Have them reflect (perhaps in writing) on what they understood. In the two-circle technique, for example, you might tell students that the goals are to allow them to have discussion without your assistance and to improve the quality of that discussion by focusing on how groups can work together to answer questions.

You also need to support risk and failure. Try a brainstorming technique where students need to come up with a long list of potential uses for used cars or 10 different interpretations of a story. The point is to create a long list, not to worry about the quality of the list. Getting students used to errors and mistakes as a part of the process and getting them comfortable with each other's failures will create the sort of relaxed environment where risk can occur.

Faculty can also support risk (and civility) by asking students to relate new comments to old ones. Ask students to start with a summary and a compliment ("What I like about your idea is . . .") before they disagree or digress. It is also useful to ask students to paraphrase and then ask for clarity about a point. Help students understand the different types of disagreement: is there a difference of facts, interpretations, belief systems, cultural assumptions, or type of discourse? Ask a third student to summarize a disagreement and a fourth student to articulate the nature of the disagreement. Understanding the rules of academic discourse is difficult, and I make this a topic in and of itself.

Implementation: What Is Discourse?

I ask students to read a short definition of discourse and then engage in a group discussion about an inconsequential topic or popular argument just to demonstrate the different modes of argument and how academic discourse tries to encompass multiple modes at once. How to find the best pizza is a topic of at least some interest on most campuses.

How to Find the Best Pizza

Different modes of discourse *is a fancy way of saying there are different ways of talking about something: criticism, history, technical analysis, cultural analysis, or return on investment, for example. Some ways of knowing are better suited to some kinds of knowledge. Descartes, for example, tried to prove logically that God existed, but most people think faith is separate from logic. Are you more likely to be converted by a logical argument or an enthusiastic sermon?*

You should by now have a large body of opinions and ideas. While fact versus opinion is a useful dichotomy, most things are rarely just one or the other. How can you identify better opinions? When you want to find the best pizza, do you assume this sort of knowledge does not exist? In other words, is everything you can know about the best pizza just opinion, or are there useful things you can discover about where the best pizza might be found? Think of at least three different modes of discourse you could use to demonstrate which is the best pizza, and be prepared (1) to argue in each mode and (2) to discuss the strengths and weaknesses of each mode.

If students are stumped or slow to respond, then feeding them one mode at a time can get them started:

1. Survey: This is empirical data, but does your survey distinguish different cultural responses? Chicagoans and New Yorkers

have different pizza preferences. How is it useful (or useless) to determine which Dallas pizza tastes best to New Yorkers?

2. Expert: Does a food critic have taste better than you? Maybe she just has more experience (i.e., has been to all of the pizza shops on campus)?

3. Deduction: Do the best ingredients make the best pizza?

4. Value: Is there a price point at which there are diminishing returns? Or is best an absolute standard?

5. Cultural knowledge: Ask an Italian? Or its advertising corollary, pizza made *by* an Italian must be best. What sort of knowledge is a Chinese restaurant full of Chinese patrons or a truck stop with lots of trucks outside?

Another fun topic is the different ways you might argue with your roommate about his need to sleep with the light on.

Writing in *On Liberty*, John Stuart Mill claimed that an argument should consist of 75% counterarguments. To make your own writing and thought more persuasive, you must "know them [counterarguments] in their most plausible and persuasive form . . . must feel the whole force of the difficulty which the true view of the subject has to encounter and dispose of" (Mill, 1859, p. 67). As a discussion technique, ask a student to propose a theory or insight and then ask the remaining students for the supporting arguments, followed by a listing of the counterarguments.

In discussion, as with a lecture, a periodic change of activity to refresh the mind is a good thing. Remember that not all students thrive in the cut and thrust of heated debate. You might stop a discussion and have students take 10 minutes to write a position or create a knowledge concept map (see Hay, Kinchin, & Lygo-Baker, 2008). You can read these later or have students share with each other. The point is that if you want discussion to have an effect on their thinking, you need to provide opportunities for reflection and thinking.

Some silence is still golden. One of the hardest things for faculty to do is to remain quiet and listen. You can gauge the effectiveness of your structure by how little you have to say. There are times, of course, when even the best structure fails. Resist the temptation to fill the void with a lecture. Sitting and enduring complete silence for 10 minutes may be the hardest thing you ever have to do as a teacher, but you probably will not have to do it twice in the same class. Some prefer to dismiss class with the apology that you will try to create better conditions for discussion the next time. I prefer to wait or start again at the top: ask students to create written responses and then use these to restart discussion.

The Lab and the Studio

While large lecture halls and midsize classrooms dominate most college campuses, two common classroom models—the laboratory and the studio—lend themselves better to faculty–student interaction. Both are places where students are typically engaged in active learning and faculty and students are more likely than in the traditional classroom to be working side by side.

The student lab is a place where students practice techniques, but it is also a place of discovery. A lab or studio, whether it is dedicated to costuming, computers, or chemistry, is a combination of rules, repetition, creation, and feedback. Every lab has its rules, some for safety and others for courtesy, but labs on all parts of the campus are places where the habits of the discipline are learned. Students also learn that there is a connection between best practices and the practical success of the lab. Cutting corners results in compromised results in a more tangible way than it does in the lecture hall; students can discover for themselves the effects of dirty glassware. Most of us understand from experience the need to back up computer data; learning may take place the hard way, but experience works.

Very few students sit down in a lecture hall thinking that they might make an important (or even unimportant) discovery for the world in this place, but students enter the lab or studio with more creative ambitions. It may simply be popular mythology, but the lab conjures up images of Einstein, mad scientists, and cures for cancer. And, in truth, running experiments (if they really include an element of exploration) is creating knowledge in a way that taking lecture notes generally is not.

Studios are also places of collaboration and feedback. Like labs, studios tend to be places where the professor moves around giving individual advice and responding to student work. Studio work is likely to be project based and might be done individually or in teams; painters work individually, but dancers, scientists, actors, engineers, designers, and programmers often work in groups. In a studio, students are self-directed and self-motivated: they have a goal (often a project, performance or a design) and must try different approaches to get there. Students in a studio know they must arrive prepared; directors, conductors, and choreographers are constantly reminding students that they have an obligation to each other (and not simply to the teacher) to know their part and be ready to work when they arrive. Studios too are places where knowledge is constantly being discovered and shared. How can we make more classrooms like studios and labs?

What would happen if your English or calculus class tried to emulate the environment of a painting or dance studio, with the work ethic, focus, and potential for discovery? Perhaps every student is seated at a math easel (maybe with an iPad or a notepad) working on a series of problems. The professor could walk around and stop to help or point out an interesting error or success to the entire class. When a student comes up with a new way of solving the problem, she might get to tell the rest of the class. Or maybe students work in groups to come up with more elegant ways to retell a short story. Groups could recite their versions to the rest of the class and get feedback and then go back for more revision. No one goes home until everyone has accomplished the task.

All of our disciplines engage in some sort of research, but we often delay both the process and the excitement of research until students have plodded through introductory theory courses. But why not start with the lab and give students the motivation to learn more theory? Suppose the first semester of your engineering major were a group project to get a ping-pong ball from one side of the gym to the other using only remote control devices, with a time delay as if the students were on Earth and the ball on Mars? (This is a real example from www.smu.edu/lyle.) Modeling real-world collaboration, teams need to include students from different areas working together. Students in the performing arts want to get onstage right away, and for the most part we let them. Why not start with a real experimental question for scientists and a design problem for engineers? We know from Bain (2004, pp. 39–42) that students who think of themselves as scholars with something to contribute become deeper learners: why not harness that motivation and make discovery the core of every class?

High-Impact Student–Faculty Interaction

Studios and labs work partly because they are focused on the practical and partly because they are sites of intense student–faculty interaction. Civic engagement, study abroad, research, work experience, and internships can all work the same way: providing motivation for more theoretical work; helping complete Fink's (2003) taxonomy by stimulating application, synthesis, and caring; but also bringing students and faculty together in new situations.

Randy Bass at Georgetown University's Center for New Designs in Learning and Scholarship points out that student surveys at Georgetown consistently show that their deepest learning happens outside the classroom. He notes that four of the eight high-impact learning activities identified by students in the National Survey of Student Engagement require no classroom time at all: internships, study abroad, research, and a thesis or capstone project (Young, 2011). All of these programs have also been identified as best practices on successful college campuses (Kuh, Kinzie, Schuh, & Whitt, 2005).

Is there a service-learning project that might enhance your class and simultaneously motivate your students and provide opportunities for application of class work? Many colleges now have centers that coordinate off-campus activities, but for service learning to have maximum effect it needs to be connected to coursework and the classroom. Students can learn something dishing out food, but service learning works best when students have an understanding of a real problem, a theoretical framework, and learning outcomes that help them apply knowledge to a new context. The benefits multiply in an engaging project that matters: students learn from and inspire each other, they become self-motivated, and the various types of learning seem naturally connected.

Internships and work experience have also not been a traditional part of a liberal arts education, but when carefully integrated they also can stimulate broader self-learning. The Millennial generation is all about integration: they want it all. Millennials believe they can and should both make money and give back. They want success both in and out of the classroom (Howe & Strauss, 2000). Connecting the classroom to the workplace or the world is a natural for this generation.

One strategy could be to abandon campus class time entirely. If internships, service learning, research, and study abroad are good sites of student learning and lectures are not, we could certainly lower costs by delivering lectures online and then meeting students mostly or only in our labs or studios or off-campus at sites of internships, civic engagement, or study abroad. I suspect that the higher-education, for-profit version of the Lexus, when it arrives, will look something like this: virtually infinite online content, tutoring, and other flexible resources combined with physical faculty–student interaction, providing the most benefit with the lowest cost.

For those of us not working at the university of the future, however, is there some way to harness that same connection inside the classroom? Look for ways to bring the most pressing problems of the world and your discipline into the classroom. Create assignments that provide easy opportunities for students to connect the classroom to the outside world. Find out what grocery store clerks know about the food they sell. Research the computer needs of your local church. Ride public transportation and explain your love of Beethoven to a stranger. Are there ways to bring local problems into your classroom? Doing this creates empathy and connection with your subject.

When you do not need to see your students face-to-face, send them off-campus. When you do see them, ask yourself what situations offer the maximum student benefit. While the maximum impact situation could be active learning activities or a structured discussion, it might also be meeting in a museum or in your lab. Look for opportunities for these high-impact faculty–student experiences.

Leveraging Personal Technology in the Classroom

As a professor, you can choose not to use PowerPoint, but what do you do about all of the technology that students bring to class? Do you ban laptops or cell phones? We know that despite their deeply held beliefs students cannot actually multitask; they merely switch tasks very quickly (Marois & Ivanoff, 2005). Student technology can clearly get in the way of some classroom activities, but getting students to stop using it is challenging.

Students want respect, consistency, and professors who "get it." If you can deliver all three, you can win students over.

First, respect students enough to make class interesting and worth the time to stop texting. Collecting cell phones in every class or embarrassing a student caught texting during class ("Are you texting your girlfriend? Let's all call her!") will diminish any respect you might have earned. There are few rules about texting you can truly enforce while teaching. A class that is engaging and requires interaction is the best weapon you have. Accept that texting and posting are now a part of student life. Complain if you must, but for many students today an experience is not an experience if they cannot share it. If you have been to a wedding, art gallery, or political rally recently, you may have noticed that it is now common to see an ocean of phones held up high, as observers make and post videos and photos in real time. It is not that students are always bored; they simply want to share important experiences. If they can tear their eyes away from the IMAX 3-D screen during the climax of a *Mission Impossible* film to check Facebook, they will text during your class. Try following a few of your students on Twitter to see what they are tweeting and posting about your class. If your class is really interesting, students will post about that, and you should declare victory and move on.

Second, make some use of technology in class but have consistent policies: think about what your policies say about your attitude toward the modern world. For example, requiring students to hand in a hard copy of a paper may seem routine to you, but it can be a hardship for students who have to drive to campus. Doing so will be perceived as a lack of respect, and even the real academic world no longer works this way: when was the last time you sent a piece of paper to a journal? In the real world, there are laptops and cell phones; you have probably been in a meeting where a question about something came up, and in seconds a person with a laptop or a cell phone had the important information required. Building judicious use of personal technology into your classroom will demonstrate to students that you get it and are not simply too old to understand how technology can be helpful.

Try, for example, structuring a class around a missing piece of information that you "accidentally" forget to bring with you to class. Ask students if they can find the reference or data you need, but pick something that will result in a large number of students landing on the wrong page or getting the wrong information. (Are tomato sauce and ketchup really bad for you?) Ask students to resolve the conflicting results, and determine how they might get better information about the subject. How do they know if they have the right information, and what could you all do to establish which information is correct? A good argument that pits you and your brain against students and their cell phones can be both fun and informative, and hopefully the horse will sometimes outrun the steam engine. Since the rules of evidence are different in our different disciplines, such an activity can lead to a useful discussion about standards of information. (Without the benefit of a scholarly study or a U.S. Food and Drug Administration ruling, how might we analyze the claims that ketchup might give your baby allergies or increase your sperm count?) You can use technology and still have the essential part of the experience be about the attention and drama that happens in the physical classroom.

Third, make a contract with students to turn off all laptops and cell phones periodically and just think and be present. You will need to convince them of the benefit, but new experiences are exactly the point of college. Try allowing students to use laptops or cell phones sometimes, but as part of an activity. Ask students, for example, to open their laptops and do a short writing exercise. Then say the magic words: *please close your laptop.* If you consistently use the closed-laptop time for important engaged thinking or useful activities, students will return the respect and tune in. Make paying attention a learning outcome (and note that *paying* implies that it costs something). Helping students discover the benefits of focused dialogue and reflection is as important as any content you have to cover.

Implementation: Overcoming Student Resistance

I am often approached at workshops with a question that goes something like this: "I tried teaching naked and active learning. I stopped lecturing and completely changed my class. All of my data demonstrate that students learned more, so I know it works. But students complained to me that my class was the only one where I expected them to actually do the reading. I got slammed in my course evaluations. I have to get tenure, so do I need to go back to the traditional passive and easy lecture course for a while?"

Students are good at finding easy courses with the unstated agreement that professors will give them the minimum amount of work if they promise to leave the professors alone to do research. These courses exist at every university. Switching to active learning during class time will require that students take more responsibility and come prepared. Regardless of how well you design your course and construct your assessments to line up with your learning outcomes, some students will resent not being in an easier class. You can take heart in the expectation that as more faculty are forced into more active learning methods the situation will change.

Some of the resistance is because lectures are easy; both students and faculty understand the expectations. You know how much work you have to do to create a new lecture, and if it goes wrong you can probably fix it. It is much harder to lead a good discussion or create an activity that really delivers, and you were probably not trained to do so. Faculty should compare their first attempts at new teaching methods with their first attempts at teaching and not with their fine-tuned lecture classes. For teachers with average student evaluations, adopting active learning tends to improve ratings in the long-term (Felder, 2011).

Felder (2011) suggests a number of ways to separate real problems with pedagogy from the way you are implementing it:

- Do your students complain specifically about your pedagogy, or do they also complain about the length of your exams, the clarity of your assignments, or your lack of office hours? Try fixing those things first before you abandon the pedagogy.

- Tell students that you are using a different pedagogy that research demonstrates will lead to important job skills, and be specific about what they are.

- Be sure that you are allowing enough class time for activities to unfold productively. Not doing so is a common mistake that can kill the effectiveness of active learning (see Felder & Brent, 2009).

- Use midterm evaluations and specifically ask students if they think the active learning pedagogy is helping or hurting their learning. Share these results with the class; if students see a majority are doing well, they may give it one more try.

- Have you used this new pedagogy long enough to accommodate your own learning curve? You will get better with practice, just as you did with lecturing.

The Classroom as a Stimulating Learning Environment

We know that the atmosphere in a classroom is as important as any information available there. We used to be able to argue for lectures by saying that knowledge was available only in our classrooms or that students arrive unprepared for more in-depth learning. Even before technology eliminated both excuses, the best teachers were those whose classrooms were places of relaxed uncertainty, controversy, and discovery. Now that students arrive both bored and carrying encyclopedias in their pockets, it is imperative that we stimulate both their minds and their technology and not let them sit passively.

Creating a classroom environment that values attention, contribution, risk, evaluation, synthesis, application, empathy, and cooperation requires real work and serious change for most courses. Most of us value those things, but if we are still trying to cover the content most days then students will perceive us as out of touch with the basic fact of modern life that everything you might ever want to know is already on the Internet. Given this wealth of knowledge, application and evaluation are increasingly essential; also, no faster technology will ever eliminate the need for human attention, empathy, and thoughtfulness, essential lessons that have enduring value.

Thinking of your classroom as a lab or a studio can help start the transformation. Are there other ways you can interact with students? Can you model a different behavior? What can students do with what they are learning? Is there something we can create together with this new knowledge? While change will take work, it can be liberating and satisfying to refocus your classroom on your research, on problems that matter, or on just having more fun.

The naked classroom allows us the time to focus on creating significant learning experiences for our students. Delivering content in advance, motivating learning with multiple channels of communication, and constructing assignments that force students to prepare for class will change both your expectations and those of your students for what happens in class. Presenting interactive lectures only when it truly serves your learning outcomes, using active learning techniques, structuring focused discussions, and using technology as a deliberate tool when necessary can turn even the largest survey course into an engaging studio environment. The technology that gives us more and better useful information in more accurate, precise, and easier ways is only going to improve: Apple's Siri is already faster, more knowledgeable, and even funnier than you are. Student boredom with traditional education will only increase unless you can substitute engagement for content in your classroom. Creating an atmosphere that allows for failure and exploration will make the most use of student preparation and make your classroom a place worth visiting.

Part III

Strategies for Universities of the Future

9

The Educational Product
in the Internet Age

Competition and change are new concepts in higher education. Some in the academic ranks are surprised (or even
offended) by calls for accountability: we know that what we do is
good and important, and we like to think of students as our product rather than as our customers. We are slow to embrace change
and value our stability over the centuries, but we can no longer
afford the luxury of being stuck in the past. Part One outlined the
technological drivers of breathtakingly rapid change. Part Two
demonstrated how faculty can harness technology to improve
learning, especially the quality of the precious face time we have with
our students. Part Three will address the more administrative and
financial issues confronting face-to-face higher education and will
argue that teaching naked is a vital strategy for its survival.

Any of the challenges universities now face would be significant on their own: a long and steady decline of state funding
coupled with a prominent rise in government and public frustration
over high tuition; new global competition; a weak global economy; a demographic shift that will reduce the number of potential
applicants; a declining graduation rate from public high schools;
and a profound technological revolution that is redefining fields
of knowledge, access to knowledge, and even the importance and
meaning of knowledge. Together, however, these new pressures
will dramatically increase competition, incentives for new models, the pace of change, and the need for an institutional strategy
focused on better student learning

Delivery systems for all sorts of products have changed with technology, but changes in delivery systems also alter what is delivered and how it is consumed. It is easy to assume that education will escape such pressures because our product is so unusual. The history of music delivery is a cautionary tale for higher education partly because it is so easy to confuse the product with the packaging in both industries. Silly as it may now seem, many people believed that liner notes and album cover art were an inseparable part of selling music that would keep record stores in business. (Tower Records closed in 2006.) Similarly, universities have invested heavily in recreation centers, sports teams, and residence halls in recent years in an attempt to attract students. As a new generation looks at the costs and benefits of a university education, however, the product may be redefined as distinct from the associations of its previous packaging.

Recorded music, books, and journalism are examples of products that no longer require the same physical packaging, and this chapter begins by analyzing the recent upheavals in these industries. For music, this is the third time around: music delivery has been through two pre-internet revolutions, and each time changes in technology altered the perception of the product, created a new relationship with the consumer, and changed expectations of quality. Lessons from these three industries provide lessons for predicting how the Internet will transform our local educational product.

Music Delivery Before the Internet

Music in the 18th century was always live and almost always involved some social interaction. Musical instruments were expensive and required professional training, so courts, councils, and churches employed professionals to make music. Unless you were a professional musician who could indulge in the unprofitable luxury of playing for yourself in an empty room, music was always a social activity (Raynor, 1972).

At the beginning of the 19th century, the music publisher Breitkopf pioneered the use of a new cheap letterpress printing for music (Chanan, 1994). At the same time, an expanding middle class and reduced production costs created a market for pianos in homes. Piano makers Broadwood, Pleyel, and Erard began producing and selling thousands of pianos a year (Ehrlich, 1990). The new hardware (the piano) needed a steady flow of new software (scores or sheet music). In London there were 12 music shops in 1750, 30 in 1794, and 150 in 1824. While music catalogs in the 1700s listed no more than a few hundred compositions, the Boosey catalog of 1824 ran to 280 pages with 10,000 foreign publications (Rothstein, 1987). The opportunities and competition for sheet music became global, resulting in three important changes in the way music was consumed.

First, the change in delivery system changed the nature of the product. In the 18th century, a *Kapellmeister* (like Bach) created live music—an event. The distribution system was limited to the distance from which you could hear live music. Like most professors, Bach did not need to produce a fully notated score each week; he could perform from his own sketches or even improvise. Beethoven could also improvise, but if he wanted to capitalize on the new global market he needed to produce detailed sheet music—an annotated score. In the same way that textbooks allow students to distinguish between the course content and the quality of teaching, 19th-century listeners gradually began to distinguish between the musical work and its interpretation, between what the composer had written and the sounds made by the performer.

Second, the new technology brought music directly to the consumer in a private space. Hearing music in the 18th century was like going to college; it required a massive expense to pay for professionals and infrastructure. Few musicians were freelancers; most were full-time employees of cities, churches, or wealthy patrons. While hardware (i.e., a piano) was not initially cheap, it was now much easier to hear music in the home and in private when you could own your own piano and buy sheet music from which to play.

Third, standardization of delivery created a global market. Internationalization brought consumers both higher quality and more variety. While 18th-century English listeners would have heard some foreign music from traveling musicians, most of their musical diet was local and homegrown. By the end of the 18th century, however, English consumers could now choose from thousands of cheap editions of Italian, French, and German music. Despite the huge catalogs carried by music shops all over Europe, however, most of them carried the same music, so there was little variation of choice; from London to Vienna everyone was playing the same Beethoven sonatas.

The unification and expansion of the market, therefore, created a single huge pyramid of success. When music was an event and not a thing, there was a limit to how much music any single musician could provide. Markets for music were essentially local, with musicians competing against other local artists for the best live gigs. Music publishing, however, allowed musicians to duplicate the product beyond such limits. The standardization of delivery allowed for standardization of product; as long as Beethoven wrote piano sonatas that could be played on the standard piano with five octaves (which he did), his music could be played almost anywhere in Europe.

Remarkably, the cycle repeated with new musical technology and similar consequences at the beginning of the 20th century. This time the new technology was the phonograph, the player piano, and the radio. Again, the same three effects emerged: the change of the product, more music with less social interaction, and eventually a single global pyramid of success.

First, the nature of the product changed again. Like sheet music, a recording is software that needs hardware (in this case, a phonograph) to turn it back into sound, and it is much easier to turn a record than sheet music back into music. Sheet music had created a new category of specialized composers, and now recordings created a new category of performers like Benny Goodman, Elvis Presley, and Michael Jackson, who became famous even while few remember their associations with composers Fletcher Henderson, Jerry Leiber, Mike Stoller, and Quincy Jones. Recorded performance became the new product.

The second effect was, again, a more personalized experience. Gramophones and radios were even cheaper than pianos and required even less skill to make them play. With radio, the programs were free. You could change the station to customize to your tastes, although you had to listen to what was broadcast. With records, later headphones, and finally the Sony Walkman, music became increasingly private and personalized.

The third effect, the creation of a single global market, again allowed a small number of musicians (now performers), previously limited by the speed of international travel and their own stamina, to be around the world all at once. Like Beethoven, opera singer Enrico Caruso recognized the potential of the new technology. He made more than 260 recordings, including the first million seller, his 1904 recording of "Vesti la giubba." He raised expectations of quality for millions of consumers who would never visit the Metropolitan Opera House to hear him sing in person. Local musicians (i.e., the vast majority of all musicians) had to adapt to the new standards of professionalism.

The same three trends can already be seen in higher education. First, the nature of our product is changing. Students no longer need to spend four years on a leafy campus to get an education. The potential market is large, so there is a huge incentive to create new products. Cheap pianos created a new demand for method books, so Carl Czerny could give up doing gigs and instead teach piano lessons and sell didactic piano etudes like "The Art of Finger Dexterity." Similarly, the Khan Academy and the University of Phoenix have taken advantage of the opportunities for new products afforded by the new environment.

Second, the new products are not just spectacularly cheaper but more private, more convenient, and more personalized. We can now listen or watch the lectures we choose whenever and wherever we want.

Third, the market has become more standardized. Nationally distributed textbooks have made most Chemistry 101 courses more alike, and the new global market for video lectures will further increase standardization. At the moment, thousands of faculty design and teach unique versions of Chemistry 101, but in the future there will be less variety and probably wider distribution of the very best versions. As with music, increased professionalism and standardization will improve quality and reduce choice.

The Internet brought yet a third revolution in music delivery, and record companies were slow to refashion themselves as music companies. Record companies had seen formats change before—LPs replaced 45's, and CDs replaced LPs—so they assumed that this change would be similar. Few anticipated that the change from physical storage devices to digital files would so radically alter the product itself and the way it was consumed (Bowen, 1998). Yet once again, a shift in the delivery technology altered the nature of the product, brought consumers more privacy, and expanded the global market.

The Internet Transformation in Books and Journalism

The Internet and mobile wireless devices have altered the delivery and hence the nature of even more industries, especially those focused on intellectual property. All of these industries have felt the same three effects on the distribution system: a change in the nature of the product; more customization and social isolation; and a global market of infinite choice.

Borders assumed that selling books required both the traditional shopping environment (coffee, overstuffed chairs, and a huge selection) and the traditional physical product (paper pages bound together). When Borders first arrived in small towns or suburbs during their expansion in the 1990s, their thousands of square feet focused on customer service and selection were greeted with joy. Louis Borders developed a precomputer inventory system on square three-inch punch cards that became a separate business, Book Inventory Systems, and was used by other major independent booksellers (Leopold, 2011). The Internet, however, radically altered the concept of *inventory*: it is important only if you want to try before you buy or you need the product today. Once consumers got used to trading a few days of waiting in exchange for convenience, lower prices, and even more selection, the expense of maintaining inventory in multiple locations became a drag on the business.

Borders, however, also confused the packaging with the product: books, it turns out, are really just format neutral sequences of words. Seeing Barnes & Noble (and not Amazon) as the real threat, Borders missed the importance of both the Internet and e-books. After launching its website in 1998 (the same year as the film *You've Got Mail* featured a small bookstore battling against a chain bookstore), Borders outsourced its online business to Amazon in 2001 and did not return to the Web until 2008. Amazon introduced the Kindle in 2007, and by July 2011 Amazon announced it was selling 105 Kindle books for every 100 print books (Amazon, 2011). Barnes & Noble stock fell 75% between 2006 and 2011 and then banked on a strategy that its own e-reader, the Nook, would allow it to survive (Mangalindan, 2011). Printed books are almost as old as universities, but almost everything about the industry has changed overnight.

Journalism is another intellectual property-based industry where the Internet has transformed the product. Your local newspaper used to offer something you could not get anywhere else: access to expert analysis on both local and international issues. Newspapers were part of larger networks that allowed the product to be tailored and delivered to individual regions, and local advertising and classified ads paid the bills. Now that cars, apartments, and everything else can be more efficiently bought and sold on the Internet, movie times are on your phone, and the news of the world is streamed to your iPad, the regional newspaper that includes world news (now hours old) is a dinosaur. Newspapers in every small town now print the same national and international news from the Associated Press, Reuters, or one of the major newspapers that still deploys correspondents. Newspapers are cheap, but people cancel their subscriptions when they can get the information elsewhere for free. The problem is that the local paper was really a combination of products. When some of those products became redundant, newspapers failed to understand the part that still had commercial value. When the business model for classified ads or world news collapsed, newspapers made the mistake of giving away their most important product—the work of local reporters—for free on the Internet. The major brand-name players (e.g., the *New York Times*, *Washington Post*, and the BBC) will survive and find new ways to deliver their content to a worldwide audience. Regional papers, however, have had to become more local and more focused in mission.

Compared with what has happened to music, bookstores, and journalism, higher education has changed remarkably little so far. If university budgets continue to tighten, then universities may do what newspapers did: look for efficiencies. Every major newspaper used to employ a bevy of foreign correspondents. That was a good thing for the world and for democracy, but just as people were not willing to pay for a variety of opinions about Middle East politics, they won't pay for a medieval history professor at every college. There is a huge scholarly benefit to having lots of different professors teaching lots of individualized classes on European history, but, when serious cost-cutting begins, small departments and redundant courses like foreign correspondents will be cut. Universities might consider getting ahead of this curve by outsourcing a few specialized upper-division courses to another institution. This is a bit like using Associated Press as your international news source and eliminating the jobs of your foreign correspondents. Asking what your local population most needs (and will pay for) is a good financial move. But it is also a threat to many of the values most dear to academics.

If all we see in new technology is a threat, however, then we will make the same mistake journalism made by not thinking soon enough about both the possibilities of the new technology and alternative ways to package and focus our core product. Speed is an important part of the news, and currency is an important part of teaching; however, since there is still a need for investigative reporting there is also deep and abiding value in thoughtfulness and careful analysis. Like professors, journalists are hired to discover and make sense of information. Note that while newspapers are in trouble, magazines that focus on analysis (the *New Yorker*, the *Atlantic*, and especially the *Economist*) are doing well (Pew, 2009). A four-year full-time degree will retain the power to change lives, but we will need to be willing to let some of the content come from other sources and to focus on developing graduates who can think, reflect, create meaning, and apply information.

Lesson 1: The Product Can Change

In all of the examples cited, the technology of the delivery method changed the product, and in several of these cases failure to anticipate which parts of the product were worth the new and now relatively higher cost had devastating consequences. As with any new technology or market disruption, radical innovation will (and should) characterize higher education for some time to come. When the playing field changes, competitors immediately reevaluate their strengths and look for new advantages. New products will appear that, initially, might not appear at all as competitors. Free noncredit courses or online degrees might seem like very different products than a campus experience, but with lower cost, greater convenience, and more marketing supporting these products, colleges will need to reevaluate what consumers want and are willing to pay for.

Expect chaos, innovation, new types of competition, and even new types of fraud as characteristics of an industry are undergoing rapid change. Haydn's early symphonies were circulated only in manuscript, but music printing gradually replaced manuscripts and spread Haydn's fame across Europe. Publishing presented an economy of scale for the publisher and a chance for artists to reach a greater public, but it also brought a potential loss of revenue and control. A composer could sell a limited number of manuscripts and collect a fee for each, but the publisher would pay the composer only once. New technologies and new economies also create new opportunities for fraud. As Haydn's reputation increased, publishers not only reprinted his works (Symphony no. 101 in D was published almost a dozen times by 1800) but also published fakes.

College is a combination of products: learning, experiences, personal growth, connections, and a degree. At some point, however, free courses from Yale or MIT will start to count toward degrees, or employers will realize that the product is learning and not the degree, in which case free content on the Internet will become a real source of competition. As with newspapers, the challenge for each institution is to determine the aspects of its product that retain commercial value.

Lesson 2: Customization and Social Isolation Will Increase

For better or for worse, Americans have adjusted to shopping in social isolation and will adjust even more rapidly to learning alone. Borders thought the experience of buying books would have value, and it is easy to assume that the experience of college has the same kind of special value. It might. The decision, how-ever, will be made by parents and students, who will consider cost and convenience.

Shopping online (or buying sheet music or records) offers the advantages of privacy and customization, and as we have seen these advantages are powerful industry changers. For some stu-dents, maybe those who do not always have the right answer, an endlessly patient computer, a tutor in India, or a private text mes-sage from the professor in a large class will be preferred and will even increase learning (see Chapter Three).

Students are already more likely to combine courses from mul-tiple colleges as they assemble a degree in the same way that many of us already use Google Reader or Fluent News to combine multiple news sources into one metasource. Look for a new indus-try of degree aggregators, a service that will repackage courses and degrees from other institutions into highly individualized new accredited programs and degrees. Students will be able to search catalogs on multiple campuses for just the course they want. Less radically, virtual seminars will allow students from different insti-tutions to take more specialized courses. Students will be able to study whatever language they want at any university and not just the languages offered at one institution.

Implementation: Sister Schools

New international markets and online technology make a tempting combination, but most of the benefits and little of the risk of a large international program can be reaped if colleges and universities limit their distance learning programs to a small number of geographic locations, foreign or domestic. The benefit of having a single virtual campus in another country is obvious. Marketing can be concen-trated in one location without having to compete with every univer-sity in the world, and local trust between real people can be built through face-to-face meetings and experiences.

Look for a city or region that has something in common with your own geographic area and for schools with a similar mission. If you specialize in urban part-timers who work, disciplines related to agriculture, or residential liberal arts, look for a sister institution or two where missions overlap and resources might be shared. Now your faculty and students can benefit from a variety of global perspectives in the classroom, but without having to change completely the financial model of your institution. That foreign tuition is generally much lower than American tuition makes it easier for lower-priced community and state colleges to participate in such alliances.

Groups of colleges banding together can reduce costs, eliminate redundancy, and increase the choices of courses and majors, bringing economies of scale to fresh design of standard courses (Bates & Sangra, 2011). Students will demand easy transfer of credits and more customization, and consortia will allow individual colleges to specialize but still attract local students based upon the offerings of the other members of the group.

By limiting your strategy to a few places with common interests, you greatly reduce marketing and travel costs, and your investments in people and equipment stay focused. At the same time, having additional students will bring the economies of scale that most administrators are seeking.

Accepting the new reality of social isolation will require significant rethinking. For many of our students, college is an important time of socialization and social growth. Traditional American higher education is built around notions of public discourse. We are hesitant to believe that online discussion (which certainly creates time for more thought) is as useful as the ability to think on your feet. Our classrooms and assignments were meant to create habits that could be transferred to the real world, but that real world has changed.

College has been focused on individual work and social interaction, but the world is becoming a place of collaborative work and social isolation. Should we resist this change or embrace it? The Internet creates new ways of working, new ways to be successful, and maybe even new ways to be happy. We need to consider how these trends might alter our mission.

Lesson 3: More Choices Create New Gatekeepers

In all of these examples, and even without the Internet, when distribution moves from highly diverse local suppliers to fewer national or international sources, competition moves from the fringes to the central space, and the competition for the center creates new gatekeepers.

Initially, sheet music and Borders provided the consumer with more choices, but they also killed off some of the local providers, which eliminated a different sort of choice. English music consumers in the 19th century largely exchanged Potter, Cramer, and Bennett for Haydn, Mendelssohn, and Beethoven. Big-box chain grocery stores and bookstores replaced the local competition in the same way, by offering (in one store) more variety, lower prices, and sometimes even higher quality. The paradox is that more immediate variety for the consumer does not always mean more total variety. If your small town gets a multiplex, it gets more local variety; if the same 10 Hollywood films are playing in every neighborhood multiplex in every city in every state, though, that is less total variety. More importantly, the four major groups of multiplex theaters in the United States—Regal, AMC, Cinemark, and Carmike—became gatekeepers for about half of the movie screens in the United States.

The nationalization of American radio market had a similar effect on regional dance bands. By the 1920s every town had its dance hall and plenty of local bands to fill the new demand for public dance music. Competition was local and based upon the audience response to live performance. While the best bands moved to New York or Chicago, most bands operated within territories within a day's drive from their home base. These bands brought music to towns too far from major cities to have access to the major bands and too small to support their own local music. Broadcasting on a local radio station helped bring in local gigs but didn't bring national fame. During the 1920s, however, radio stations were absorbed into national networks. The Radio Corporation of America (RCA) founded the National Broadcasting Company (NBC) in 1926. The Columbia Broadcasting System (CBS) became NBC's smaller rival in 1928. The depression reduced the multiplicity of record companies to a Big Three: Victor, Columbia, and the upstart Decca. Listeners in the far corners of America could now listen to the best bands from New York on any radio; a number of overlapping regional markets had been turned into a single national market. For listeners and musicians in Texas, for example, the reference point shifted from Don Albert, Troy Floyd, and Alphonse Trent (who led territory bands of mostly regional fame) to Benny Goodman, Count Basie, and Duke Ellington.

As choice proliferates, so do gatekeepers. In the 1950s, with thousands of new singles arriving each year, disc jockeys and payola became the most important gatekeepers. Expert advice, or at least popular endorsement, becomes more important as competition intensifies. Since Oprah first mentioned that she was enjoying Jacquelyn Mitchard's *The Deep End of the Ocean* in September 1996, every book she featured on Oprah's Book Club (a once-a-month program) became a best seller. Oprah became the most important book critic in America overnight.

Until now, most universities (even the large state institutions) have been the educational equivalent of territory bands or independent movie theaters. We deliver live education to a regional audience. Consumers have heard of the more famous competition, but Yale remains out of reach for most of the local audience. Most students both commute and work and largely attend community, regional, or state colleges. The Internet, however, could create national networks and a similar Big Three (or Four) group of national providers. For college, most parents can grasp the local market through connections and friends. The national market is too complex and data too scattered, so most people look for some help. Imagine if Oprah were to rank colleges. Instead, college rankings have worked as a type of gatekeeper for higher education. Who will be the new gatekeeper?

As choice proliferates, there will be more and different gatekeepers, more marketing, and more ranking systems. Learning will become more important, as gatekeepers begin to rank learning and output measures rather than input measures. As technology increases the accessible audience for education, the importance of marketing will also increase. Many universities already spend huge amounts on marketing, disguised as college football and basketball programs. These reach a wide audience, but their message about the school is extremely limited. A focused product and a distinctive brand will become more important as the marketplace fills.

Our Product Is an Experience

Higher education needs to distinguish the real product from its unnecessary packaging, and the distinction will not be the same for every institution. For some students, the sports teams, the diversity of clubs, or the connections formed in Greek life are an essential part of the product. For these students (and their parents who will pay), college is an experience. For average or working students, however, only the degree (and eventually the learning) matters. Convenience will be paramount, and most of our current packaging will be irrelevant.

Like music, higher education will almost certainly move forward as competing live and recorded products. Like live music, live higher education can be an experience that remains unique, varied, social, and highly customized to individual audiences. On the other hand, online education is like recorded music: cheaper and more private but with higher expectations of quality. None of the new delivery systems for music killed live performance: the experiences are different, and they appeal to different people at different times. Similarly, live and online higher education can coexist.

However, online education will alter live education. Both stage and film are viable art forms, but they are suited to different situations and types of stories. Film forced theater to do what it could do best (intimate personal experience) and not compete with what film could do better (epic spectacle and special effects): science fiction, for example, works best onscreen where all of the technology is most effective. (We won't see *Star Trek: The Musical* anytime soon.) Still, even live theater has had to adjust to audiences that are used to the spectacle of film by incorporating more multimedia and spectacle. Like live theater, live higher education can be more interactive and more engaging than its recorded counterpart, although current data suggest it is neither.

If on-campus learning remains not at all or only marginally better than online learning, then the justification for the massive difference in cost can be only the experience. In this case, investment in residence halls, recreation centers, and sports teams will prove to be the right strategy: if we cannot stock more books than Amazon, we can at least have better coffee and couches. This strategy might work for a few football-driven institutions, but even the most jaded parent still wants college to deliver learning.

Recorded music had a profound effect on the quality of live music. While there are more important things in musical performance than the correct notes, recorded music steadily raised the bar for precision and accuracy in live music. New technologies made it easier to fix mistakes on records, and the absence of mistakes on recorded music forced live performers to increase their accuracy. The increasingly lower cost and higher quality of online learning is unbeatable. If higher education cannot improve the amount of learning on campuses, then lower-cost and higher-efficiency products will continue to take market share, and future generations may miss the seminar room in the same way we miss our record stores.

Our Product Is Local

For many products, consumers can now decide between lower prices on the Internet and perhaps a short delay for shipping or getting in the car to go shopping now. Food needs to be consumed locally, so restaurants and grocery stores will not go away unless someone discovers a way to beam food directly into the microwave. Gas stations too are safe—until we all get electric cars.

University administrators have long been aware that our product (for all but the elite brands) was mostly local. Like the music industry, we realized that there were two strategies to extend our reach. First, we could go on tour and move the live product to the audience, so we built regional or satellite campuses. Second, we tried various combinations of recorded education to deliver the product to a wider audience. In higher education, these were initially called correspondence school (delivered through the mail) and later distance learning (using a variety of media). The Open University in England, established in 1969, initially used radio and television to deliver courses. The Internet eliminated the delivery costs, and more universities have joined the now global competition for online students.

Some of the biggest brands, like MIT, Yale, and Stanford, created websites and distribute lots of material but did not create any mechanism for turning these courses either into degrees or revenue. Open Yale Courses and MIT Open CourseWare are free and available worldwide, but without any grades or feedback. (Sebastian Thrun's free Introduction to Artificial Intelligence course at Stanford in fall 2011 is a notable new exception, www .ai-class.com.) State and community colleges have moved their distance learning programs into online education and offer accredited degrees with robust feedback. Few of these institutions have international brands, and few have good business reasons or the resources to create them. MIT, however, is enhancing its brand with free online content and even free certification through MITx (see Chapter Eleven) and thereby increasing demand for its expensive degrees. MIT's efforts are certainly good for the world, but they are not good news if your institution wants to find new sources of revenue on the Internet.

The future will bring new global universities, but most traditional universities are ill-equipped to gamble on a high-risk investment to compete in large-scale online education that will put every institution of higher learning into the same global market. For most institutions, online courses remain a small endeavor or a contingency plan: the Sloan Survey shows only 33% of baccalaureate institutions considering online as an integral part of their long-term strategy, while 67% reported that online courses were part of their H1N1 contingency planning (Allen & Seaman, 2009).

Online courses might reduce costs and improve learning, but not both at the same time. A study of courses in the University of North Carolina System found that online courses cost more to develop but had the same delivery costs as on-campus courses (Program Evaluation Division, North Carolina General Assembly, 2010). In the short-term and on a small scale, developing new online courses will not reduce costs. Unless you are a leading brand and want to leverage your investment worldwide or you are willing to sell off your physical campus, developing a new introductory course seems pointless. Soon you will be able to go to a central marketplace to buy outstanding online introductory courses that you can customize for your campus.

If your institution has a campus, then you are a little like Borders. You might want to get into the online book sales business, but Amazon is already there and has lower overhead. And your investment in campus experience will be wasted online. You will need to justify the higher costs of your place-based education with benefits of increased learning or a better experience. The rewards for the next Beethoven will be great, but the risks are equally enormous; therefore, most colleges should probably continue to limit their online strategies to discrete local regions. Rather than trying to compete directly with the big name online providers, take advantage of the wide range of supplemental possibilities that the Internet offers. Universities that thrive will be those that use both the power of the Internet and the power of the classroom to offer better learning.

Implementation: Increasing Diversity

Technology offers an easy and cheap way to increase the diversity of our student populations with real educational benefits. Online discussion boards and virtual classrooms make it easier to hear directly from distant students with alternative perspectives. Cheaper online courses might also invite more diversity in the economics, age, and cultural backgrounds of our students.

Getting students with different assumptions to interact in the virtual classroom will be a good thing, but these different assumptions will present new administrative and pedagogical challenges. Are faculty ready to navigate a wide variety of student needs for communication, style, support, feedback, interaction, and even time zones? Are Christian students ready to interact with Hindu and Muslim students at the same time? Can students have a respectful dialogue about gender roles with a woman who wears a hijab?

Further, students from other cultures or educational systems bring different assumptions about how learning works, when it is appropriate to talk to the teacher, and what constitutes appropriate course content. Such differences can be invaluable educational experiences, but faculty and students will face cultural and practical hurdles.

Our Product Is a Hybrid

Our students want the convenience of some online content, but few prefer totally online courses (Walker & Jorn, 2009b). Most of our teaching is already blended or hybrid courses—courses that have online content but also meet face-to-face. For traditional courses this means a regular class meeting three times a week, but with some content distributed online, a learning management system (LMS) website, and perhaps a discussion board or some online feedback. For regional institutions to which students commute, hybrid courses may meet only once a week or month. Most of the growth in higher education will occur in hybrid courses that meet equally online and face-to-face, where we can increase both learning and convenience.

A totally online course can be taken anywhere, so the competition is global. In other words, unless your Chemistry 101 course is better or cheaper than all the others, what is your market? Why not, instead, simply piggyback on the existing free courses from major institutions? If Stanford and MIT are willing to give away the lectures and exams for Chemistry 101, why not offer complementary face-to-face study sections and labs? At the best institutions, most small class interaction for introductory courses will be with a teaching assistant. Less prestigious institutions can increase quality and efficiency by putting professors in the most critical part of the process: naked interaction with students.

Every course with a textbook is already a hybrid of sorts: students get a hybrid of perspectives between the textbook and the teacher, and that is a good thing. Most courses also use an LMS to supply even a few readings and other opinions online. For most institutions it makes sense to shift the balance to a little more online content. Replace large lecture sessions with brand-name online podcasts and instead have local faculty interact with students in smaller face-to-face sessions (see Chapter Eight). This hybrid approach will improve learning and leverage both our local strengths and what the brand names are giving away for free.

The best education of the future will be a hybrid. There is value in physical contact with teachers, but there is also potential learning and real convenience in online coursework. Most musicians both perform live and make recordings in different balances. The skills are different, but they enhance each other. Most faculty have been performing only live, but they do not have to stop doing so to embrace online education. For most institutions, the primary question will be one of balance between face-to-face interaction and online resources.

Implementation: Summer School

Schools with large residential populations that are physically absent in the summer might try out their online efforts with summer school. Many students go home for the summer, take a general course at a local community college, and then transfer the credit back to their home institution. Being at home may be a financial decision, but these students trust your brand and know the names of their favorite professors. Taking an online course from their home institution will eliminate any hassle of transfer of credits and might be worth some additional expense. Be aware, though, that any online venture has high start-up costs that might not justify the return, and that there will soon be competition in the online summer school market as well.

Our Product Is Unique

Gasoline, movies in theaters, and groceries are still locally distributed, but most are no longer independently owned: they are chains with national or even international brand names. Universities will have many of the same incentives to grow and improve efficiency by aggregating smaller campuses. Already, state legislatures demand articulation and transfer agreements within state systems and some require sharing of new online courses. The logic is that the University of Texas at Arlington should not need to design a new calculus course when the University of Texas in Austin already has one. That is a reasonable stance, but smart global corporations also allow for local customization.

In business, adapting a global product to fit local customs and needs is called *glocalization*. McDonald's is a global company known for the consistency of its products, but in India it offers mostly chicken, lamb, and vegetarian food. In Israel there is a kosher Big Mac (with no cheese), and in Japan McDonald's offers shrimp nuggets and the Koroke Burger (with mashed potatoes, cabbage, and katsu sauce). In France there is the McCroissant. Likewise in education, there is always going to be a need to localize the material, and colleges will need to capitalize on this.

The global universities of the future will offer standardized and consistent products like McDonald's does. They will start with introductory courses and outsource tutoring to India, but in an effort to glocalize to American English your tutor will be named Steve. Some of the best brands are already exploring expansion, either with foreign regional campuses (New York University at Abu Dhabi), partnerships (Stanford and King Abdullah University of Science and Technology in Saudi Arabia), or hybrid products (Cornell-Queens MBA offered locally in a dozen large American and Canadian cities and in Monterrey, Mexico). These will be tailored to the local communities and compete against local products.

In *The Lexus and the Olive Tree*, Thomas Freidman (1999) argues that the world is being shaped by the simultaneous desires for prosperity (the Lexus) and the preservation of cultures (the olive tree). Glocalization is seen as a form of resistance to the pressures of globalization. Why would the French need an American company to bring them a McCroissant or the McBaguette? (This is really a form of globalization.) If we want a good croissant in Paris, most of us would look for a patisserie; most academics cannot imagine a global university that did not destroy the individual cultures of most departments and campuses. The French, however, have embraced their 1,100 McDonald's restaurants, where they are much more likely to sit and linger than Americans, making France the second largest consumer of McDonald's in the world after the United States.

Most universities will want to stay independent. Like the independent movie theaters or bookstores that have persisted, colleges will need a loyal local consumer base and a focus. The usual business rules apply: we will need to be better, cheaper, more convenient, or more specialized to survive. One long-term strategy might be to carve out a regional or even national niche as the premed school or the writing school, for example. A further strategy will be to emphasize the naked human connection across the curriculum and in all learning.

Students are increasingly comfortable interacting online, but a body of literature suggests that the human connection remains an important part of online education. We know that atmosphere is an important part of any learning environment, so it should come as no surprise that emotion and style of interaction still play a role in online learning (Lehman & Conceicao, 2010).

The same sense of connection that helps in a physical classroom is important online as well. As far back as 1976, Short, Williams, and Christie found that distance learners who could watch the instructor on video cassettes as a supplement to correspondence study felt a greater sense of presence. Connecting to your professor or fellow students as real people matters just as much online as it does in the physical classroom (Garrison, Anderson, & Archer, 2003). Creating a sense of community and shared mission needs to be a part of any online strategy but also of any campus.

Lombard and Ditton (1997) find that the less we focus on the technology and the more it becomes transparent, the better the learning experience. Both in the classroom and online, technology is a means to an end. Whether in person or online the emotional power of our subject and its human connection is an important part of what we teach. This means that face-to-face instruction will always have deep value and that even in an online classroom the art of teaching will still be at a premium.

Finding the Right Hybrid

Like the market for new recordings of Beethoven's Fifth, the market for large introductory courses is already crowded. With Beethoven or Chemistry 101, live is still better, but most professional performances sound about the same to most people. Like future musicians, college administrators will need to understand new distribution systems, differentiate missions and products, and create a strategy for navigating both local and global competition. If you play your own songs or offer courses locally, you will still need some online services. If you really want to record Beethoven or teach Chemistry 101, you had better have something truly new to say. The Internet, however, will make it easier to sell more specialized courses.

The strategy of focusing on the more obscure product was popularized in the book *The Long Tail: Why the Future of Business Is Selling Less of More* (Anderson, 2006). Traditional retailers could (and will) focus on the most popular products: Pareto's principle (Pareto & Page, 1971) is that 80% of sales come from 20% of products. As the Internet increased the size of the market, however, the least frequent sellers (the other 80% of your products) become proportionally more important. In 2008, for example, Amazon sold fewer copies of popular books than it did in 2000 but saw sales of niche books (defined as books not typically carried in bricks-and-mortar stores) increase fivefold to account for 36.7% of total sales in 2008 (Brynjolfsson, Yu, & Smith, 2010). The Internet will continue to increase the market for obscure products that can be easily found and cheaply delivered widely (Brynjolfsson, Yu, & Simester, 2011). So while the Internet increases the competition in the center, it also provides an alternative strategy for the fringes. There might not be enough local interest at your own university for a particular niche course, but offer it on the global market and it might become your university's best seller.

Every institution is a little different, and your institutional strategy for responding to the new delivery system will depend on your current position. Is your institution more like live or recorded music? Are you more like Borders, with enormous local presence and physical overhead, or an independent e-publisher that can distribute niche products around the globe? Are you a regional city newspaper with local reporters or a global brand like the BBC? Which of your products are local, and which (if any) of your niche products might be global?

Like most colleges, the vast majority of musicians are focused locally. While few of either have any global reach, everyone needs a website to connect with prospective local customers. Making use of online tools does not make you an online company, but it is impossible to compete for business or students without leveraging the ever-changing technology that is now in everyone's hands. With the lower cost of online delivery, there will be pressure to meet more often online and less often on campus, so it will be crucial that we make the best use of more expensive face-to-face instruction. The best courses of the future will combine both online and physical instruction, but in different amounts. The best curriculum will combine common courses from cheap online sources and physical courses that are offered only locally. The key will be discovering the right hybrid for your institution.

The parallels with art are important: most of the popular music consumed today cannot be reproduced live. Bach's music, by contrast, was available almost exclusively in live performances by him. When he died, his music vanished with him (to be revived only generations later). New technology enabled Beethoven to sell sheet music in countries he never visited, and suddenly local pianists and composers had international competition. Education faces the same paradigm change. Is it better to sit in a large class-room and listen to a local professor or to watch the world's great-est teacher on video? Film changed the expectations for live events. We want something extra from the big screen. Some films deserve to go straight to video. Most faculty can give up lecturing.

The courses that remain on your physical campus will need to emphasize naked teaching. It may make sense for you to originate some obscure courses that you can sell globally, but it makes more sense for common lecture courses that feature international lec-tures and local professors as curators to be hybrids for your students. Newspapers already follow this model. Local newspapers now curate a selection of national and international news from other sources and focus their own correspondents on local news. We have lost something by not having more redundancy in the sys-tem, and there are fewer reporters on national stories; the upside, though, is that newspapers have become more localized, varying even by neighborhood. The idiosyncratic American history course on every college campus will not disappear; however, only the best will be offered globally, and only those that capitalize on internet resources, leverage local interest, and engage local students will be offered at all. Face-to-face universities that remain indepen-dent will have a unique mission and offer personalized on-campus learning.

Higher education has, until now, delivered a complex mix of information and services through a highly variable and localized delivery system. In this new world, the market for our face-to-face educational product will remain mostly local but with increas-ingly global online competition. College administrators (like those in other changing industries) will need to balance what must be delivered locally and what can or should be done, or at least sourced, online. Higher education will need to morph from a locally delivered product to a hybrid model that includes both online resources and classroom interaction.

10

The Naked Curriculum

The search for food is one of the oldest human endeavors, yet it has been utterly changed by technology and computers. Precision farmers now plant and plow their fields with automated GPS trackers, fertilize with computerized sprayers that vary the amounts of nitrogen applied in four-inch grids, record the volume harvested from each plant to calculate profitability by row, and use sophisticated software to decide what, where, and when to plant or sell (Nash, 2006). The farming industry is now driven by data and information.

Food may not seem much like higher education, but it is fundamentally local. Surely the idea of global competition for food seemed far-fetched to farmers 40 years ago, yet the three lessons of internet transformation (from Chapter Nine) apply to both food and higher education. Faster modes of transportation and technologies allowing food to be frozen, canned, or pasteurized so it could be moved farther before it was eaten, raised standards and created new markets for new foods. The result was massive change in the scale and economies of the food industry. Even the smallest local grocery store had to respond to customer expectations of blueberries and sushi every day of the year, just as students in even the smallest college are now demanding more language and subject choices.

Food, too, is now more customized, and customers want convenience and social isolation. Eating your burger your way in your car was not enough. Frozen, prepared, and take-out food choices have exploded, so you can go home and eat exactly what you want—alone. Students are also increasingly concerned about convenience of class times, want customized instruction and degrees, and are often less interested in the social packaging of college.

With more choices, there are new gatekeepers. In food, the gatekeepers are grocery store chains and national advertising dollars. You can sell bread locally by finding a small market and delivering a product consumers want. But if you want to sell bread nationally, you need a national marketing campaign and shelf space at Wal-Mart. This requires a different scale of business infrastructure: the chief executive officer of Wonder Bread does not make any of the bread. In American education, athletics have served as a gatekeeper by providing the national marketing for most universities, but none of that will transfer to the global marketplace.

Technology has greatly expanded the food industry and created new choices for existing businesses. Do you want to operate restaurants, write cookbooks, or sell frozen food? (If you are Wolfgang Puck, you can do all three.) Do you want to grow high-yield global products or local organic produce? (Doing both is not an option.) Farmers in the middle, where most universities are, had to choose whether to become part of a larger supply chain or grow a more unique local product. The food industry has learned the lessons of internet transformation and has adapted successfully by enhancing, readjusting, and extending its products (an organic salad kit?), while music, books, and journalism have all been too slow to change and thus have struggled. Which path will higher education take?

Universities are about to experience the same pressures of new products, more customization, and global competition. Most universities, however, currently have little flexibility. We have expensive campuses and a fixed work force. We are the equivalent of the local expensive French restaurant that serves plenty of thick sauces to a customer base who is used to cheap, frozen meals. Unless we want to go into a distance food business, we had better refresh our menu frequently, serve consistently delicious food, provide exemplary personalized service, offer weeknight specials, provide reward points, find local sources of food, create online buzz, hire a harpist, and examine our pricing. Like a masterful meal under ideal conditions, there is nothing quite like the experience of great naked teaching. The campuses that survive will offer learning that can't be provided any other way, and the administrators who can create conditions that transform the learning will help their campuses prosper.

Turn Professors into Curators

Low tuition and a winning football team will always attract (mostly local) students, but academic success is what retains them (Pascarella & Terenzini, 2005). We know that academic challenge, active learning, a supportive environment, high-quality faculty–student interaction, and diverse experiences will engage students and encourage them to stay (Kuh, Kinzie, Schuh, & Whitt, 2005), but we have plenty of evidence that such is not the current state of affairs (Arum & Roksa, 2011). Low graduation rates are a problem for all stakeholders in higher education, and for institutions they represent a huge financial loss; even a slight increase in your retention rate will greatly improve the bottom line.

However, faculty and administrators alike get squeamish when the conversation turns to making structural changes that improve learning. For all the good aspects of tenure and academic freedom, the idea that what goes on in the classroom is sacrosanct is not spurring innovation or improving our institutions. We know that learning matters, and we have a mountain of research on how to improve it. It is time we had the courage to start putting it at the center of our mission.

Although I am a dean and an active faculty member, I am also a parent of a college student, and I am beginning to understand why the public perceives higher education as broken. I, too, am shocked when I learn that even the most respected teachers routinely show movies for entire class periods, ignore the syllabus, cancel class, admit they are bored, fail to discuss required readings, mumble at the chalkboard, let students out an hour early, allow students to talk and shop in back of class, forget to post online tests, or require students to copy from PowerPoint. As a parent, I want to get my money back, but as a dean I know I have to think very carefully about how to encourage tenured faculty to change their ways.

Faculty all say that we don't just lecture, but the research contradicts this. One very large survey of almost a third of U.S. faculty (172,000) found that 76% identified lecture as their primary instructional method (Finkelstein, Seal, & Schuster, 1998). Another study that actually observed faculty found that, on average, students participated for 3 minutes per 50 minutes of class time (Nunn, 1996). As discussed in Chapter Eight, there is a place for lectures, but they should be used only sparingly and only when there is evidence that they are really the best pedagogy. They also need to be deeply inspiring, challenging, interactive, motivating, and geared to exactly the audience present. An hour sampling the videos on iTunesU will convince you that, as in most things, the vast majority of lectures are at best average and many are much worse: meandering, boring, and incomprehensible. We lecture by default. The *sage on the stage* is a hard habit to break, and deans need new tactics to stimulate change in the classroom.

The job of faculty needs to become more focused on designing learning experiences and interacting with students. While we, as faculty, consider ourselves as course designers, we still mostly deliver content. Most faculty have little or no training in pedagogy or adolescent psychology and view *course design* as ordering topics and assembling resources in a syllabus. Now that technology has created a cheaper way to deliver content, faculty should spend more time finding the right entry point, creating a supportive environment, communicating high standards, and guiding student learning.

Faculty must become curators, performers, directors, assemblers, and pedagogues. In the same way that some actors do better in Hollywood or on Broadway, some faculty will be better on iTunesU and some better live. Some will be better in small groups and others in large.

We also need to rethink the idea that all faculty must be involved in every aspect of course design and delivery. It is a cliché that everyone in the theater wants to direct. Some bad actors become good directors, but other actors blossom with the right direction and should keeping acting. Faculty have different strengths, but few have the inclination to master the research on pedagogy and course design. Deans and provosts need to work with faculty to come to a completely new understanding of how best to design and deliver courses, engage students, and create new curricula.

Implementation: How Deans Can Foster Better Teaching

As with most change, no single approach will inspire everyone. Changing the culture requires a complex set of new initiatives, support, encouragement, rewards, and modeling, listed here from cheapest to most expensive.

Set the Tone

I invite all incoming new faculty (regardless of rank) to my house for dinner each year. With the invitation, I send a copy of a book on teaching and ask new faculty to read it. Before we eat, I ask them to talk about it for an hour. First impressions matter, both in the classroom and in life.

Promote the Scholarship of Teaching and Learning

Many disciplines now have journals and conferences dedicated to pedagogy in the discipline, and the Web offers many ways to publish teaching innovations. Faculty who contribute to Merlot or who create and distribute new teaching materials need to be celebrated and promoted. There needs to be a consistent message that teaching is valued. Revising tenure and promotion guidelines to include pedagogical research is an essential part of creating an honest reward system.

Be Flexible About Faculty Work Contracts

Teaching assignments should be based upon where faculty can be most effective. Automatically giving every faculty member a 2+3 or a 3+3 teaching load does not reward quality or even quantity: a new course of 200 students is hardly the same as a seminar of 5. Instead of trying to balance course loads with teaching assistants (TAs), which provides no incentive to improve learning, design a better bureaucracy. Offer flexibility and support excellence: allow an inspiring and inspired teacher to teach more and do less research, and be sure that the merit review process is appropriately adjusted. Most of us would do better to replace course "loads" (a pejorative term that we apply only to teaching and not research) with some more refined system of points, where a course with more students, more writing assignments, a new pedagogy, a new topic, or a more important spot in the curriculum (like a freshman introductory course) is worth more points. Getting TAs or a two-day a week schedule might subtract points. I've encountered systems where the number of students was a direct multiplier and other factors were additive. Chairs often do this in their heads or in negotiations ("If you will teach Intro, I will let you have a Tuesday-only schedule next semester"), but a more transparent system would allow everyone to be a part of matching mission and rewards. Eventually, we will need a system that distinguishes course design, delivery, and grading and allows different faculty to have different roles.

Improve Learning Outcomes

Most accreditors now require learning outcomes on every syllabus and at least some demonstration that they are measured. Deans can use this requirement as an external stick. Although accreditors are never going to check every syllabus, your chairs should. Start by enforcing the need for learning outcomes on every syllabus: no outcomes, no pay increase. But also offers workshops and meetings on how to write meaningful learning outcomes.

Require Evidence-Based Pedagogy

It is hard to measure the most important learning outcomes, but it is still better to have high aspirations. The point of assessing learning outcomes is to improve both teaching and learning outcomes, but given the choice I would rather have ambitious learning outcomes with imprecise assessments. There is, however, one caveat: the teaching methods and course design must meet the standards of pedagogical research. In other words, deans must hold faculty accountable to the same standards of proof in teaching as they do in disciplinary research. If you are going to lecture, then present evidence to demonstrate that lectures are the best method for your learning outcomes. If you are willing to design your course using Fink's (2003) model of integrated course design or other research-based pedagogy, then the dean will cut you some slack on the need to demonstrate that it worked. My reasoning is borrowed from Nelson (2010; see Chapter Five). We have enough research demonstrating the effectiveness of active learning that the burden of proof has shifted. I believe you can improve teaching faster by encouraging new pedagogy than by insisting on stricter use of assessment. Eventually you will need both, but try starting with the carrot and not the stick.

Redesign Course Evaluations

Student course evaluations are an imprecise but necessary tool, so they should be as good as they can be. Most of us endure terrible systems because the process to change them is so fraught with emotion and tension. A redesign, however, is an opportunity to demonstrate how existing research can save us time and provide practical improvement: just because we are smart does not mean we need to reinvent the wheel to prove it. Professionally developed and tested systems exist: you can, for example, try out the student ratings process from the Idea Center for free (www.theideacenter .org). Creating an inclusive revision process, however, is a chance to reinforce the importance of teaching. Ultimately, course evaluation should reflect the core mission of the institution: if your mission is to teach students to see the world in new ways, then that should be the first question on every evaluation. Support teaching risks in the course evaluations by asking students if the teacher used innovative teaching methods.

Create Robust Teaching Reviews

Train teaching mentors to do a real 360-degree review of teaching. Instead of asking senior faculty to drop in from time to time, do a more detailed periodic review (e.g., once every three years for all faculty). A senior distinguished teacher from another discipline might, during the course of a semester, visit several class sessions, review syllabi and assignments, read course evaluations, have a focus group with a few students, sample some final projects, and talk to the faculty member under review about goals before writing a useful but official teaching review. Use one of the excellent existing peer-to-peer systems that combines robust analysis with positive feedback—just as you would to help any student (see, e.g., Chism, 1998).

Support Teaching Risks

Changing your teaching style or redesigning courses is a colossal risk. It takes time that could be spent on research, and students may initially rebel (see Chapter Eight). While student evaluations of a new course are critical as feedback for faculty, administrators need to read them in the context of experimentation. If you use course evaluations for merit raises or promotion, offer to eliminate the course evaluations for a redesigned course from that year's numerical analysis. Doing so costs you nothing and demonstrates that risk is supported and failure is tolerated. Almost all courses are better the second time they are offered. If you can, offer guaranteed credit toward merit review for redesigned courses: for example, redesigning a course counts like an article in a major journal. Combine support for experimental teaching with an efficient bureaucracy that supports risk, and you will increase innovation.

Start a Lending Library

Buy two dozen books on teaching, and place them in your faculty lounge. Let people steal them. (See www.teachingnaked.com for links and lists.)

Distribute Innovation Grants

Distribute small grants for new technology, equipment, learning, or support for people to help with new course designs. Often faculty just need training or want an iPad. We are trying to make our students into lifelong learners, so we should model this by taking courses and training. Most universities have money for research equipment but not for improving our primary mission. We all have money to send faculty to disciplinary conferences, so divert a little of that to send faculty to teaching conferences like the Lilly Conference on College Teaching or one of the many disciplinary society conferences on pedagogy.

Find Redesign Time

Faculty need time to rethink courses and teaching: time off to design new courses, time to work together on important issues and time to hear new ideas. Most universities offer leaves only for research, but why not offer the same deal for professors who will return with the same level of tangible results for course redesign? A cheaper way is to offer course relief or a small stipend for a redesign project.

Advocate for a Teaching Center

The bigger the change, the more support faculty will need. That means technical support and emotional support but also staff members who really understand course design. A teaching center is the gold standard, but start with free lunches if you have to: convene a weekly or even daily gathering of small groups talking about new teaching ideas to build a culture of teaching. Our commitment to teaching is emotional, and it is easily frustrated. Feed the passion for teaching. If you want to create a new teaching center, start with the POD network (www.podnetwork.org).

All of these strategies are wasted unless the departmental, school, or university mission is clear about the importance of student learning and unless the systems of support and rewards back up the lofty statements. Most universities have teaching critical thinking or expanding horizons as explicit goals. The overwhelming research consensus is that lecture courses do not deliver these skills and that student-centered instruction can. It is time for honest talk about how and if what is being done in the classroom actually aligns with institutional promises. Universities often send mixed messages. Without teaching professorships, visible institutional investment in teaching, and tenure for faculty who put teaching first, faculty will assume (correctly) that research is the real mission.

Implementation: Naked Meetings

Consider the analogy of the *naked* meeting: when is it worth your time to go to a physical meeting, and how is it best organized? In both meetings and class sessions, we want an informed and moderated discussion that allows conversation to flow freely, stimulates and engages everyone, and keeps the discussion safe. We also want to know what the goal of the meeting is and that we will accomplish something in our time in this place. Showing up unprepared and listening to a PowerPoint presentation is easy, but we could do that online. Just talking for an hour about the new curriculum is equally likely to be neither motivating nor fruitful. Meetings are your chance to model the behavior you want to encourage in class:

- Send a detailed briefing in advance that contains all of the announcements.

- Avoid PowerPoint, send it in advance, or at least allow plenty of time for discussion and interaction.

- Try alternative venues: seat faculty at round tables in the cafeteria—like at a conference—instead of in a lecture hall. Serve refreshments.

- Demonstrate a more active seating strategy. Barbara Davis (2009, p. 127) suggests asking students to refrain from sitting in some rows as this allows you to walk among students. It also works for faculty meetings and will demonstrate how you can change the environment without new furniture.

- Create a culture of cooperation and innovation. I routinely add some group work to meetings where we solve specific problems. One year the entire school faculty worked at tables to create new minors, and in another we wrote new learning outcomes. We have built shared grading rubrics and redesigned our teaching evaluations, and sometimes committees prepared research or created templates. Doing substantive work together models the power of the naked classroom.

- Respond and follow up. Demonstrate that you do not have to say everything in the meeting. Follow up, but reference the discussions and ideas from the meeting.

Rethink the Units of Learning

For many children of the 1960s and 1970s, the record album remains a unit of artistic expression. How could *Sgt. Pepper's Lonely Hearts Club Band* or *Songs in the Key of Life* be seen as mere collections of songs? The idea of a collection of songs grouped together as a record album, however, is inextricable from the technology of storage. As the technology has changed, the unit of expression has changed.

Records that were 78 rpm were originally sold separately in paper or cardboard sleeves, usually with a big hole in the middle so consumers could read the record label. Records could be stored horizontally or vertically, but as your collection grew so did your pile of broken records. Paper or leather folios, similar to photo albums, began to be sold in the 1910s as a way to store 78s, but the idea of a collection by one artist or one type of music with cover art did not become common until the 1930s. By 1949, however, when the LP took over, the idea of a collection of six to eight songs in an *album* (of three to four double-sided 78s) had become the standard, so LPs that could play four songs on a side were called albums. In a rare technological concession to classical music, the size and length of the CD was expanded to hold a complete performance of Beethoven's Ninth Symphony (about 70 minutes). The Internet and iTunes shattered that album concept. While artists and record companies will be experimenting with different amounts and pricings of music for some time to come, the smaller *song* seems to have become the new unit of artistic expression for now.

Units of university curricula are also historical holdovers: no research demonstrated that a 15-week semester with courses meeting three times a week was the best unit of learning. The medieval university was designed to educate an elite class of church leaders in the trivium (i.e., grammar, logic, and rhetoric, the three modes of expression) and the more advanced quadrivium (i.e., arithmetic, geometry, astronomy, and music, the four types of calculation). The point was to acquire skills (job skills at that), and students left when they had them. The curriculum was entirely portable and was the same at all schools throughout Europe, so there was no difficulty starting in one place and finishing in another. Degrees, courses, semesters, and even research—a new idea of Humboldt at Berlin University in the 19th century—all came later.

We have kept the semesters and the courses, much like record companies continued selling LP-length CDs, because they are convenient for our current infrastructure. Discussions about changing the length or number of semesters inevitably break down, often along disciplinary lines, with the engineers wanting shorter terms and the humanities wanting longer ones, and the practical and administrative challenges of any change on a university campus come into painful full view. For example, I work on a campus where the different graduate schools run different terms and schedules. The Theology School has semesters, whereas the Business School has six-week modules, each starting at different times.

Online education will challenge all of our packaging units, and now would be a good time to rethink some better ways to organize our product. Even if the model that taught all of us is a good one, there must also be other units in which to package learning, especially with new technology. We need lots of new models, and we need to apply the same rigorous methods we use in our disciplinary research to determine which of them will most enhance learning.

Why are all courses the same length? They should last as long as they need to; does anyone really believe that one semester of a foreign language makes any long-term difference? Do courses need to be the same length for every student? Semesters make little sense in an online world, and future students will look at semesters and album jackets in the same way. Part of the Khan Academy's success is the use of very short, song-length videos organized into *playlists*. Although it is set up this way because Millennials understand those units, I suspect that they are also better for learning.

There is no evidence that 50-minute lectures or discussions are optimized units of learning. Some people like going to class, but as learning improves on the flat screen will the social experience of sitting silently in a lecture hall really have more market value?

Perhaps Randy Bass is right that the age of courses is over (Young, 2011). Certainly, there will be more choices.

The for-profit college industry has demonstrated that students want to start courses and programs at multiple times throughout the year. One of the main predictions from the *Chronicle of Higher Education* report on the students of 2020 (Van Der Werf & Sabatier, 2009) is that they will demand more choices and seek fewer four-year degrees. Hybrid class schedules with night and weekend meetings and more online learning are already a given, but future students will want even more flexibility and convenience and lower cost (Van Der Werf & Sabatier, 2009). We need units of curriculum that reflect learning.

The degree, of course, is our largest product unit. While we have graduate degrees of various lengths as well as some variations in the number of courses required for different majors, the 120-credit bachelor's degree remains standard. There are already opportunities (and pressures) for other credentials and certificates. However, we have massive sunk costs in our current infrastructure, and the bachelor's degree has market benefit: whereas the overall unemployment rate in the United States was 8.6% in November 2011, only 4.4% of college graduates were unemployed compared with 8.8% of those with only a high school diploma and 13.2% of those with neither (Bureau of Labor Statistics, 2011).

So the short-term change will be in new three-year and five-year degrees. Experiments with three-year degrees have already begun, for example, at Bates College. And with so many academic high-flyers arriving at college with a year of more of advanced placement and other transferrable credits, a 25% discount on price will continue to be attractive for some.

The five-year degree will be a necessity, too (Van Der Werf & Sabatier, 2009). A demographic shift has halted the steady climb in 18–24-year-olds that has fueled an expansion of higher education, so there will be fewer students in that age group and even fewer students qualified to start a four-year degree. The over

600,000 students who drop out of high school every year represent a huge market of potential students who can most benefit from a college degree. A five-year degree with a preliminary first year to finish high school will make not only recruitment but also social sense.

A potential new unit in the online world is the educational *badge*. In keeping with the idea (from both gaming and educational research) that smaller rewards and less distance between levels increase success and motivation, badges are awarded for specific skills in smaller increments of learning (Young, 2012). The Khan Academy has an intricate reward system of points, patches, and badges. Meteorite badges are awarded for *persistence* (answering a problem correctly after struggling) or a *nice streak* (20 correct answers in a row). Moon badges are better and require proficiency.

At the end of 2011, MIT announced MITx, a new learning platform that will provide courses, learning tools, and an open-source scalable software infrastructure for any educational institution to use. Most importantly, MITx will "allow for the individual assessment of any student's work and allow students who demonstrate their mastery of subjects to earn a certificate of completion awarded by MITx" (MIT, 2011). These certificates may not (initially) have the value of a complete MIT degree, but they will allow students to demonstrate proficiency.

Employers like the idea of certifying specific skills, and Mozilla has created an open-badges infrastructure to both verify awards and allow for their display on Web pages. Badges could recognize online courses but also peer mentoring or work experience. With $2 million from the MacArthur Foundation, Mozilla, the University of California Humanities Research Institute, Duke University, and Humanities, Arts, Science, and Technology Advanced Collaboration award grants for research into badges, ranking, and other nondegree certification systems that foster lifelong learning and track and promote feedback regarding competencies and skills. The aim is to create a "robust badge ecosystem, where traditional and 21st century skills and achievements are inspired, recognized, translated across contexts, and displayed and managed across the web" (www.dmlcompeti tion.net).

Badges represent an attempt to align units of learning with rewards as well as a direct application of an important lesson learned from gaming: lots of small rewards foster intrinsic motivation. British universities that still rely only on comprehensive final exams in the third year can at least claim that the unit of learning aligns with the reward of the degree. American degrees are broken down into smaller units of courses and even smaller learning modules, but currently only the entire degree has value in the marketplace. If employers start not only valuing badges or other skills certifications but also even requiring them, the traditional degree could be in trouble.

E-portfolios are a kind of badge system in the making. The point of an e-portfolio is to demonstrate the real skills you have learned, and universities have been thinking of them as an additional way to demonstrate currency and potential job performance. But suppose we looked at the e-portfolio as an alternative credential entirely and created learning units that had market value? While this could work for specific content skills like video editing or computer skills (where Microsoft certifications are already a common job requirement), it could also work for the more general skills employers say they want most: writing and critical thinking.

At the very least we need to ensure that a college degree delivers these writing and critical thinking skills. Since both are best developed through naked faculty–student interaction, traditional colleges should be leading the charge. Sadly, the opposite is true. Universities have been creating more specialized majors to try to produce graduates with the job skills that students, parents, and employers want, but most of these represent only a third of the course work needed for a degree. What is the value of the rest of the curriculum if it does not deliver writing and critical thinking? Like most employers, many universities now use skills tests to measure competency in writing, math, or software before hiring staff—even when they are college graduates. We don't even trust our own graduates. If employers begin to waver even a little about the market value of a BA and start to consider badges or other skills-based competencies, it will be too late for most of us. We need to start today to offer the right units of learning and to demonstrate—maybe even guarantee—what our graduates have accomplished.

Record companies fought the demise of the CD because they mistook the delivery system for the product. The real product was recorded music, but familiarity with the physical copy confused some into thinking music was a thing, even though the hard copy was only the delivery mechanism. Like the record companies, we've become confused: the degree is a unit of packaging, not the product. The real product is learning.

Implementation: Preparing for New Faculty Models

The new model for faculty will separate course design from course delivery and will open possibilities for new economic models. At the moment, textbooks are produced by third-party publishers, not by universities. Many publishers already offer the other pieces of the course: PowerPoint presentations, online learning tools, and even learning management systems with grade books. So we already outsource a large part of course design to a for-profit business; with new technology, we could instead design courses ourselves and distribute or sell them to each other directly. Merlot (www.Merlot .org) has been doing this for learning modules, and now MITx will do it for courses. Some faculty will be fine with teaching or facilitating ready-made courses—if there were no market for these, publishers would not be offering them. Who better to design new courses than college faculty? Publishing may be a higher-risk business than universities are ready to accept; however, there is no longer any need for printing and distribution, and iBooks 2 has made it significantly easier to publish a new e-textbook.

For example, some universities and faculties will be better suited to designing and selling courses, and others will want to buy and deliver. It seems unlikely that the current elite schools will be the best suppliers of course designs. The elite institutions are clear that research is the most important part of faculty work. Further, writing textbooks has not been rewarded for tenure at many elite institutions, so they tend already to come from universities with more focused teaching missions and more average students. There will be a new market for the faculty and universities who can deliver excellent teaching materials.

Implementation: Team Teaching

Team teaching has never caught on, in part, because it is more work (initially) and more expensive. Some of that, though, is because we always assume that team teaching means two professors and no one else. Cancer care is now delivered by teams because it saves lives. Good teams bring complementary skills together that exceed those of any individual. Why is teaching mostly a solo act? Bates and Sangra (2011) suggest that very large courses (250+) could be taught with multiple professors working with graduate students and off-campus graduates of the program now in the workforce, an instructional designer, and digital technology support staff. Some teachers can do it all, but we can probably improve both efficiency and effectiveness by redesigning the work flow as well as work distribution.

Improve Curricular Progression

Whatever units of learning you choose, the total will need to be more than the sum of its parts. The current assumption in American higher education is that the course is the learning unit and that courses are additive and interchangeable: 30 credits makes you a sophomore, and 120 credits means you can graduate. That would be a fine model if learning were simply about the addition of linear knowledge chunks: Contracts + Constitutional Law + Torts + Criminal Procedure = Lawyer. A little bit of history, a dash of political science, exposure to science and math, plus a dab of the arts add up to a liberal arts degree. As most cooks understand, though, the order in which we add the ingredients usually matters too.

Although most majors require some courses to be taken in sequence and foundation and capstone courses are increasingly common, American higher education is deeply committed to electives, choices, and the ability to take courses in almost any order. Perhaps we require or at least recommend the surveys before the seminars, but we give students too many choices. Even if the college major is sequential, few general education programs are: most consist of single courses from a list of areas. We routinely allow freshmen and seniors to enroll in the same class and then require the same assignments and use the same grading formulas for students at every level of intellectual development.

What this says about American education is that we are focused on content. If all we require is that any student complete the final exam to a sufficient standard in a certain *quantity* of courses, we signal that there is only a single level of thinking available or required. If a freshman and a senior can write the same paper about the same content and get an A, then we don't require the analytical or writing skills of our seniors to improve from their freshman year. We also send the message to freshmen that with an A they have mastered college writing. Our credit as currency model says that the number of hours you spend on a subject is the most important criterion and that we trust that you will integrate the knowledge. Once you have passed a course, you are rarely accountable for that material again. Most of us recognize this problem, but we are loath to require a sequential curriculum or an integrated final exam (as is common in most countries) and trust instead to systems of advisors who guide students through the maze of choices.

Sequence, of course, is critical. No one would suggest that math or language courses could be taken out of sequence or that we should mix 3rd and 10th graders in subject-based courses. Most of us spend a great deal of time in our individual courses thinking about the progression of topics. Why would it not matter, then, if you take American or European history first in college? More importantly, why would we not require juniors to have better writing skills than sophomores in every class?

A curriculum can indeed add up to more than the sum of its courses, but only if faculty work together to create a sequential curriculum that builds upon previous course skills and not just content. Getting an entire campus to agree upon the learning outcomes for freshman English (and even beyond) is hard, but also invaluable. Imagine being a student at the end of your sophomore year with all A's but knowing that the grading rubrics for papers would all get harder next year and that your junior courses will require more and better conceptual thinking than you did as a sophomore.

Creating rubrics and clear pathways for the development of skills as students progress through college will mean a radical shift for American higher education. Since different countries have degrees of different lengths, how does an employer know how a three-year degree from one country compares with a two-year degree in another? Since the Bologna Accords in 1999, 47 countries (excluding the United States) have tried to harmonize their higher-education systems by focusing more on learning outcomes and standards and less on hours of content. The aim is to make degrees more portable in a new world economy, but focusing more on what students can do and less on how many hours of classes also puts the emphasis on learning. The Lumina Foundation has started the ball rolling in America with its collaborative Degree Qualifications Profile (Lumina, 2011), but there is no time to waste. The American brand still has considerable cache in higher education, but the higher-education versions of Lexus and Toyota are on the way.

Another manifestation of this recent emphasis on sequenced skills and capacities is the Association of American Colleges and Universities Project LEAP Liberal Education and America's Promise (www.aacu.org/leap). Introducing essential skills at a foundational level early in the college career and then periodically revisiting and building on that foundation at increasingly sophisticated levels in subsequent years requires a more linear curriculum. It does not have to be regimented—there can be enormous breadth of content—but it does take collaboration and planning.

Implementation: Stimulating Curricular Revision

Start with Learning Outcomes

The best place for departments to start is by creating learning outcomes for each major. Then they can use a curriculum mapping process (www.performancepyramid.muohio.edu/pyramid/curriculum-mapping.html) to determine how courses in the major fit together to achieve the outcomes, which in turn informs discussions about curricular progression and revision. If your entire department's curriculum is structured to teach writing or critical thinking and teachers in more advanced courses build upon skills introduced in beginning courses, everyone will be working together. If all faculty expect students to be prepared for, and actively engaged in, class activities, there will no longer be just one teacher who is trying to teach higher-order thinking and suffering for it in course evaluations.

Create Rubrics

Next, introduce rubrics and get faculty to try them out. Then design rubrics for the major learning outcomes. If you promise that graduates will be able to write well, what does that mean? How far along will they be as juniors? Perhaps the department can create rubrics for papers in 100/200 level courses and a more advanced one for papers in 300/400 courses. It will not be easy to get faculty to grade with a shared rubric, but at least the process of trying to come up with one will validate the student assumption that college is just about navigating individual idiosyncratic professor preferences rather than about learning a progressive set of critical skills. Another tactic can be to separate the rubric from grading and to create a rubric for accreditation assessments. Doing so will set goal posts, and gradually the department will align its curriculum to ensure its own success. They will teach to the test, as they should, since they get to write the test.

Create a Nimble Curriculum Review Process

A dean's or provost's job is to create a bureaucracy that rewards risk and tolerates some failure, which requires being nimble enough to accommodate rapid change. If it takes years to process curricular changes or if hundreds of revisions are requested, then departments will be too deliberate. If you encourage faculty to make little changes in the curriculum as needed and you can enact those changes quickly, then your system will be more dynamic. The risk of change in curriculum then becomes lower than it seems: if a new course does not work, you can always change it back. Constant change might seem like a burden on students, but a curriculum that changes too slowly is an even worse problem. Most universities have a slow and cumbersome curricular review process that works like a no-returns policy at a department store. People buy less when they know they cannot return something, so encourage returns.

Invent New Interdisciplinary Minors

The risk, cost, and bureaucracy for minors are much lower than for majors. Faculty will be more willing to invest real energy, which can then lead to other things. Emphasizing interdisciplinary minors creates opportunities for cross-departmental collaboration and thinking, and it is also where most new programs belong. Most of your faculty work in existing fields, most of which are not going away. Minors allow faculty to investigate the spaces in between that might be fruitful, without having to give up anything. The process will stimulate and encourage innovation and can lead to bigger things (like new majors).

The Naked Curriculum

Many of the tactics suggested here are indirect ways of getting faculty to teach naked. Faculty hate to be forced to do anything: we all became academics, in part, because we like the independence of learning new things and exploring beyond the current reaches of knowledge. We are contrarian by nature, and we like to argue every side of an issue, just in case there is something interesting on the other side. Being collaborative and seeing the larger picture has generally not been rewarded, so we are unlikely to be convinced that anything suggested by administrators is in the best interests of the institution.

We do, however, value our students and genuinely care about what they are learning. We'd all like to be better teachers—even if we feel the university does not reward us for doing so. Creating a shared sense of mission about teaching, therefore, is more motivating than almost anything else. Faculty, like students, are motivated by autonomy, mastery, and purpose because intrinsic rewards are the ones that really change behavior (Pink, 2011). Building a shared mission around students is a powerful force for change.

Working backward from learning outcomes will prove motivating. Departmental or major learning outcomes are unlikely to focus on only content. When faculty declare that they want students to be able to think or write, that is the moment to ask if our teaching methods, course design, student–faculty interaction, curricular progression, and degrees deliver these skills.

I have not made many specific curricular recommendations beyond those that increase the best sort of faculty–student interactions. In general, I think we need fewer large survey courses: if they survey content, there are better ways to memorize dates or pictures. If they survey concepts, there are certainly better ways to teach those concepts. When large classes are necessary, I would delay them until the second year or beyond. We need more mobile learning in our courses as well, but all of these things will work out if we concentrate on the really big battle. Delivery and course design influence learning, and I believe that faculty will find unique and better solutions for content once they are focused on learning outcomes, progression, and innovation.

The most important things we want to teach are best taught in the classroom. Getting faculty to learn new technology or redesign curriculum are means to an end: everything we do should be designed around fostering better and more meaningful student–faculty interaction. If we are not focused on enhancing the experience of learning in every way, then we should get online and start selling frozen food.

11

The Naked Campus

An important part of an administrator's job is creating a responsive bureaucracy that stimulates innovation and motivates faculty to improve learning. With new curricula and better teaching we will have products that more students will want to buy. Most of us, however, have to accommodate new goals and initiatives within the constraints of our existing campus infrastructure.

The campus experience can be life-changing, and face-to-face classes are a magnificent teaching tool. At the moment, though, the public sees college as an increasingly expensive product that is not delivering on its full potential (a finding confirmed by our own research), even while they learn things on their cell phone every day. Even if the top 50 schools delivered little deep learning, there will still be demand for the lifelong networking and the elite brand they offer. That leaves a stark choice for the rest of American higher education.

Some colleges will be able to run like a themed spa or cruise, where learning about the Civil War or classical music is interspersed with great food and service: many colleges already run trips like these with faculty for alumni. Such experiences are an excellent opportunity for learning, but a guided trip to the Galapagos with Stanford faculty is out of reach for most people. In addition, although it is a learning trip, the experience is primary. The competition for the college as spa experience is another college spa. If your neighbor builds a bigger climbing wall or has a better football team, your applications will go down.

The college as spa experience is a perfectly reasonable business model, but does it fit with the core mission of the institution?

It evades the issue to say that the students demand these amenities. Which students? We all want students who want to learn. Most of us prefer students who are good at school. Many students with good grades and high SAT scores are smart, but mostly they are good at school. Many of those students can pay, but in our arms race to be more like Harvard, we often provide scholarships for the very students who least need the money. The truth is that we mostly need the campus spa to attract the most privileged students who will move us up the rankings.

But there are more students who want to learn, and some of them can even pay. Our other choice is to be clear that education is our product and to deliver it. Lots of schools talk about preparing students to get jobs, and that is fine, even though first jobs are often awarded based on whom you know. Second jobs, however, go to those who have strong basic skills, know how to learn, are comfortable with risk, have persistence, and can adapt. This is especially true in a period where jobs are changing rapidly. A recreation center, residence halls, and stadiums may also be places for learning, but if we are to survive, we need to figure out how we can leverage them to increase learning and change lives.

We've all learned similar lessons in the realm of time management. If you want to finish your dissertation, work on it every day—first—before you open your e-mail. Everything that happens on a college campus needs to be rethought for how it affects learning. From classrooms to pricing, we need to integrate infrastructure decisions with our learning strategy.

Integrate Your Infrastructure

Unless you are about to build a new building, most of us are presented with an existing set of architecture and furniture. We've probably also got an aging set of computers and a class schedule that is almost sacred. When the roof leaks, you will have to fix it, but there is a complex relationship among the parts of our infrastructure.

The type of furniture, the size of classrooms, when classes meet and with what sorts of technology are all related decisions. Integrating your infrastructure and putting learning at the center is complicated, but it will keep you from competing with the spas.

There is little you can do immediately about having too many lecture halls, but, faced with old lecture halls in need of new seats, consider new flexible seating. This option may be cheaper than replacing fixed theater-style seating and has pedagogical benefits. You will also encounter pressure to put the latest technology in every classroom. Most faculty waste time trying to use advanced technology in class, which is actually a major student complaint (Walker & Jorn, 2009b). It may be more efficient to move classes into a more technological space only on the days when it is necessary: it is certainly not necessary to give to everyone what only a few really need. Your technology investment may be better spent on improving mobile learning or on training your faculty to use the technology you already have. The basic question remains: will a bigger or faster (and surely more expensive) piece of equipment improve learning?

You can encourage better pedagogy and more faculty–student interaction by creating attractive low-tech classrooms. Instead of rows of chairs with desks facing in one direction, provide moveable chairs and tables and install lots of whiteboards. Such a classroom will still need technology, but good Wi-Fi and projectors should do the job. (Portable projectors have become fairly cheap and may reduce issues of theft.) The flip side is that everyone will want a laptop. A pilot program with a class set of iPads might just satisfy that hunger for new technology and still allow for active learning.

Implementation: Distributing Technology Differently

Technology and pedagogy are interrelated. You can save money by taking computers out of most classrooms and faculty offices and giving all your faculty laptops instead. Laptops are only slightly more expensive, but you will make up that the difference by needing fewer of them: you will no longer need to refresh your classrooms with new computers, and laptops can easily be shared among classrooms. A very few faculty will object or want to keep their old desktops. Persist. The goal is to reduce the number of devices (which reduces support costs). One device per professor is reasonable. Explain to faculty that the money you save by having them bring a laptop to class (eliminating the need for computers in classrooms) will be used to hire more faculty technology support. The investment in teaching faculty how better to use technology will pay dividends, and eliminating computers from the classrooms will also encourage more naked faculty–student interaction.

The move to laptops should be relatively uncontroversial for most faculty; as long as you are reducing the number of devices, you are reducing costs. iPads and tablets are a harder issue. If most or even some of your faculty now get iPads as well as laptops, the number of devices your technical staff need to support will increase. In the medium-term, the move to iPads and tablets is probably unstoppable. The number of desktops has dropped dramatically as most students and faculty now use only a laptop, but tablets have raised the number back to two devices, three if you count their phones. Still, I would limit most faculty to one university device and hope that tablets begin to replace laptops fairly soon. Buying a set of iPads for classes and special projects will encourage innovation: the tactile nature of tablets can be a game changer in education. You run the risk of creating a need for more tablets, but if that is the price of innovation, that is a good problem to have.

There are, of course, enormous differences among student populations; at private schools virtually 100% of students now arrive with laptops. At state schools or community colleges there are sizable populations with no computer at all. You need detailed data about your population and their technology habits. Be aware that many students without access to any other computer use their phones for everything, including filling out their entire college application.

Recommending or even requiring that all incoming students have the same laptop model minimizes software problems and reduces support costs and creates many new pedagogical opportunities. Many parents assume that college requires a new laptop, so letting potential students know by the preceding May will at least ensure that the laptops that do arrive with new students are mostly the same platform. At many institutions, a laptop requirement will force this cost into the financial aid package, which for most will be a loan. Another option is to buy the laptops and build them into the tuition cost. A laptop is an important advantage today, and requiring one is a favor to most students.

More comfortable furniture or tables and chairs will probably reduce the seating capacity of some of your classrooms. If that is all you do, then making classes smaller will cost money. However, if you connect better furniture and some smaller classes with some larger classes, you can improve learning without long-term cost increases. If faculty are really lecturing for 47 minutes of every 50-minute class, then 30 students is an ineffective class size anyway: load students into a stadium and lecture away. Every larger class you offer creates faculty time for several smaller classes. Maybe the curricular funnel for the major needs to be reshaped with a slightly larger sophomore survey course but with smaller freshmen seminars. When faculty do insist on lecturing, their classes should be larger. If faculty decide they can live without quite so many hours of lecture, then they will have more time to see students in smaller groups.

I teach a three-credit class of 100 students that would normally meet three times a week and take three hours of my time, plus preparation and grading. Once I made podcasts of all the lectures, I was able to abandon the large class meetings and meet with 20 students at a time (one hour for each group × five groups for a total of five hours per week plus grading). Five versus three hours of contact time is slightly more time each week, but it provides a dramatically different experience for each student. If I use some of that class time for guided peer-review assignments, oral presentations or graded studio, or discussion or lab time, then I can reduce outside grading time. I must make the initial investment of creating podcasts and a good course site within our learning management system, but teaching multiple small sections can be done over the long-term without increasing faculty teaching time. From a dean's perspective, of course, more small sections require more small classrooms and the lecture hall is left empty, so detailed curricular planning needs to be tied to facilities plans as well as technology.

I have also tried various hybrids of this class, in one case with one large group session a week where the big dramatic demonstrations happen and we build a larger community. I've also tried using undergraduate student teaching assistants who completed the course in a previous year or whom I interview for the position. They meet with me for one hour each week as a group and then lead one discussion section. They have to do extra work to prepare for their sections, and they get academic credit for this work. Using undergraduate assistants allows me to conduct multiple small groups at once. The model works best in a series of smaller classrooms and not in a lecture hall, but I can circulate and visit all 10 sections every other day. You can find over two dozen such models in *Student-Assisted Teaching: A Guide to Faculty–Student Teamwork* (Miller, Groccia, & Miller, 2001).

Schedule, furniture, technology, classroom architecture, student numbers, faculty teaching loads, and curriculum are all related. Rather than trying to solve one problem at a time, look for trade-offs. Some faculty will trade more students for fewer days on campus or a lighter load the following semester. If you have good data on course enrollments and smart classroom use, you can probably divide a larger room to create small rooms and recast some of the lecture classes as active learning labs. If you give faculty options to improve the curriculum and offer creative solutions for alternative class schedules, you may even be able to reduce the MWF 11 a.m. parking problem.

Implementation: Experimental Classrooms

Encourage experiments. If someone has an idea for an alternative classroom, build it quickly in a visible location. When I needed new furniture, we tried several different models in different classrooms, accommodating different tastes and also modeling a tolerance for messiness and experimentation. Some of these efforts are not as efficient as just reading all of the research and finding the best answer, but sometimes you have to learn by doing. It also models how we learn from failure and that research and change are a vital part of what we do.

Reconsider Price Discounting

Our pricing models are highly variable (from free to astronomical; see Chapter One), but our most expensive colleges engage in the most discounting. A total of 50% of students at the University of California at Berkeley and 60% at Harvard receive some form of financial aid. Both schools have launched high-profile attempts to award more money on the basis of need and family income. For families with gross annual incomes of $80,000 to $140,000, the Middle Class Access Plan at Berkeley caps the parental contribution at 15% of their household earnings (University of California at Berkeley Public Affairs, 2011). In 2007, Harvard was the first school to commit to this sort of general means test. Dozens of private schools have introduced similar programs, but Berkeley is the first public school to do so. For the vast majority of average or middle-class students, however (and surely even a few bound for Harvard or Berkeley), a final choice about college includes (and usually demands) a consideration of the actual cost.

No one wants to pay the sticker price, and college in America is always on sale. The average private school discount is 42%, and it is normally proudly presented as a financial aid budget. Some of this money goes to help poor students, but at most schools much of this spending is part of the institutional strategy for improving the quality of incoming students. Most schools offer money to their best academic applicants and make money on the bottom half of the class, whose parents can afford to forgo a scholarship at a lesser school and spend the cash to send their children to a slightly better school. Academics also matter the most to the best students, who attend the best academic institution they can get into and afford.

State schools discount even more, but only to in-state students, creating a legal in-state monopoly. There is, therefore, little competition for the vast majority of average middle-class students. Better students can get a discount at a private school or even at other state schools, but for average students the price of the best in-state schools will beat any out-of-state public competition. The in-state discount diminishes the incentive for innovation or efficiency at state schools, which are really competing only against the other schools in their state (Garland, 2009).

Understanding our product and our packaging will help us define new modes of pricing. Students and parents want recognition and exclusivity—a school that will impress their friends. They also want a bargain; some of the hardest negotiators for financial aid, in my experience, have been the parents whose children did not need the money. Increases in college tuition, especially double-digit increases at state schools, will exacerbate the cost–benefit analysis parents are already making. Though admissions officers like to brag about the exceptions, relatively few students will give up a full scholarship at an Ivy League school to attend a regional school unless there is at least a matching scholarship. The real competition is in the vast middle, where most schools and most students are. Here, location, size, type, packaging, and pricing are everything.

Admissions officers like to talk about *fit*, which includes not only class size and the programs offered but also all of the packaging that has little to do with academic quality: beautiful grounds, dorms, recreation centers, coffee shops, and sports teams. The majority of students who were not academic superstars in high school want to go to football games and enjoy Greek life: for them, the product is the experience.

The importance of the packaging will be put to the test by a new budget degree. Coventry University in England already prices its degrees differently: £7,500 ($11,250) for classroom-based degrees like business, English, or history; £7,900 ($11,850) for activity-based degrees like the arts and music; and £8,300 ($12,450) for laboratory-based degrees like biology and computer science. For specialist degrees in fashion or engineering, Coventry will charge the government maximum of £9,000 ($13,500) in 2012. (American universities already do some of this, but most of them hide the additional costs for arts or laboratory courses in fees.) These prices are relatively new and high by English standards, so the university will offer no-frills courses in a new Coventry University College "designed for students who want to focus on their studies and live at home without worrying about accommodation" (wwwm.coventry.ac.uk/cuc). Tuition will be reduced to £4,800 ($7,200) for professional courses in accounting, law, information technology (IT), marketing, and engineering, but with no access to the university's library, IT, or sporting facilities. Classes will be offered at more flexible hours, from 7 a.m. to 10 p.m. on weekdays, and until 4 p.m. on weekends, in 6-week blocks for 42 weeks a year, without the long summer holiday. Students can complete a degree in either less time (as little as two years for what is normally a three-year BA in England) or more. The university guarantees 20 hours of contact time a week: 18 hours in a group of 25 and 2 hours in a group of 5 (Vasagar, 2011).

Coventry is quickly going to discover what students think the recreation center is worth. While it might seem like a risk, implementing a new pricing system is a good way to discover what the market wants. Part of the problem is that we are all chasing the same high-end students who do not need the discounts but want the recreation centers. Imagine if you were running a spa, but instead of simply trying to be the best spa you could be you offered discounts to the most physically fit customers. Having more demand from elite customers is a way to build a more exclusive brand (move up the rankings), but it is hardly a requirement for a strong business.

Most universities have a local population that will pay for learning. Serving that community efficiently can also pay the bills. All of the money that is currently going to price discounts for students with academic ability but not financial need could be redirected to building a better learning product.

The one certainty is that choice is proliferating. There will be even more new pricing models in the future, and both the environmental packaging (i.e., the campus) and the academic packaging (i.e., the courses, credits, and degrees) will affect our pricing strategies. The extension of the Coventry model will be convenience pricing, but will it cost more or less to take courses at night or on the weekends? Most businesses would want to use resources such as classrooms as often as possible and charge market value for different times of the day. They would, similarly, charge more for the premium product (e.g., better professors, smaller classes, or more feedback). That won't feel right for most academics, but if we are honest, our current pricing system makes even less sense.

In the end, both the curriculum and pricing of American higher education is based upon seat time. You pay to sit in the chair, and if you sit in the chair long enough (120 credit hours at most places) and pass only a minimum standard you get a degree. That approach is focused on the wrong part of the body. Surely we can do better.

Create Learning-Based Pricing

Faculty are fond of saying that students are the product and not the customer, but that is not how we charge them. Prices are based upon contact hours and not on learning. If we were serious that student growth and learning were the benefit and result of college, then what would happen if we charged students only if they learned?

Think of the difference between visiting your doctor for a sinus infection (covered by your insurance) versus getting Lasik to fix your eyes (for which you will pay yourself). For the sinus infection, even with a copay or a deductible both you and the doctor know that someone else will pay most of the bills. While there is a shared goal of curing the problem, there is little incentive on either side to do fewer tests. In fact, since most patients get better on their own and it is hard to know when to give the doctor credit for a speedy recovery or long-term health, most doctors err on the side of spending more (insurance company) money. If you want antibiotics, you can probably get them cheaply. Even if you don't get them, you will still probably feel better in a week. If you feel worse, you can come back and pay another small copay. If you do get antibiotics and you feel better, you will probably attribute the improvement to the treatment. It is hard to measure efficacy among doctors, and thus there is almost no competition.

Getting Lasik is another world entirely. Here the patient is spending real money and wants a result that only the doctor can deliver. The doctor's success or failure is immediately obvious. There is intense competition among Lasik providers, and consumers demand comparison of results. Since patients are spending their own money, the cost must guarantee the benefit. But most importantly, there is a single cost for the desired benefit: if retreatment or multiple post-op visits are necessary, there are no additional fees. Even if the patient causes a problem to the eye within a year, many surgeons will correct vision again with no further charge.

Imagine if higher education worked this way. Instead of a system where most people pay a fraction of the cost for a benefit that is hard to evaluate, universities could charge a single flat fee for a package of learning outcomes. Instead of charging the student for repeat visits (i.e., credits), the onus would be on the school to deliver the learning in the most efficient way. I don't want to return to my eye doctor for additional surgery; we both have an incentive to accomplish the goal in the least number of visits. Ultimately, I want the outcome and will go back if I need to, but I don't want to pay each time. (My vision is now 20/20 once again, thank you.)

There is little logic in charging students by contact hours. Yes, in theory, you will progress faster with a better piano teacher, basketball coach, or therapist, but wouldn't you rather pay a fee and know that the teacher will deliver your ability to play a sonata, make more free throws, or have less anxiety? Note that learning-based pricing is consistent with the model of making college more like a computer game (see Chapter Four). Computer games make themselves easier to learn by inviting infinite failure at virtually no cost (low-stakes assessment). In contrast, our current model of charging students for failure is an incentive for success, but it also raises the stakes. A learning-based policy may not be in the immediate interest of the service provider, but in a competitive market, a defined cost for a defined benefit makes sense.

Colleges, like most doctors, decide whom they will teach. Our current system is blunt, but it does have a mechanism for charging more for a student who will need more—as long as the *more* is measured in course enrollments. We do not charge students more if they argue about every grade, and we offer no discount for avoiding office hours. I am not arguing that only the professor is responsible for learning, but our current system creates an incentive to admit at least some students who will not complete their degree. While ranking systems punish this strategy and some for-profits have exploited it to the extreme, the financial incentive to admit students unlikely to succeed still exists because of our pricing strategy.

The Bologne Convention and most U.S. accreditation agencies are now using outcome standards to determine if a degree has intellectual value. Faculty fear that calls for efficiency will always mean more students, but if we really can find reliable ways to measure learning, then we also need to examine our pricing incentives. If higher education priced its product like eye surgeons do and delivered guaranteed learning for a fixed price, we would at least be consistent in our logic that educated students are the product.

Specialize: Identify Your Market and Serve It

The fact that American colleges are highly standardized makes it easy to transfer credits, but it also makes us relatively undifferentiated in the marketplace. We all offer the same basic degrees in the same subjects on the same sorts of campuses. Once students have selected the basic category (urban–rural, public–private, small–large, 2- or 4-year, none of which we can really change), they are left with a large body of very similar choices. There are still dedicated liberal arts colleges, and a smaller group of military academies or Historically Black Colleges and Universities. However, everyone wants to be a research university, and too many universities are chasing recognition in the same top 50 or top 100 list, a trend Rosen (2011) calls *Harvard envy*. We all have the same mission and audience, and there is too much competition for the middle.

Prospective students understand the economic or societal benefits of a college degree: better jobs, less unemployment, and higher lifetime earnings (and recent data even breaks this down by major: Carnevale, Cheah, & Strohl, 2012). Students want personal growth (learning to be independent, finding your passion), social benefits (friends and lifelong memories), and entrees to careers (making connections) along with academics and opportunities for real-world learning and internships. The problem is that most schools have the same marketing data, so all of our brochures and mission statements tout the same benefits and characteristics.

For our part, we all want more diverse students and students with slightly better academics than the ones we have. Almost no (not-for-profit) schools have a chief marketing officer, which means we are all relatively unsophisticated in how we segment our market. One of the main differentiators is location—exactly the thing that the Internet makes irrelevant. Virtually all schools, even in the Ivy League, have a higher local profile and a higher percentage of local students. Schools that survive only on local students are at risk from new Internet competitors. Schools that try to become more national or improve SAT scores will have to offer greater discounts as they compete with the schools that have higher rankings. And there are, of course, fewer total students in each higher SAT category.

Such undifferentiated competition has not been good for students or universities. Leveraging state pride will not be sustainable against rising in-state tuition and cheaper internet alternatives. The middle is about to get even more crowded, and not everyone can be in the top 50. Just as sheet music or the radio introduced audiences to broader competition, the Internet makes local inventory obsolete. As basic courses are offered online in cheaper and better forms, we will need fewer comprehensive research universities. Market differentiation will play a much big role in higher education.

It is a lot easier to be the best in a subcategory. As choices expand in one category, the market (and that means marketers) often subdivide the categories. In the early days of pop music, there were three categories (really ways to segregate the audience and not the music): pop, hillbilly, and race records. Today, pop, rock, country, soul, and hip-hop are only the most general categories. A subcategory like electronic dance music, for example, is subdivided into further sub-subcategories, like ambient, drum and bass, electronica, freestyle, jungle, house, techno, and trance, to name only a few. Most of these exist in further sub-sub-sub-categories as well (e.g., acid house, Chicago house, deep house). As choices grow, we will see more subcategories of university, as we should.

Universities are already segmented by types of students and areas of content, especially in the arts and professional areas like nursing or business. We have not seen as much segmentation for undergraduate science or premed, but we will. Again, the long tail suggests that even more segmentation and more niche markets will emerge. In addition to specializing in content areas or even broad types of students (like commuter vs. residential or part-time vs. full-time), schools could focus on even smaller subcategories or a combination of them. One school might focus on the creation of excellent first-year graduate courses in the humanities that it designs but does not deliver, while a second develops rich online programs for part-time lawyers who want to learn psychology, and a third looks at practical degrees for students in developing nations. With the competition mostly headed toward the research goal, there is a great opportunity for institutions focused on teaching and more focused teaching at that.

One of the lessons of Borders is to leverage your assets. When Borders arrived, it had something the smaller independents did not have: inventory. As Amazon began to compete with Borders for inventory, Borders should have found some other way to stay vital that leveraged its other assets and market position. Borders had loyal customers who liked to visit. Instead of reducing staff and letting the stores get run-down, Borders should have invested in programming (live music, book discussions, yoga, or local services) that might have given people more reasons to visit. Borders is gone, but many of the more idiosyncratic independent booksellers that once feared Borders survive. We each need to find our niche.

There is a reason there is only one Amazon: it is the best and cheapest at what it does. If you want to compete, you need to offer something better, unique, or cheaper. Higher education has become too generic. With the same increasingly expensive products on every campus, we compete only through discounting. While online degrees won't affect the best brands or appeal to the best students, they will carve into the market share in the middle. For those middle universities, a new culture of innovation and change will be required. Most institutions will be forced to look for new revenue from part-time or nontraditional students, but there are many different ways to go about this.

Implementation: Online Courses

Putting courses online in hopes of a global market is far worse than a waste of time for most universities: it will divert important resources that should be focused on the local customers. At the same time, however, local students will want more technology. Universities can be more like Google.

At the moment Google is the world's most important sorter of knowledge. Since there are far too many YouTube videos of and about Shakespeare, most people want some guidance. Google provides one sort of guidance, but it does not create courses. Curating and sorting the existing resources into courses will be important and valuable. (Imagine your life without any search engines.) Offering courses tailored to local students and college mission combined with face-to-face discussion and lab sections will provide a much better opportunity for both financial and educational success.

Let Princeton and Stanford slog it out for the national market. For-profit education is on average more expensive than private college and with less financial aid, but it is results focused and growing exponentially. While the for-profit sector is currently only 4% of all BA degrees, they have proved that students seem willing to go into debt for convenience. For-profit colleges also spend 33% of their budget on marketing versus 4% for traditional colleges (Van Der Werf & Sabatier, 2009).

Not-for-profit higher education will need to offer a much wider range of options of all sorts (degree types and lengths, units and styles of learning, types of content and students, and even pricing), but individual colleges will each need more focus. Universities have been like gas stations: we are all pretty similar, but we survive because we have a local advantage and have not had much competition (except for the best students). Market differentiation will be essential in the future. Focus on the intersection of your core strengths and your core market and find something to do well.

Implementation: Invest in Advising and Learning Support

There are two extreme models of student advising: on one end, some universities employ a staff of professional advisors; on the other, faculty do all of the student advising. Most universities are someplace in the middle. However you deliver advising, you need more of it, and it needs to be better.

Given the multiplicity of options, the standardization of content, and the lack of progression at American universities, advising is the place where customization and service occur. Once students get to higher-level seminars, professors also customize, but at most universities first-year students are at an enormous disadvantage. The norm for most is large introductory courses in widely different fields with widely different styles of teaching and grading systems and little personalized help. Few schools will be able to reduce class size across the board quickly, so the only possible personalization will come from an adviser or learning coach. This might be delivered in the residence halls or an advising center, but it is an investment that will be repaid in retention.

Getting faculty involved also pays dividends. Making advising an important part of campus life puts learning back at the center. Faculty often feel isolated on campus. Learning about the general education curriculum and other majors requires exactly the kind of investment we want faculty to make.

Become a Curator of Risk

In the end, deans, provosts, and presidents are curators of risk. We do not deliver curriculum or grade exams, but we are responsible for creating the conditions to encourage risk and change. A school bureaucracy should do what good bankruptcy laws should do: reward success but not punish failure so much that risk is eliminated.

Risk involves the potential for failure, and surely some of our institutions and colleagues will not survive. Higher education, however, has artificially created one of the most secure job environments in history. While tenure has done its job by protecting research agendas, it has not fostered innovation in teaching, which we now need if we are to prosper.

If IBM can change, so can we. IBM no longer makes PCs or hardware. Chief executive officer Samuel J. Palmisano turned the company from a slow but steady hardware company into a software and services company because he concluded that the corporate market for personal computers would not present long-term opportunity for innovation. In 2004, he sold off all of the IMB hardware businesses, giving up $20 billion a year in sales, and instead bought $14 billion worth of data-mining companies and invested in research to interpret data. Palmisano focused on what was unique about what they did, why it was a good place to work, and why society should care (Lohr, 2011). IBM moved boldly to remake itself. While HP is still struggling with PCs, IBM is now worth more than four times what HP is worth.

For universities, having a shared mission, a social conscience, and an ability to make a difference can create a great working environment and can foster risk and change. Looking for where the innovation will be is another important tactic: it is simply more motivating to work in an area that has potential. Innovative companies are fun places to work, but leadership has to propose bold steps. Could we change schedules, majors, or degrees? Do we need different departments or structures? Do we need a satellite campus, a different incentive program, or even a new mission? Change, especially in universities, can be uncomfortable, but bringing everyone into the process, listening hard, being transparent, and making everyone responsible for innovation can create a culture of transformation.

Integrate Learning

Most faculty spend a lot of time thinking about content and what to cover, but content delivery is not the core strength of a university, just as it is not for newspapers. The core strength of a university is integration.

American college campuses bring together a variety of ideas, disciplinary thinking, people, problems, new situations, and activities. When we separate student activities, faculty–student interaction, community engagement, study abroad, or even athletics from academic learning, we diminish the potential for lifelong change. Developing new values and interests, learning about yourself, encountering new ideas, and learning to apply new skills are critical parts of significant learning. College campuses are ideal for the integration of these different sorts of learning. Lectures may be poor at transmitting content, but they can be excellent at motivating new learning and connecting ideas and people. Universities are good (but can be much better) at integrating the human and personal significance of content, enhancing intellectual curiosity, increasing personal investment in the material, negotiating difference, and connecting information across disciplines.

The physical universities that survive and prosper will be those that best use their expensive facilities to integrate content from multiple sources in classroom discussion and active learning and serve a regional population with hybrid classes that are unavailable elsewhere. Universities have the potential to be excellent accelerators of change, but with decreasing budgets and increasing accountability and competition most will need to outsource some course content and focus on motivation, student engagement, and the integration of academic and other student growth. Colleges and universities will need to make significant structural changes.

In hard times, organizations need to get more from less. Higher education is no stranger to this problem. The question, however, is more what? While there will be pressure for more students or more graduation, our focus needs to be on more learning. As competition increases, our long-term viability will be tied to the demonstration of more learning on our campuses. In practical terms this means that a naked campus will increase both the quantity and the quality of classroom use.

It turns out that recorded music did not actually need any of the packaging. People liked the immediacy of retail shopping, but when it was replicated online Tower Records was finished. Online learning is getting better, and new high-quality online courses and degrees are inevitable. Without expensive campuses to maintain and a huge global market, someone will offer an online Lexus-like degree that will be attractive to many students. If we cannot increase and leverage the best faculty–student interaction on our campuses to outperform online learning, then most of us will end up like Borders or Tower Records.

Since our costs go up with every new square foot on campus, we need to maximize the learning per square foot: it all needs to be naked. If students are going to come to campus, there must be something more on campus than is available online, and that can only be faculty interacting with students in powerful and meaningful ways. It may seem ironic that reducing technology in the classroom should be a core strategy for higher education in a new century, but it is exactly what we all want from our doctors, our arts, our religious organizations and even our restaurants. We want the power of a global economy, but customized and delivered in person. Teaching naked to maximize learning needs to be at the core of the mission and behind everything we do on campus.

Abraham Lincoln's tyranny of common sense presents the greatest challenge for our future. We cling to the dogma that higher education is working and that students are learning because of how we teach. There is, however, overwhelming evidence that this is a completely false assumption. Without new forms of competition and learning and with parents willing to pay ever-higher tuition, we might have been able to survive without real change. But the present perfect storm demands that we strip away the past and look honestly and deeply at how we can improve student learning.

We need to apply Fink's (2003) triangle of goals, assessment, and methods to everything we do. The new common sense needs to start with a greater sense of progressive curriculum and shared mission. Once we have identified what students will learn on our particular campus, we then need to look at all activities as potential sites of learning. Individual courses and activities may change a few lives, but integrating the learning objectives and activities across four years will dramatically increase the effect. If we can further integrate learning across campus life, we will have an even more powerful product. We need, in other words, not simply more naked teaching but also more coordinated approaches to creating encounters with faculty and reinforcing campus activities that link to our learning outcomes.

The new common sense needs also to be that college should be more like a video game, where everything is designed to promote learning and change. Surely we can do a better job of finding the right entry point for all students, building a curriculum of constant but small challenges, allowing performance before competence, requiring mastery before moving forward, encouraging risk and more play with intellectual ideas, and fostering internal motivation. If video games continue to do all of these things better than colleges, then future graduates will continue to learn more from video games than newspapers or books. It should indeed be common sense that faculty must first interest, motivate, and excite our students about learning.

The new common sense, then, should include integration, video game design as a model, and naked teaching. But mostly, it should include innovation and risk as a necessity for success. There are more and better ideas than those included here. Our students and the world have changed. Success in the future will depend on our ability to adapt and find new ways to connect with students. As Abraham Lincoln reminds us, "We must think anew and act anew. We must disenthrall ourselves, and then we shall save our country."

Bibliography

AACU. (2007). *College learning for the new global century, a report from the leadership council for liberal education & American's promise.* Association of American Colleges and Universities. Retrieved from http://www.aacu.org/leap/documents/GlobalCentury_final.pdf

Allen, E., & Seaman, J. (2009). *Learning on demand: Online education in the United States, 2009.* Babson Survey Research Group and Sloan Consortium. Retrieved from http://sloanconsortium.org/publications/survey/learning_on_demand_sr2010

Allen, E., & Seaman, J. (2010). *Class differences: Online education in the United States, 2010.* Babson Survey Research Group and Sloan Consortium. Retrieved from http://sloanconsortium.org/publications/survey/class_differences

Allen, E., & Seaman, J. (2011). *Going the distance: Online education in the United States, 2011.* Babson Survey Research Group and Sloan Consortium. Retrieved from http://sloanconsortium.org/publications/survey/going_distance_2011

Amazon. (2011). Amazon media room [Press release]. Retrieved from http://phx.corporate-ir.net/phoenix.zhtml?c=176060&p=irol-newsArticle&ID=1565581&highlight

Ambient. (2009a). The worldwide market for self-paced eLearning products and services: 2009–2014 Forecast and analysis. Ambient Insight Research. Retrieved from http://www.ambientinsight.com/Reports/eLearning.aspx-section3

Ambient. (2009b). The worldwide market for English language education self-paced eLearning content: 2009–2014 Forecast and analysis. Ambient Insight Research. Retrieved from http://www.ambientinsight.com/Reports/eLearning .aspx-section2

Anderson, C. (2006). *The long tail: Why the future of business is selling less of more.* New York: Hyperion.

Anderson, L. W., & Krathwohl, D. R. (Eds.). (2001). *A taxonomy for learning, teaching and assessing: A revision of Bloom's taxonomy of educational objectives.* New York: Longman.

Angelo, T. A., & Cross, P. K. (1993). *Classroom assessment techniques: A handbook for college teachers* (2nd ed.). San Francisco: Jossey-Bass.

Argyris, C. (1982). *Reasoning, learning, and action: Individual and organizational.* San Francisco: Jossey-Bass.

Argyris, C., & Schön, D. (1974). *Theory in practice: Increasing professional effectiveness.* San Francisco: Jossey-Bass

Arnett, J. J. (2004). *Emerging adulthood: The winding road from the late teens through the twenties.* New York: Oxford University Press.

Arum, R., Cho, E., Kim, J., & Roksa, J. (2012), Documenting uncertain times: Post-graduate transitions of the *Academically Adrift* Cohort. New York: Social Science Research Council. Retrieved from http://highered.ssrc.org/wp-content/ uploads/2012/01/Documenting-Uncertain-Times-2012.pdf

Arum, R., & Roksa, J. (2011). *Academically adrift: Limited learning on college campuses.* Chicago: University of Chicago Press.

Astin, A. W. (1977). *Four critical years: Effects of college on beliefs, attitudes, and knowledge.* San Francisco: Jossey-Bass.

Astin, A. W. (1993). *What matters in college: Four critical years revisited.* San Francisco: Jossey-Bass.

Bagley, E.A.S., & Shaffer, D. W. (2009). When people get in the way: Promoting civic thinking through epistemic gameplay. *International Journal of Gaming and Computer-Mediated Simulations, 1*(1), 36–52.

Bain, K. (2004). *What the best college teachers do*. Cambridge, MA: Harvard University Press.

Baird, A. A., & Fugelsang, J. A. (2004). The emergence of consequential thought: Evidence from neuroscience. *Philosophical Transactions of the Royal Society of London, Series B: Biological Sciences, 359*, 1797–1804.

Bandura, A. (1977). *Social learning theory*. New York: General Learning Press.

Barkley, E. F. (2010). *Student engagement techniques: A handbook for college faculty*. San Francisco: Jossey-Bass.

Barr, R. B., & Tagg, J. (1995). From teaching to learning—a new paradigm for undergraduate education, *Change, 27*(6) (November–December), 12.

Bask, K. N., & Bailey, E. M. (2002). Are faculty role models? Evidence from major choice in an undergraduate institution. *Journal of Economic Education, (33)*2, 99–124.

Bates, A. W., & Sangra, A (2011). *Managing technology in higher education: Strategies for transforming teaching and learning*. San Francisco: Jossey-Bass.

Baxter Magolda, M. B. (1992). *Knowing and reasoning in college: Gender-related patterns in students intellectual development*. San Francisco: Jossey-Bass.

Bean, J. C. (2011). *Engaging ideas: The professor's guide to integrating writing, critical thinking, and active learning in the classroom* (2nd ed.). San Francisco: Jossey-Bass.

Belenky, M. F., Clinchy, B. M., Goldberger, R. N., & Tarule, J. M. (1986). *Women's ways of knowing: The development of self, voice and mind*. New York: Basic Books.

Big Bang Theory. (2011). "The infestation hypothesis." Season 5 (2011–12), Episode 2. CBS TV.

Blackburn, R. T., Lawrence, J. H., Bieber, J. P., & Trautvetter, L. (1991). Faculty at work: Focus on teaching. *Research in Higher Education, (32)*4, 363–383.

Blaich, C., & Wise, K. (2011). The Wabash National Study—The impact of teaching practices and institutional conditions on social growth. 2011 American

Education Research Association Annual Meeting, Wabash College, Center of Inquiry in the Liberal Arts. Retrieved from http://www.liberalarts.wabash.edu/storage/Wabash-Study-Student-Growth_Blaich-Wise_AERA-2011.pdf

Bloom, B. S. (Ed.). (1956). *Taxonomy of educational objectives. The classification of educational goals—Handbook 1: Cognitive domain.* New York: David McKay.

Bonawitz, E., Shafto, P., Gweon, H., Goodman, N. D., Spelke, E., & Schulz, L. (2011). The double-edged sword of pedagogy: Instruction limits spontaneous exploration and discovery. *Cognition, (120)*3, 322–330.

Bongey, S. B., Cizadlo, G., & Kalnbach, L. (2006). Explorations in course-casting: Podcasts in higher education. *Campus-Wide Information Systems, (23)*5, 350–367.

Bonwell, C. C., & Eison, J. A. (1991). *Active learning: Creating excitement in the classroom.* ASHE-ERIC Higher Education Report 1. Washington, DC: George Washington University, School of Education and Human Development.

Boroch, D., Hope, L., Smith, B., Gabriner, R., Mery, P., Johnstone, R., et al. (2010). *Student success in community colleges: A practical guide to developmental education.* San Francisco: Jossey-Bass.

Bossert, S. T. (1988–89). Cooperative activities in the classroom. *Review of Research in Education, 15,* 225–250.

Bowen, J. A. (1998). Listening: The history and future of music delivery. Presented at the International Recording and Music Technology Conference at the Jerusalem Music Centre, Israel.

Bowen, J. A., & Carr, B. (2005). "Jazz by Ear" and "Bandstand" games for learning jazz. Available free at josebowen.com

Bowen, J. A. (2006). Teaching naked: Why removing technology from your classroom will improve student learning. *National Forum for Teaching and Learning, (16)*1 (December), 1–5. Retrieved from http://www.ntfl.com (with an additional appendix "Top ten ways to improve student learning using technology outside of the classroom").

Bowen, J. A. (2011). Six books every college teacher should know: A review essay. *Journal of Music History Pedagogy, (1)*2, 175–182. Retrieved from http://www.ams-net.org/ojs/index.php/jmhp/article/view/23

Bowen, W. G., Chingos, M. W., & McPherson, M.S. (2009). *Crossing the finish line: Completing college at America's public universities*. Princeton, NJ: Princeton University Press.

Bransford, J., & Brown, A. L. (2000). *How people learn: Brain, mind, experience, and school* (exp. ed.). Washington, DC: National Research Council, Committee on Learning Research and Educational Practice.

Brembs, B., Lorenzetti, F. D., Reys, F. D., Baxter, D. A., & Byrne, J. H. (2002). Operant reward learning in aplysdia: Neuronal correlates and mechanisms. *Science, (296)*5573, 1706–1710.

Brittain, S., Glowacki, P., Van Ittersum, J., & Johnson, L. (2006). Podcasting lectures. *Educause Quarterly, 3*, 24–31.

Brotherton, J. A., & Abowd, G. D. (2004). Lessons learned from eClass: Assessing automated capture and access in the classroom. *Transactions on Computer-Human Interaction (11)*2, 121–155.

Broussard, J. E. (2011). Playing class: A case study of ludic pedagogy. Doctoral dissertation, Louisiana State University. Retrieved from http://etd.lsu.edu/docs/available/etd-11092011–154402/unrestricted/jbroussard_dissertation.pdf

Brynjolfsson, E., Yu, J. H., & Simester, D. (2011). Goodbye Pareto principle, hello long tail: The effect of search costs on the concentration of product sales. *Management Science, (57)*8, 1373–1386.

Brynjolfsson, E., Yu, J. H., & Smith, M. D. (2010). The longer tail: The changing shape of Amazon's sales distribution curve. Social Science Research Network (Sept. 10, 2010) Working paper. Retrieved from http://ssrn.com/abstract=1679991

Bureau of Labor Statistics. (2011). The employment situation. U.S. Department of Labor News Release USDL-11–1691, November. Retrieved from http://www.bls.gov/news.release/pdf/empsit.pdf

Carnes, M. C. (2011). Setting students' minds on fire. *Chronicle of Higher Education*, March 11, A72. Retrieved from http://chronicle.com/article/Setting-Students-Minds-on/126592/

Carnevale, A. P., Cheah, B., & Strohl, J. (2012). Hard times: College majors, unemployment and earnings: Not all college degrees are created equal. Georgetown University Center on Education and the Workforce, pp. 1–17. Retrieved from http://www9.georgetown.edu/grad/gppi/hpi/cew/pdfs/Unemployment.Final.update1.pdf

CDW-G. (2011). 2011 CDW-G 21st-century classroom report. Industry online survey of 1209, students, faculty and IT staff conducted by O'Keeffe & Company for CDW-G. Retrieved from http://webobjects.cdw.com/webobjects/media/pdf/newsroom/CDWG-21st-Century-Campus-Report-0711.pdf

Chanan, M. (1994). *Musica practica: The social practice of Western music from Gregorian chant to Postmodernisp*. London: Verso.

Chickering, A. W., & Gamson, Z. F. (1987). Seven principles for good practice in undergraduate education. *American Association for Higher Education Bulletin*. Retrieved from http://www.aahea.org/bulletins/articles/sevenprinciples1987.htm

Chism, N. V. N. (1998). *Peer review of teaching: A sourcebook*. San Francisco: Jossey-Bass.

Christensen, C. M., & Horn, M. B. (2008). How do we transform our schools?: Use technologies that compete against nothing. *Education Next, (8)*3, 12–19. Retrieved from http://educationnext.org/how-do-we-transform-our-schools/.

Christensen, C. R., Garvin, D. A., & Sweet, A. (1992). *Education for judgment: The artistry of discussion leadership*. Cambridge, MA: Harvard University Press.

Cialdini, R. B., Borden, R. J., Thorne, A., Walker, M. R., Freeman, S., & Sloan, L. R. (1976). Basking in reflected glory: Three (football) field studies. *Journal of Personality and Social Psychology, (34)*3, 366–375.

Cochran, H. H., Hodgin, G. L., & Zietz, J. (2003). Student evaluations of teaching: Does pedagogy matter? *Journal of Economic Educators, (4)*1 (Summer), 6–18.

Coghlan, E., Futey, D., Little, J., Lomas, C., Oblinger, D., & Windham, C. (2007). ELI discovery tool: Guide to podcasting. Retrieved from http://www.educause.edu/ GuideToPodcasting/12830

Copley, J. (2007). Audio and video podcasts of lectures for campus-based students: Production and evaluation of student use. *Innovations in Education and Teaching International, (44)*4, 387–399.

Couturier, L., Newman, F., & Scurry, J. (2004). *The future of higher education*. San Francisco: Jossey-Bass.

Csikszentmihalyi, M. (1990). *Flow: The psychology of optimal experience*. New York: Harper & Row.

Csikszentmihalyi, M., & Larson, R. (1987). Validity and reliability of the experience-sampling method. *Journal of Nervous and Mental Disease, 175*, 526–536.

Csikszentmihalyi, M., Rathunde, K., & Whalen, S. (1993). *Talented teenagers: The roots of success and failure*. New York: Cambridge University Press.

Csikszentmihalyi, M., & Schneider, B. (2000). *Becoming adult: How teenagers prepare for the world of work*. New York: Basic Books.

Dale, C. (2007). Strategies for using podcasting to support student learning. *Journal of Hospitality, Leisure, Sport and Tourism Education, (6)*1, 49–57.

Damasio, A. R. (1994). *Descartes' error: Emotion, reason, and the human brain*. New York: Avon Books.

Davis, B. G. (2009). *Tools for teaching* (2d ed.). San Francisco: Jossey-Bass.

Dey, E. L., Burn, H. E., & Gerdes, D. (2009). Bringing the classroom to the web: Effects of using new technologies to capture and deliver lectures. *Research in Higher Education, 50*.4, 377–393.

Diamond, R. M. (2008). *Designing and assessing courses and curricula: A practical guide* (3rd ed.). San Francisco: Jossey-Bass.

Draganski, B., Gaser, C., Busch, V., Schuierer, G., Bogdahn, U., & May, A. (2004). Neuroplasticity: Changes in grey matter induced by training. *Nature, (427)*6972, 311–312.

Dubner, S. J. (2010). How is a bad radio station like the public school system? [Radio series episode] *Freakonomics Blog Radio*. New York: New York

Times. Retrieved from http://freakonomics.blogs.nytimes.com/2010/05/12/
freakonomics-radio-how-is-a-bad-radio-station-like-the-public-school-system/

Duke University Center for Instructional Technology. (2005). Duke University
iPod first-year experience final evaluation report. Retrieved from http:// cit.duke
.edu/pdf/reports/ipod_initiative_04_05.pdf

Edirisingha, P., & Salmon, G. (2007). Pedagogical models for podcasts in
higher education. LRA/ BDRA demonstration file, conference pre-print copy.
Retrieved from http://www2.le.ac.uk/projects/impala

Ehrlich, C. (1990). *The piano: A history* (rev. ed.). Oxford: Oxford University Press.

Entertainment Software Association. (ESA). (2010). Essential facts about the
computer and videogame industry: 2010 Sales, demographic and usage data:
Entertainment Software Association. Retrieved from http://www.theesa.com/
facts/pdfs/ESA_Essential_Facts_2010.PDF

Entertainment Software Association. (ESA). (2011). Essential facts about the
computer and videogame industry: 2010 Sales, demographic and usage data.
Retrieved from http://www.theesa.com/facts/pdfs/ESA_EF_2011.pdf

Epting, L. K., Zinn, T. E., Buskist, C., & Buskist, W. (2004) Students perspectives on the distinction between ideal and typical teachers. *Teaching of
Psychology, (31)*3, 181–183.

Erickson, B. L., Peters, C. B., & Strommer, D. W. (2006). *Teaching first-year
college students.* San Francisco: Jossey-Bass.

Ericsson, K. A., Krampe, R. T., & Tesch-Römer, C. (1993). The role of deliberate practice in the acquisition of expert performance. *Psychological Review,
(100)*3, 363–406.

Evans, C. (2007). The effectiveness of m-learning in the form of podcast revision lectures in higher education. *Computers & Education, 50,* 491–498.

Fahey, R. (2008). It's inevitable: Soon we will all be gamers. *The Times,* July 7.
Retrieved from http://www.timesonline.co.uk/tol/comment/columnists/guest_
contributors/article4281768.ece

Felder, R. (2011). Hang in there! Dealing with student resistance to learner-centered teaching. *Chemical Engineering Education, (43)*2, 131–132.

Felder, R. M., and Brent, R. (2009). Active learning: An introduction. *ASQ Higher Education Brief*, 2.4. Retrieved from http://www.ncsu.edu/felderpublic/Papers/ALpaper(ASQ).pdf.

Fernandez, V., Simo, P., & Sallan, J. M. (2009). Podcasting: A new technological tool to facilitate good practice in higher education. *Computers & Education, 53*, 385–392.

Festinger, L. (1957). *A theory of cognitive dissonance*. Evanston, IL: Row, Peterson.

Fink, L. D. (2003). *Creating significant learning experiences: An integrated approach to designing college courses*. San Francisco: Jossey-Bass.

Fink, L. D. (2004). Self-directed guide for designing courses for significant learning. [Free online 37-page do-it-yourself handbook] Retrieved from http://www.deefinkandassociates.com/GuidetoCourseDesignAug05.pdf

Fink, L. D., & Fink, A. K. (Eds.). (2009). *Designing courses for significant learning: Voices of experience. New Directions for Teaching and Learning*, No. 119. San Francisco: Jossey-Bass

Finkelstein, M. J., Seal, R. K., & Schuster, J. (1998). *The new academic generation: A profession in transformation*. Baltimore: John Hopkins University Press.

Flanagan, B., & Calandra, B. (2005). Podcasting in the classroom. *Learning & Leading with Technology, (33)*3, 20–25.

Franklyn-Stokes, A., & Newstead, S. E. (1995). Undergraduate cheating: Who does what and why? *Studies in Higher Education, (20)*2, 159–172.

Freeberg, N. E., Rock, D. A., & Pollack, J. (1989). *Analysis of the revised student descriptive questionnaire, phase II: Predictive validity of academic self-report*. College Board Report No. 89–8. New York: College Entrance Examination Board.

Friedman, T. (1999). *The Lexus and the olive tree*. New York: Farrar, Strauss and Giroux.

Froh, R. C., Menges, R. J., & Walker, C. J. (1993). Revitalizing faculty work through intrinsic rewards. In R. M. Diamond and B. E. Adam (Eds.), *Recognizing faculty work: Reward systems for the year 2000*. San Francisco: Jossey-Bass, 87–96.

Gadamer, H. G. (1975). Hermeneutics and social science. In *Philosophy social criticism/cultural hermeneutics 2 D*. Dordrecht, Holland: Reidel, 307–316.

Gadamer, H. G. (1876). *Hegel's dialectic: Five hermeneutical studies*. Trans. P. Christopher Smith. New Haven, CT: Yale University Press.

Garland, J. C. (2009). *Saving alma mater: A rescue plan for America's public universities*. Chicago: University of Chicago Press.

Garrison, D., Anderson, W., & Archer, W. (2003). A theory of critical inquiry in online distance education (pp. 113–127). In M. G. Moore and W. G. Anderson (Eds.), *Handbook of distance education*. Mahwah, NJ: Erlbaum.

Gee, J. P. (2003). *What video games have to teach us about learning and literacy*. New York: Palgrave Macmillan.

Gee, J. P. (2004). *Situated language and learning: A critique of traditional schooling*. London: Routledge.

Gee, J. P. (2005a). Good video games and good learning. *Phi Kappa Phi Forum*, (85)2, 33.

Gee, J. P. (2005b). *Why video games are good for your soul: Pleasure and learning*. Melbourne: Common Ground.

Gee, J. P., & Hayes, E. R. (2010). *Women and gaming: The Sims and 21st century learning*. New York: Palgrave Macmillan.

Gladwell, M. (2008). *Outliers: The story of success*. New York: Little, Brown & Co.

Glazer, F. S. (2011). *Blended learning: Across the disciplines, across the academy*. Sterling, VA: Stylus.

Glenn, D. (2011). Online learning portals: Customizing colleges right out of higher education. *Chronicle of Higher Education*, p. A22–23.

Golden, D. (2010). Online schools market to the military. *Bloomberg BusinessWeek*, Department of Psychology, University of California, Berkeley.

Goldstein, R., Almenbergb, J., Dreberc, A., Emersond, J. W., Herschkowitscha, A., & Katza, J. (2008). Do more expensive wines taste better? Evidence from a large sample of blind tastings. *Journal of Wine Economics*, (3)1, 1–9.

Gordon, J. A., Shaffer, D. W., Raemer, D. B., Pawlowski, J., Hurford, W. E., & Cooper, J. B. (2006). A randomized controlled trial of simulation-based teaching versus traditional instruction in medicine: A pilot study among clinical medical students. *Advances in Health Science Education*, 11, 33–39.

Goswami, U. (2008). *Neuroscience and education. Jossey-Bass reader on the brain and learning*. San Francisco: Jossey-Bass.

Gottschalk, K., & Hjortshoj, K. (2004). What can you do with student writing? In *The elements of teaching writing: A resource for instructors in all disciplines*. Boston: Bedford/St. Martin's.

Growth in for-profit colleges' proportion of students and federal aid. (2010). *Chronicle of Higher Education*, June 22, p. A3. Retrieved from http://chronicle .com/article/Chart-Growth-in-For-Profit/66016/

Grunert-O'Brien, J., Cohen, M. W., & Millis, B. J. (2008). *The course syllabus*. San Francisco: Jossey-Bass.

Hake, R. (1998). Interactive-engagement vs. traditional methods: A six-thousand-student survey of mechanics test data for introductory physics courses. *American Journal of Physics*, (66)1, 64.

Harnish, J. (2008). What's in a seminar? Seminar process to encourage participation and listening. Identifying good seminar behaviors. Collaborative Learning Conference II: Working Together, Learning Together. Everett Community College, Everett, WA.

Hartley, J., & Davies, I. (1978). Note taking: A critical review. *Programmed Learning and Educational Technology*, 15, 207–224.

Harrity, M. B., & Ricci, A. (n.d.). How course lecture capture can enhance student learning. Retrieved from http://www.wpi.edu/Academics/ATC/ Collaboratory/News/NERCOMPHandout.pdf

Hay, D., Kinchin, I., & Lygo-Baker, S. (2008). Making learning visible: The role of concept mapping in higher education. *Studies in Higher Education, (33)3*, 295–311.

Heidegger, M. (1927). *Being and time.* (Trans. J. Macquarrie & E. Robinson.) Oxford: Basil Blackwell.

Hertz-Lazarowitz, R., Kirkus, V. B., & Miller, N. (1992). Implications of current research on cooperative interaction for classroom application (pp. 253–280). In R. Hertz-Lazarowitz and N. Miller (Eds.), *Interaction in cooperative groups: Theoretical anatomy of group learning.* New York: Cambridge University Press.

Hofer, B. K., & Pintrich P. R. (2002). *Personal epistemology: The psychology of beliefs about knowledge and learning.* Mahwah, NJ: Erlbaum.

Howe, N., & Strauss, N. (2000). *Millennials rising: The next great generation.* New York: Vintage.

Hudson, C., & Smith, J. (2011). Inside virtual goods: The US virtual goods market 2011–2012. Retrieved from http://www.insidevirtualgoods.com

Hulleman, C. S., & Harackiewicz, J. M. (2009). Promoting interest and performance in high school science class. *Science, 326,* 1410–1411.

IbisWorld. (2009). Us Industry report: Language Instruction. Santa Monica, Ibis World. Retrieved from http://www.ibisworld.com/industry/default .aspx?indid=1543

Information technology on campuses: By the numbers. (2011). *Chronicle of Higher Education,* May 8, p. B233. Retrieved from http://chronicle.com/article/ Info-Tech-on-Campuses/127405/

Jensen, E. (2005). *Teaching with the brain in mind* (2d ed.). Alexandria, VA: Association for Supervision and Curriculum Development.

Jeschofnig, L., & Jeschofnig, P. (2011). *Teaching Lab Science Courses Online: Resources for Best Practices, Tools, and Technology.* San Francisco: Jossey-Bass

Johnson, D., & Johnson, R. (1999). *Learning together and alone: Cooperation, competition, and individualization* (5th ed.). Boston: Allyn & Bacon.

Johnson, D. W., Johnson, R. T., & Smith, K. A. (1991a). *Active learning: Cooperation in the college classroom*. Edina, MN: Interaction Book Company.

Johnson, D. W., Johnson, R. T., & Smith, K. A. (1991b). *Cooperative learning: Increasing college faculty instructional productivity*. ASHE-ERIC Higher Education Report 4.

Johnson, D. W., Johnson, R. T., & Smith, K. A. (1998). Cooperative learning returns to college: What evidence is there that it works? *Change Magazine*.

Junco, R., Heiberger, G., & Loken, E. (2011). The effect of Twitter on college student engagement and grades. *Journal of Computer Assisted Learning, (27)*2, 119–132.

Kamenetz, A. (2010). *DIY U: Edupunks, edupreneurs and the coming transformation of higher education*. White River Junction, VT: Chelsea Green.

Khatib, F., DiMaio, F., Group, F. C., Group, F. V. C., Cooper, S., Kazmierczyk, M., et al. (2011). Crystal structure of a monomeric retroviral protease solved by protein folding game players. *Journal of Nature Structural & Molecular Biology, 18,* 1175–1177.

Kierkegaard, P. (2008). Video games and aggression. *International Journal of Liability and Scientific Enquiry, (1)*4, 411–417.

King, A. (1997). ASK to THINK-TELL WHY: A model of transactive peer tutoring for scaffolding higher level complex learning. *Educational Psychologist, 32,* 221–235.

Kohn, A. (1993). *Punished by rewards: The trouble with gold stars, incentive plans, a's, praise, and other bribes*. Boston: Houghton Mifflin

Kolb, A. Y., & Kolb, D. A. (2005). Learning styles and learning spaces: Enhancing the experiential learning in higher education. *Academy of Management Learning and Education, (4)*2, 193–212.

Kuh, G. D., Kinzie, J., Schuh, J. H., & Whitt, E. J. (2005). *Student success in college: Creating conditions that matter*. San Francisco: Jossey-Bass.

Kuhn, D. (1999). A developmental model of critical thinking. *Educational Researcher, (28)*2, 16–46.

Kuhn, D., Cheney, R., & Weinstock, M. (2000). The development of epistemological understanding. *Cognitive Development, (15)*3, 309–328.

Kulturel-Konak, S., D'Allegro, M. L., & Dickinson, S. (2011). Review of gender differences in learning styles: Suggestions for STEM education. *Contemporary Issues in Education Research, (4)*3, 9-18. Retrieved from http://journals.cluteon line.com/index.php/CIER/article/view/4116 .

Lachenmayer, D. (1997). Learning styles: A handbook for teachers to identify and teach to all learning styles. M.Ed. dissertation, Pennsylvania State University Graduate School.

Lage, M. J., & Platt, G. (2000). The Internet and the inverted classroom. *Journal of Economic Education, (31)*11 (Winter), 11.

Laird, T. F. N., Chen, D., & Kuh, G. D. (2008). Classroom practices at institutions with higher-than-expected persistence rates: What student engagement data tell us (pp. 85–99). In J. M. Braxton (Ed.), *The role of the classroom in college student persistence.* San Francisco: Jossey-Bass.

Lane, C. (2006). Podcasting at the UW: An evaluation of current use. Retrieved from http://catalyst.washington.edu/research_development/papers/2006/podcasting_report.pdf

Laws, P., Sokoloff, D., & Thornton, R. (1999). Promoting active learning using the results of physics education research. *UniServe Science News*, 13, July. Retrieved from http://sydney.edu.au/science/uniserve_science/newsletter/vol13/sokoloff.html

Lehman, R. M., & Conceicao, S.C.O. (2010). *Creating a sense of presence in online teaching: How to "be there" for distance learners.* San Francisco: Jossey-Bass.

Leopold, T. (2011). The death and life of a great American bookstore. CNN. Retrieved from http://www.cnn.com/US/

Levi, A. J., & Stevens, D. D. (2005). *Introduction to rubrics.* Sterling, VA: Stylus.

Lewis, J., Coursol, D., & Khan, L. (2001). College students@tech.edu: A study of comfort and the use of technology. *Journal of College Student Development*, *(42)*6, 625–631.

Lewis, S. E., & Lewis, J. E. (2005). Departing from lectures: An evaluation of a peer-led guided inquiry alternative. *Journal of Chemical Education*, *(82)*1, 135–139.

Light, R. J. (2001). *Making the most of college*. Cambridge, MA: Harvard University Press.

Lincoln, A. Annual message to Congress, December 1, 1862. *The Collected Works of Abraham Lincoln* (ed. Roy P. Basler), vol. 5, p. 537.

Linnenbrink, E. A., & Pintrich, P. R. (2002). Motivation as an enabler of academic success. *School Psychology Review*, *(31)*3, 313–327.

Liu, E., & Noppe-Brandon, S. (2009). *Imagination first*. San Francisco: Jossey-Bass.

Loesser, A. (1954). *Men, women and pianos*. New York: Simon and Schuster.

Lohr, S. (2011). Even a giant can learn to run. *New York Times*, Business Day, December 31. Retrieved from http://www.nytimes.com/2012/01/01/business/

Lombard, M., & Ditton, T. (1997). At the heart of it all: The concept of presence. *Journal of Computer-Mediated Communication*, *(3)*2. Retrieved from http://www.ascusc.org/jcmc/vol3/issue2/lombard.html

Lumina. (2011). The degree qualifications profile, defining degrees: A new direction for American higher education to be tested and developed in partnership with faculty, students, leaders and stakeholders. Lumina Foundation for Education. Retrieved from http://www.luminafoundation.org/publications/The_Degree_Qualifications_Profile.pdf

Lund, C. R. F. (2008). Moving lectures out of the classroom to make room for learning. [PowerPoint slides] Retrieved from http://www.ubtlc.buffalo.edu/workshops/handout.asp?titleID=170&eventID=639

Lyman, F. (1981). The responsive classroom discussion. In A. S. Anderson (Ed.), *Mainstreaming digest*. College Park: University of Maryland College of Education.

Mangalindan, J. P. (2011). Why Barnes & Noble should go from bookstore to nookstore. *Fortune*, April 13. Retrieved from http://tech.fortune.cnn.com/2011/04/13/

Mangan, K. (2011). U. of Texas adopts plan to publish performance data on professors and campuses. *Chronicle of Higher Education*, August 25. Retrieved from http://chronicle.com/article/U-of-Texas-Adopts-Plan-to/128800

Marois, R., & Ivanoff, J. (2005). Capacity limits of information processing in the brain. *Trends in Cognitive Sciences*, (9)6, 296–305.

Mazur, E. (1996). *Peer instruction: A user's manual.* Upper Saddle River, NJ: Prentice Hall.

McCabe, D. L., Trevino, L. K., & Butterfield, K. D. (1999). Academic integrity in honor code and non-honor code environments: A qualitative investigation. *Journal of Higher Education*, (70)2 (March–April), 211–234. Retrieved from http://www.jstor.org/stable/2649128

McCeary, C. L., Golde, M. F., & Koeske, R. (2006). Peer instruction in general chemistry laboratory: Assessment of student learning. *Journal of Chemical Education*, (83)5, 804–810.

McGonigal, J. (2010). Gaming can make a better world. TED talk February 2010. Retrieved from http://www.ted.com/talks/jane_mcgonigal_gaming_can_make_a_better_world.html

McGonigal, J. (2011). *Reality is broken: Why games make us better and how they can change the world.* New York: Penguin Press.

McHaney, R. (2011). *The new digital shoreline: How Web 2.0 and millennials are revolutionizing higher education.* Sterling, VA: Stylus.

McKeachie, W. J., & Svinicki M. (2010). *McKeachie's teaching tips: Strategies, research and theory for college and university teachers* (13th ed.). Belmont, CA: Wadsworth.

McKenzie, W. A. (2008). Where are audio recordings of lectures in the new educational technology landscape? In *Hello! Where are you in the landscape of educational technology?* Proceedings from ascilite conference 2008, Melbourne, 628-632. Retrieved from http://www.ascilite.org.au/conferences/melbourne08/procs/mckenzie-w.pdf

Mill, J. S. (1859). *On liberty* (2nd ed.). London: John W. Parker and Son.

Miller, J. A., & Peterson, S. E. (2004). Comparing the quality of students' experiences during cooperative learning and large-group instruction. *Journal of Educational Research, (97)*3, 123–133.

Miller, J. E., Groccia, J. E., & Miller, M. S. (2001). *Student-assisted teaching: A guide to faculty–student teamwork*. San Francisco: Anker.

Miller, C., Donofrio, N., Duderstadt, J. J., Elliott, G., Grayer, J. N., Haycock, K., et al. (2006). *A test of leadership: Charting the future of U.S. higher education*. Report of the Commission Appointed by Secretary of Education Margaret Spellings.

Millis, B. (2010). *Cooperative learning in higher education: Across the disciplines, across the academy. New pedagogies and practices for teaching in higher education*. Sterling, VA: Stylus Publishing.

Millis, B. J. (2002). Enhancing learning—and more!—through collaborative learning. IDEA Paper 38, IDEA Center. Retrieved from http://www.humboldt.edu/institute/workshop_materials/Millis/IDEA_Paper_38%20New%20Format.pdf

MIT, (2011) MIT launches online learning initiative: *MITx* will offer courses online and make online learning tools freely available. MIT Press Release. Retrieved from http://web.mit.edu/newsoffice/2011/mitx-education-initiative-1219.html

Nagel, D. (2008). Lecture capture: No longer optional? Campus technology. Retrieved from http:// www.campustechnology.com/Articles/2008/09/ Lecture-Capture-No-Longer-Optional.aspx?Page=1

Nash, K. S. (2006). GPS and business intelligence: Rubenacker farms makes hay with I.T. *Baseline Magazine*. Retrieved from www.baselinemag.com

Nelson, C. E. (1996). Student diversity requires different approaches to college teaching, even in math and science. *American Behavioral Scientist, (40)*2, 165–175.

Nelson, C. E. (2010). Dysfunctional illusions of rigor: Lessons from the scholarship of teaching and learning (pp. 177–192). In L. B. Nilson & J. E. Miller (Eds.), *To improve the academy: Resources for faculty, instructional, and organizational development*, Vol. 28. San Francisco: Jossey-Bass.

Nilson, Linda. (2003). Improving student peer feedback. *College Teaching, (51)*1, 34–38.

Noe, A. (2005). *Action in perception*. Cambridge, MA: MIT Press.

Novak, G., Gavrin, A., Christian, W., & Patterson, E. (1999). *Just-in-time teaching: Blending active learning with web technology*. Upper Saddle River, NJ: Prentice Hall Series in Educational Innovation.

Nunn, C. E. (1996). Discussion in the college classroom: Triangulating observational and survey results. *Journal of Higher Education, (67)*3, 243–266.

Ory, J. C. (2001). Faculty Thoughts and concerns about student ratings. *New Directions for Teaching and Learning, 83,* 3–6.

Palloff, R., & Pratt, K. (2007). *Building online learning communities: Effective strategies for the virtual classroom*. San Francisco: Jossey-Bass.

Palmer, P. (1999). *The courage to teach: Exploring the inner landscape of a teacher's life*. New York: Wiley.

Palmer, P., Zajonic, A., & Scribner, M. (2010). *The heart of higher education: A call to renewal*. San Francisco: Jossey-Bass.

Pascarella, E. T., & Terenzini, P. T. (2005). *How college affects students: A third decade of research*. San Francisco: Jossey-Bass

Pareto, V., & Page, A. N. (1971). Translation of *Manuale di economia politica* (*"Manual of political economy"*). New York: A.M. Kelley.

Pearson, I. (2011). The 2030 Future of Sleep Report. [commissioned by Travelodge] Retrieved from http://rss.hsyndicate.com/file/152004621.pdf

Perreault, W. D., Cannon, J. P., & McCarthy, E. J. (2010). *Basic marketing*. New York: McGraw-Hill.

Perry, R. P. (1985). Instructor expressiveness: Implications for improving teaching. *New Directions for Teaching and Learning*, 35–49.

Perry, W. (1999). *Forms of intellectual and ethical development in the college years.* San Francisco: Jossey-Bass. (Original work published 1970)

Peterson, S. E., & Miller, J. A. (2004). Quality of college students' experiences during cooperative learning. *Social Psychology of Education*, (7)2, 161–183.

Pew. (2009). The state of the news media: An annual report on American journalism. Pew Project for Excellence in Journalism. Retrieved from http://stateofthemedia.org/2011/methodologies/authors-collaborators/

Piaget, J. (1970). *The science of education and the psychology of the child.* New York: Grossman.

Pinder-Grover, T., Millunchick, J. M., & Bierwert, C. (2008). Work in progress: Using screencasts to enhance student learning in a large lecture material science and engineering course. Proceedings of the 38th IEEE/ASEE Frontiers in Education Conference, Saratoga Springs, NY. Retrieved from http://fie-conference.org/fie2008/papers/1362.pdf

Pinder-Grover, T., Millunchick, J. M., Bierwert, C., & Shuller, L. (2009). The efficacy of screencasts on diverse students in a large lecture course. Paper presented at American Society for Engineering Education, Austin TX. Retrieved from http://soa.asee.org/paper/conference /paper-view.cfm?id = 11305

Pink, D. H (2011). *Drive: The surprising truth about what motivates us.* New York: Riverhead Books.

Pintrich, P. R. (1988). A process-oriented view of student motivation and cognition (pp. 55–70). In J. S. Stark and R. Mets (Eds.), *Improving teaching and learning through research.* San Francisco: Jossey-Bass.

Pintrich, P. R. (1989). The dynamic interplay of student motivation and cognition in the college classroom (pp. 117–160). In C. Ames and M. Maehr (Eds.), *Advances in achievement and motivation*, Vol. 6. Greenwich, CT: JAI Press.

Pintrich, P. R., & De Groot, E. (1990). Motivational and self-regulated learning components of classroom academic performance. *Journal of Educational Psychology*, 82, 33–40.

Pintrich, P. R., Marx, R. W., & Boyle, R. A. (1993). Beyond cold conceptual change: The role of motivational beliefs and classroom contextual factors in the process of conceptual change. *Review of Educational Research, (63)*2, 167–199.

Pintrich, P. R., & Schunk, D. H. (2002). *Motivation in education: Theory, research, and applications* (2nd ed.). Upper Saddle River, NJ: Merrill Prentice-Hall.

Prensky, M. (2007). *Digital game-based learning.* St. Paul, MN: Paragon House.

Prensky, M. (2010). *Teaching digital natives: Partnering for learning in the real world.* Thousand Oaks, CA: Corwin Books.

Prince, M. J. (2004). Does active learning work? A review of the research. *Journal of Engineering Education, (93)*3, 223–231. Retrieved from http://www4 .ncsu.edu/unity/lockers/users/f/felder/public/Papers/Prince_AL.pdf

Prince, M. J., & Felder, R. M. (2006). Inductive teaching and learning methods: Definitions, comparisons, and research bases. *Journal of Engineering Education, (95)*2, 123–138. Retrieved from http://www.ncsu.edu/felder-public/Papers/ InductiveTeaching.pdf.

Program Evaluation Division, North Carolina General Assembly. (2010). University distance courses cost more to develop overall but the same to deliver as on-campus courses. Final Report to the Joint Legislative Program Evaluation Oversight Committee, Report Number 2010–03. Retrieved from http://www .ncga.state.nc.us/PED/Reports/Topics/Education.html

Quinn, C. N. (2011). *The mobile academy: mLearning for higher education.* San Francisco: Jossey-Bass.

Raynor, H. (1972). *A social history of music from the middle ages to Beethoven.* New York: Taplinger.

Redish, E., Saul, J., & Steinberg, R. (1997). On the effectiveness of active-engage ment microcomputer-based laboratories. *American Journal of Physics, (65)*1, 45.

Reyna, V. F., & Farley, F. (2006). Risk and rationality in adolescent decision making: Implications for theory, practice, and public policy. *Psychological Science in the Public Interest, 7,* 1–44.

Reyna, V. F., & Lloyd, F. (2006). Physician decision making and cardiac risk: Effects of knowledge, risk perception, risk tolerance, and fuzzy processing. *Journal of Experimental Psychology: Applied, 12*, 179–195.

Rigby, S., & Ryan, R. (2011). *Glued to games: How video games draw us in and hold us spellbound.* Westport, CT: Praeger.

Rosen, A. S. (2011). *Change.edu: Rebooting for the new talent economy.* New York: Kaplan Publishing.

Rothstein, E. (1987). The new amateur player and listener (pp. 529–544). In Joan Peyser (Ed.), *The orchestra: Origins and transformations.* New York: Schirmer Books.

Ruhl, K., Hughes, C., & Schloss, P. (1987). Using the pause procedure to enhance lecture recall. *Teacher Education and Special Education, 10*, 14–18.

Ruiz, R. (2011). Twitter: The new rules of engagement. *New York Times,* Lifestyle, p. 4.

Schell, J. (2010). Design outside the box. Talk presented at the Design Innovate Communicate Entertain (DICE) summit Las Vegas . Retrieved from http://www.g4tv.com/videos/44277/dice-2010-design-outside-the-box-presentation/

Schultz, D. E, Tannenbaum, S. I., & Lauterborn, R. F. (1993). *Integrated marketing communications.* New York: NTC Business Books.

Schutz, A. (1944). The stranger: An essay in social psychology (pp. 91–105). In A. Schutz and A. Brodersen (Eds.), *Collected papers: Studies in social theory,* Vol. 2. The Hague: Martinus Nijhoff.

Shaffer, D. W. (2004). Pedagogical praxis: The professions as models for post-industrial education. *Teachers College Record, (106)*7, 1401–1421.

Shaffer, D. W., & Gee, J. P. (2009). *How computer games help children learn.* New York: Palgrave MacMillan.

Shaffer, D. W., Gordon, J., & Bennett, N. L. (2004). Learning, testing, and the evaluation of learning environments in medicine: Global performance assessment in medical education. *Interactive Learning Environments, (12)*3, 167–179.

Sheldon, L. (2010). Syllabus. T366: Multiplayer game design, section 13353. Indiana University–Bloomington, Department of Telecommunications. Retrieved from http://gamingtheclassroom.wordpress.com/syllabus/

Sheldon, L. (2011). *The multiplayer classroom, designing coursework as a game*. Boston: Course Technology PTR, Centage Learning.

Short, J., Williams, E., & Christie, B. (1976). *The social psychology of telecommunications*. London: Wiley Press.

Shulman, L. S. (2005). Signature pedagogies in the professions. *Daedalus, (134)3*, 52–59.

Skinner, B. F. (1953). *Science and human behavior*. New York: Macmillan.

Skinner, B. F. (1954). The science of learning and the art of teaching. *Harvard Educational Review, (24)2*, 86–97.

Slavin, R. E. (1995). *Cooperative learning* (2nd ed.). Boston: Allyn & Bacon.

Slavin, R. E. (1996). Research on cooperative learning and achievement: What we know, what we need to know. *Contemporary Educational Psychology, 21*, 43–69.

Smallwood, S., & Richards, A. (2011). How educated are state legislators. *Chronicle of Higher Education*, June 12, A14. Retrieved from http://chronicle.com/article/How-Educated-Is-Your/127845/

Smith, L. F., & Smith, J. K. (2002). Relation of test-specific motivation and anxiety for test performance. *Psychological Reports, (91)3*, 1011.

Soong, A. S. K., Chan, L. K., Cheers, C., & Hu, C. (2006). Impact of video recorded lectures among students (pp. 789–794). In L. Markauskaite, P. Goodyear, & P. Reimann (Eds.), *Who's learning? Whose technology?* Sydney, Australia: Sydney University Press.

Springer, L., Stanne, M. E., & Donovan, S. S. (1999). Effects of small-group learning on undergraduates in science, mathematics, engineering, and technology: A meta-analysis. *Review of Educational Research, 69*, 21–51.

Sternberg, R. J. (1989). *The triarchic mind: A new theory of human intelligence.* New York: Penguin

Sternberg, R. J. (2008). *The balance theory of wisdom. The Jossey-Bass reader on the brain and learning.* San Francisco: Jossey-Bass.

Suskie, L. (2009). *Assessing student learning: A common sense guide* (2nd ed.). San Francisco: Jossey-Bass.

Svinicki, M. D. (1991). Practical implications of cognitive theories. *New Directions for Teaching and Learning, 27*–37.

Tabachnick, B. G., & Fidell, L. S. (1996). *Using multivariate statistics.* New York: HarperCollins.

Taylor, E. V., Mitchell, R., & Drennan, C. L. (2009). Creating an interdisciplinary introductory chemistry course without time-intensive curriculum changes. *ACS Chemical Biology, 4,* 979–982.

Teachout, Z. (2009). Welcome to Yahoo! U. *The Big Money.* Retrieved from http://www.thebigmoney.com

Thompson, C. (2011), How the Khan academy is changing the rules of education. *Wired Magazine.* Retrieved from http://www.wired.com/magazine/2011/07/ff_khan/all/1

Treisman, U. (1992). Studying students studying calculus: A look at the lives of minority mathematics students in college. *College Mathematics Journal, 23,* 362–372.

University of California at Berkeley Public Affairs. (2011). UC Berkeley launches groundbreaking middle-class financial aid plan. *Middle class access plan.* [Press release] Retrieved from http://newscenter.berkeley.edu/2011/12/14/berkeley-middle-class-access-plan/

Van Der Werf, M., & Sabatier, G. (2009). The college of 2020: Students, chronicle research. *The Chronicle of Higher Education.* Retrieved from http://www.collegeof2020-digital.com (A subscription is required to view this report)

Vasagar, J. (2011). No frills university college offers half price degrees. *Guardian*, October 17. Retrieved from http://www.guardian.co.uk/education/2011/oct/17/coventry-university-college-half-price-degree

Veeramani, R., & Bradley, S. (2008). U-W Madison online-learning study: Insights regarding undergraduate preference for lecture capture. Retrieved from http://www.uwebi.org/news/uw-online-learning.pdf

Vogele, C., Garlick, M., & the Berkman Center Clinical Program in Cyberlaw. (2006). Podcasting legal guide. Retrieved from http://wiki.creativecommons.org/Podcasting_Legal_Guide

Walker, J. D., & Jorn, L. (2009a). 21st century instructors: Faculty technology survey. University of Minnesota Twin Cities, Office of Information Technology. Retrieved from http://www.oit.umn.edu/prod/groups/oit/@pub/@oit/@web/@evaluationresearch/documents/content/oit_content_177145.pdf

Walker, J. D., & Jorn, L. (2009b). 21st century students: Technology survey. University of Minnesota Twin Cities, Office of Information Technology. Retrieved from http://www.oit.umn.edu/prod/groups/oit/@pub/@oit/@web/@evaluationresearch/documents/content/oit_content_177146.pdf

Walvoord, B. E. (2010). *Assessment clear and simple: A practical guide for institutions, departments, and general education* (2nd ed.). San Francisco: Jossey-Bass.

Walvoord, B. E., & Anderson, V. J. (1998). *Effective grading*. San Francisco: Jossey-Bass.

Walvoord, B. E., & Poole, K. J. (1998). Enhancing pedagogical productivity. *New Directions for Higher Education*, 35–48.

Wankat, P. (2002). *The effective efficient professor: Teaching, scholarship and service*. Boston: Allyn and Bacon.

Waters, J. K. (2011). For-profit schools: They get it. *Campus Technology*, September 1, pp. 30–34.

Webb, N. M., Farivar, S. H., & Mastergeorge, A. M. (2002). Productive helping in cooperative groups. *Theory into Practice, 41*, 13–20.

Webb, N. M., Nemer, K., Chizhik, A., & Sugrue, B. (1998). Equity issues in collaborative group assessment: Group composition and performance. *American Educational Research Journal, 35,* 607–652.

Webb, N. M., & Palincsar, A. S. (1996). Group processes in the classroom (pp. 841–873). In D. Berliner and R. Calfee (Eds.), *Handbook of educational psychology.* New York: Macmillan.

Weber, A. (2011). Tax preparation industry report 2011. Retrieved from http://www.franchisehelp.com/industry-reports

Weeks, W. (2003). Incorporation of active learning strategies in the engineering classroom. In *Proceedings of the 2003 ASEE Midwest Section Meeting.* Rolla: University of Missouri.

Weimer, M. (2002). *Learner-centered teaching.* San Francisco: Jossey-Bass.

Weiner, B. (1990). History of motivational research in education. *Journal of Educational Psychology, 82,* 616–622.

Wertheimer, M. (1923). Laws of organization in perceptual forms. *Psycologische Forschung, 4,* 301–350.

Wiggins, G. (1998). *Educative assessment: Designing assessments to inform and improve student performance.* San Francisco: Jossey-Bass.

Winterbottom, S. (2007). Virtual lecturing: Delivering lectures using screencasting and podcasting technology. *Planet, 18,* 6–8.

Wise, S. L., & DeMars, C. E. (2005). Low examinee effort in low-stakes assessment: Problems and potential solutions. *Educational Assessment, 10,* 1–17.

Wolf, L, F., & Smith, J. K. (1995). The consequence of consequence: Motivation, anxiety, and test performance. *Applied Measurement in Education,* (8)3, 227–242.

Wolf, L. F., Smith, J. K., & Birnbaum, M. E. (1995). Consequence of performance, test motivation, and mentally taxing items. *Applied Measurement in Education, 8,* 341–351.

Wolfe, P. (2001). Brain research and education: Fad or foundation? *Mind Matters, Inc.* Retrieved from http://patwolfe.com/2011/09/brain-research-and-education-fad-or-foundation/

Young, J. (2010). College 2.0: A self-appointed teacher runs a one-man "academy" on YouTube: Are his 10-minute lectures the future? *Chronicle of Higher Education*, June 6. Retrieved from http://chronicle.com/article/College-20-A-Self-Appoint/65793/

Young, J. R. (2012). "Badges" earned online pose challenge to traditional college diplomas. *Chronicle of Higher Education*, January 8. Retrieved from http://www.http://chronicle.com/article/Badges-Earned-Online-Pose/130241/

Young, J. W. (1993). Grade adjustment methods. *Review of Educational Research*, 63, 151–165.

Young, Jeffrey R. (2011). Actually going to class, for a specific course? How 20th-century new learning technologies prompt a rethinking of traditional course structure. *Chronicle of Higher Education*, February 27, p. A14.

Zull, J. E. (2004). The art of changing the brain. *Educational Leadership*, (62)1, 68–72.

Zull, J. E. (2006). Key aspects of how the brain learns. *New Directions for Adult and Continuing Education*, No. 110, 3–9.

Index